New Public Architecture

New Public Architecture

Jeremy Myerson

Co-ordinating researcher: Jennifer Hudson

LAURENCE KING

Published 1996 by Laurence King Publishing
an imprint of Calmann & King Ltd
71 Great Russell Street
London WC1B 3BN

A catalogue record for this book is available from the British Library.

ISBN 1 85669 083 0

Designed by Richard Smith and Cara Gallardo of Area, London

Printed in Hong Kong

Acknowledgements. The author and the publishers would like to thank Phyllis Richardson for editorial work on the book; Noriko Takiguchi who researched projects in Japan; Otto Riewoldt for his help and advice on projects in Germany; all the designers and architects involved and the photographers whose work is reproduced. The following photographic credits are given, with page numbers in brackets: Toshihiro Abe (42, 44); Agassi Prod. (94-97); Arcaid/Paul Rafferty (14-17); Archipress/Luc Boegly (70-73, 102-105); Archipress/Robert Cesar (24); Archipress/Paul Denance (9, 25-27, 212-213); Nicholas Borel (50-53); Santi Caleca (152-155); Lluis Casals (187, 196-199); Niall Clutton (192-195); Peter Cook (90-93, 214, 216-217); G. Dagon (115, 117); Carl Victor Dahmen (178-181); Kate Derby (206-207); Jan Derwig (59, 74-77); Patrick Drickey (156, 158-159); Strode Ekhert (66-69); Esto © Jeff Goldberg (32-35); Esto © Scott Frances (106-109); Georges Fessy (208, 210-211); Mitsumasa Fujitsuka (54, 221); Aki Furudate (64 right-65); Fumiko Futai (56-57); Dennis Gilbert (78-81); Timothy Hursley (10-13, 110-113, 138-141, 188-191); Fujio Inamura (55); Michael Jentsch & Axel Thünker (47, 49); Christian Kandzia (200-201); Nick Kane (60, 62-63); C. Kicherer (114, 116); Toshiharu Kitajima (43, 182-185); Balthazar Korab (222-225); Kozlowski (64-65); Berhard Kroll (21-23); Actividades I Servios Fotogaficos Jose Latova (144-146); John Edward Linden (170-171); Satoru Mishima (45, 219); Anna Muller (147); Osamu Murai (118-121); Nacasa & Partners (6); Wolfgang Neeb (20); Voitto Niemelä (143, 166-167, 169); Shigeo Ogawa (18 left, 19, 148-151); Tomio Ohashi (5, 130-133, 172-177, 202-205); Courtesy of Dominique Perrault Architecte (136); Naomi Pollock (227); Harald Raebiger (168); Christian Richters (36-41, 82-89, 99, 126-129); Philippe Ruault (134-135, 137); Daria Scagliola & Stijn Brakke (28-31); Service Departemental Archéologique Arièges (64 left); Shinkenchiku-sha (18 right, 160-165, 218, 220); Margherita Spiluttini (100); Studio W. Täubner Fotografie (46, 48); Valokuvaamo Jussi Tiainen (122-125); Courtesy of X-Com GmbH (226).

Contents

Introduction

The Kunibiki Messe, Matsue, Japan, designed by architect Shin Takamatsu to sell the industries of Simane Prefecture. The design considerations of this building – a sci-fi-styled conference and exhibition centre – reflect a new spirit in public architecture that provided the inspiration for this publication.

This book sets out to explore a new spirit in the design of public buildings and interiors through a selection of more than 50 outstanding works of public architecture completed around the world since January 1993. These projects, diverse in scale and type, from the smallest police booth to the grandest opera house, have been chosen because they demonstrate radical new approaches to the design of the public landmarks and facilities that give cities, regions and nations their identities. Though primarily concerned with new public libraries and museums; town halls and seats of regional government; art centres, media centres and convention centres; school and university buildings; theatres and concert halls, the selection also includes many other less traditional examples of public architecture – swimming baths and a synagogue, an aquarium and an embassy.

Deliberately excluded is any reference to the new wave of public building in the area of transport, such as rail and road terminals and airports. I see this as an independent phenomenon worthy of a book of its own, and have concentrated instead on those hitherto monolithic statements – the city library, town hall, regional museum, university campus, and so on – which historically have comprised the civic realm and are now being reinvented in clever and surprising ways.

The richness and complexity of so many of the chosen schemes reflect a remarkable resurgence of interest and investment in public architecture. The deep recession of the early 1990s left private business in a cautious mood towards new architecture and design. But public authorities, faced with the challenge of regenerating rundown cities, regions and prefectures, and of attracting inward investment and jobs to their areas, have responded with imagination and enthusiasm. The result is the development of a new generation of 'magnet' buildings and interiors that communicate the aspirations of urban and rural communities that are in the process of being recast and reinvigorated.

Enlightened public sector patrons in America, Japan, Germany, The Netherlands and France are responsible for the lion's share of the projects shown in this book. But the selection actually includes schemes from 14 different nations. Projects from Taiwan, Ireland and Israel, for example, indicate just how widespread the new spirit in public architecture has become.

But what is driving this 'new spirit' and what are its characteristics? To answer that, I need to explain my reasons for compiling this book. The defining ideas that underpin its approach can be traced directly to two independent events, both of which occurred in 1993. The first was the staging of a major design conference in Scotland; the second, the completion of an important new public building in Japan.

'Design Renaissance', a world design congress hosted by the city of Glasgow, was attended by a thousand architects and designers. One of its main themes was the future of the 'city-state' and a keynote speaker was Stuart Gulliver, head of the Glasgow Development Agency. Gulliver described, with more force and candour than any other city chief I have heard, the level of commercial competition that exists today between cities and regions.

Gulliver argued that 'Glasgow is only one of a raft of cities in the industrialized world undergoing radical change – to its economy, to its built form and social patterns.' And he likened the provincial city-states of Europe – non-capital cities with around a million inhabitants, the Milans, Marseilles, Manchesters, Lilles, Antwerps, Barcelonas and Birminghams of this world – to football teams organized in leagues: first division, second division, third division, and so on. Each is striving desperately for promotion and to avoid relegation during a period of transition, with new public architecture and design a major weapon in the battle for status.

'In this transitional period, cities will follow different paths,' Gulliver explained. 'There will be reactive or "accidental" cities which take their futures for granted and simply react to changing external forces. But other cities will be proactive – "intentional". Those cities that are successful will see the city take shape around profound qualitative rather than quantitative change ... successful cities will be good places to live, work and visit. Increasingly, those cities where people of talent and skill choose to live will be the places where businesses will want to be.'

That, in a nutshell, provided a coherent explanation for the intense new focus on public architecture, which is increasingly evident in the mid-1990s. But another event on the other side of the world drew my attention to its precise design characteristics. In Japan in 1993 architect Shin Takamatsu put the finishing touches on the Kunibiki Messe, a major conference and exhibition centre in Matsue, capital of Simane Prefecture. This extraordinary six-storey building – with its 'garden of abstract geometric forms' seemingly floating in a 24-metre-high glass-walled public atrium – was designed specifically to market the industries of Simane Prefecture, using a science-fiction-style appeal to the senses as part of the big sell.

Here was an innovative form of public building – more lightweight in appearance, more ironic in style, more proactive in its engagement with visitors, more ambiguous in its definition of interior and exterior space and more overt in its competitive aims than any other civic centre I had seen. It still possessed the imposing values of the public landmark. Yet, somehow its spirit – embodied in those light-filled, aluminium-clad cones and tunnels,

a self-conscious poetry of technological forms – was new and different.

It is from the example of the Kunibiki Messe, with its grand statement, its mission to educate, its structural theatricality, its more tranquil areas for quiet reflection and its concern to interact with its users, that I have derived the key themes of this book. Arranged thematically, rather than according to building type, this volume illuminates some of the most important preoccupations of the public architecture now being designed and built around the world.

Accordingly, the book is organized in five groupings of ten or more projects. The first section, 'Grand Statements', looks at how, in an age less certain of the survival of civic values and acutely aware of the speed of economic and social change, architects and designers are reinterpreting the monolithic traditions of the public building without sacrificing an immense scale or intent. 'The Spirit of Learning' explores the ways in which the architecture of schools, universities, libraries and museum exhibits is having an impact on the entire process of education often in schemes that make fresh and dynamic use of visual metaphors. 'Dramatic Interventions' presents a selection of new projects which, through their contemporary vitality and the insertion of modern elements into or alongside older structures, significantly enhance the popular standing of cities and regions.

'The Tranquil Space' takes us into those calming public places and galleries that provide an antidote to the frantic consumerism of contemporary life and allow us to enjoy quiet contemplation of art, artefacts or music away from everyday pressures. And, finally, 'The Art of Interaction' looks at public architecture that seeks to engage and interact with people, and not simply impose civic values and symbols on them. Often this is done by arousing curiosity in a place or building through the use of contrasts, such as hard and soft, light and shade, old and new, transparent and opaque. (For ease of reference, the project information – architect, interior designer, client, size and scale, date of completion, and wherever available, the total cost – is outlined for each scheme.)

Of course, some of the projects in the book share more than one defining characteristic, even while confined to a single section. But this is to be expected. Other projects almost defy categorization, as one would also expect from a selection of the best recent ideas in the field. Above all, this is a body of design work which, I hope, will intrigue and invite comment; a selection that will inspire architects and designers to create public monuments that are about the future, not the past, and will encourage public sector clients who believe that investment in architectural creativity will yield swift and handsome economic and social returns. ●

1

Grand Statements

Dominique Perrault's Bibliothèque Nationale de France adopts the metaphor of the open book on a grand scale. One of the last of Mitterrand's *grands projets*, it is also one of the most controversial.

Grand statements have been a part of public architecture for as long as public authorities have had the will and the money to build. The imposing town hall, the dominating law court, the stately civic library – these landmarks have been a feature of urban development ever since people began flocking in large numbers from the countryside to the towns over 200 years ago.

But whereas their original purpose was to signal that a city, region, prefecture or state had arrived in terms of wealth and prestige, the 1990s generation of public buildings and interiors are sending a different message. They appear more concerned with travelling hopefully towards a better future, making a grand statement of intent, rather than simply reflecting status or basking in municipal glory.

Indeed, many of the 12 schemes chosen for this section are especially designed to avoid the tradition of monumentalism associated with grand public buildings of the past. Richard Rogers' choice of lightweight-looking stainless-steel drums for the cylindrical court and commission rooms of his expressive European Court of Human Rights at Strasbourg shows the desire to escape the ritualistic pomp and ceremony of the judicial process. In a similar vein, the architects of a new Bonn museum dedicated to the history of the Federal Republic of Germany transcend the intimidating solemnity of its subject matter by turning the building into an urban thoroughfare and flooding it with daylight beneath three glass vaults.

Michael Graves' extension of the Denver Central Library is very much in the tradition of the great American city library institutions that led Andrew Carnegie to declare in 1900: 'I choose free libraries as the best agencies for improving the masses of people ... they only help those who help themselves.' But in scale, geometry and colour, it creates an entirely new composition for Denver's historic city centre, allowing room for growth and change.

Several of the schemes shown here are about reinventing institutions – the Tokyo Tatsumi International Swimming Centre, for instance, recasts the local city swimming baths in a futuristic form – just as they are about remodelling sections of the city. The twin pavilions of James Ingo Freed's much-expanded Los Angeles Convention Center impose light-filled landmarks on the downtown skyline, reinterpreting the tradition of the soaring public room in a new glazed form and reflecting a more general preoccupation among public architects with transparency and with dissolving boundaries between the building and the street. 'To me', says Freed, 'light is the essence of a great public room. If you don't have light, you don't have a great public space.'

The four open-book towers of Dominique Perrault's national library of France similarly impose themselves on the east end of Paris, although this scheme is more ambivalent about transparency. Perrault describes his work as an attempt to 'rediscover emotions built on paradoxes between presence and absence, human and monumental, opaque and luminous'. Three of the projects in this section are French, revealing the country's investment in *grands projets* – from the new east wing of the Cité de la Musique (a spreading mini-city at the entrance of the Parc de la Villette in Paris) to Will Alsop's iconoclastic 'Grand Bleu' town hall at Marseilles. Almost everywhere, it seems, the grand public design statement is still on the agenda, but it has been reinterpreted with certain ironic overtones for an age less certain of the survival of civic values and acutely aware of the speed of social and economic change. ●

The Denver Central Library

Denver, Colorado, USA

Michael Graves has renovated and massively extended Denver's central library, using bold geometry and colour to make a strong statement about the city's forward-thinking civic values.

Design Architect
Michael Graves, Architect
Architect of Record
Klipp Colussy Jenks
DuBois Architects

Interior Designer
Michael Graves, Architect

Client/Commissioning Body
City and County of
Denver Department of
Public Works

Total Floor Space
584,000 square feet

Number of Floors
8

Total Contract Cost
US $48 million

Date of Completion
Autumn 1995

Western Reading Room of the Denver Central Library. The warm focal point is a wooden 'derrick' structure made from reclaimed Oregon timbers. The wood used is a mix of stained plain-sliced, straight-grain maple and curly maple veneers and solids.

View from the south of Michael Graves' massively extended library. A coloured stone rotunda topped with a square crown on copper trusses signals a grand appearance in Denver's Historic District. The external finish is a combination of cast and natural stone, and includes an unusual blue stone, a true dolomite from central Europe called German Anrochter.

A distinctive square crown held by copper trusses on top of a coloured stone rotunda provides a powerful new civic landmark on the skyline of Denver's City Center Historic District. Burnham Hoyt's original Denver central library, built in 1956, has been skilfully renovated and massively extended by Michael Graves in a scheme designed to make an overt statement about Denver's architecture and community. As Graves remarks, 'It's rare that you have a chance to design a significant cultural monument in the heart of a great American city.'

Hoyt's library was only intended to serve for a decade but it was still in use in 1990 when the city fathers decided that urgent action was needed to improve library facilities on the site. Denver has the eighth largest public library collection in the USA but, given the cramped conditions of the original building, only 20 per cent of it was accessible to the public. The brief to Graves was that the revamped and enlarged library should be durable, easy to maintain, and flexible to adjust to future advances in information technology. Also, the existing central library needed to remain functioning while the extension was built in two phases.

Graves approached the project with an accent on bold geometry and colour, clear planning and warm interior finishes. Mindful that he was creating a much larger building, Graves was careful to include many different scales of space, from grand-proportioned gathering and circulation areas to rooms with more human dimensions. The scale and colouring of the 390,000-square foot extension allows the original 150,000-square foot renovated library to maintain its own identity as one element in a larger composition. Hoyt's original building maintains the institution's presence on Civic Center Park while the new-built addition frames it to the south.

Two major public entrances establish an east-west axis through the expanded building and take visitors into a three-storey vaulted Great Hall, the central public room of the building, which provides orientation to the facilities on all levels. Special rooms at the edge of the library provide views of the city and mountains beyond. Internally, typical Graves trademarks can be seen in the soft, warm colours and finishes, from custom-designed carpeting throughout the quiet reading spaces to a 'derrick' structure in the Western History Reading Room made from reclaimed Oregon timbers. A variety of lighting solutions, including warm fluorescents, metal halide, and fixtures built into furniture, ensure that the many different types of space are well lit in ways that are energy efficient.

The public city library has a very special place in America's civic and cultural traditions. In this large, sensitively managed project, Michael Graves has captured that essence without forsaking the future. ●

Above: The main public entrance lobby establishes an east-west axis through the building.
Right: Section across a three-storey atrium looking east.

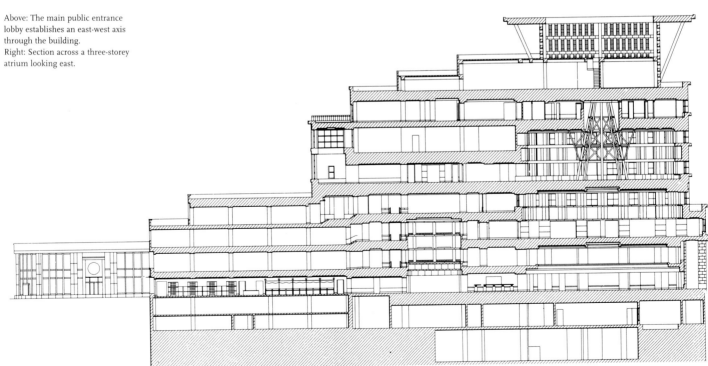

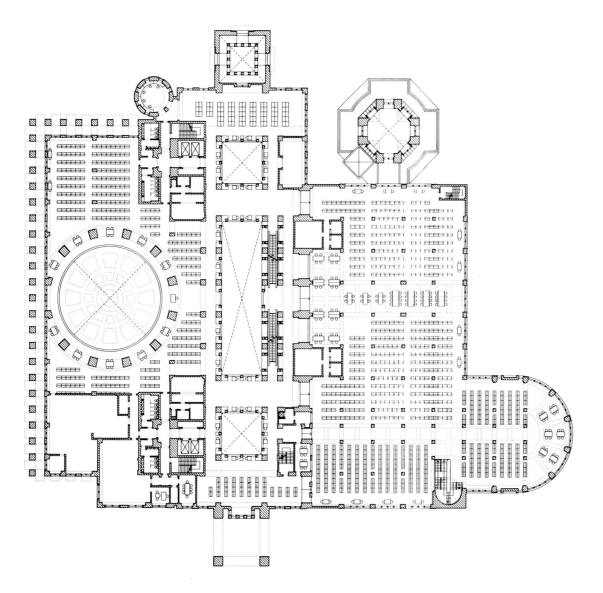

Above: Second-floor plan.
Right: Interior view of the reading rooms at second-floor level. These quiet spaces have custom-designed carpeting and ceilings made of drywall and lay-in acoustic mineralboard panels or fabric-wrapped panels. Lighting is a combination of warm-temperature fluorescent and custom-designed indirect lighting, including some metal halide.

Hôtel du Département des Bouches-du-Rhône

Marseilles, France

Architect
Alsop and Störmer

Interior Designer
Alsop and Störmer/Ecart

Client/Commissioning Body
Conseil Général des Bouches-du-Rhône

Total Floor Space
93,500 square metres

Number of Levels
9

Total Contract Cost
£94 million

Date of Completion
November 1994

'Le Grand Bleu' is the name given to Will Alsop's stunning new seat of local government – a Mediterranean-inspired symbol of renegeration in a rundown area of Marseilles.

View of the Marseilles town hall from the south shows the relationship between the main interconnected administration blocks, topped with an aerofoil structure, and the cigar-shaped assembly hall next door, on the right. The complex presents a composition of spectacular built forms in a rundown area of the city.

Right: The assembly hall interior, designed by Ecart, extends architect Will Alsop's preoccupation with light, symmetry and texture. Below: Cross-section of the competition-winning project.

It has been called the most spectacular town hall in France. British architect Will Alsop's winning scheme to unite all the facilities of the local government of Bouches-du-Rhône in one giant building has created an arresting new civic complex in a rundown area on the outskirts of Marseilles. Its novel, even eccentric matt-blue linear forms signal a special presence beneath the Mediterranean sky, implying, says Alsop, a 'peaceful ambience for a building that will often contain frenetic behaviour'.

Will Alsop beat a field of 156 contenders in an international competition, including an egg-shaped proposal by Sir Norman Foster, to win the career-moulding job. The new centre – designed to withstand wide temperature variations and strong winds in the region – houses 2,000 staff and provides council chambers, restaurants, a library, media centre, sports centre, offices, a crèche, a visitor's centre and parking. Previously, the Bouches-du-Rhône administration was located on 26 different sites.

The external plan is deceptively simple. Two rectangular administration blocks (the *Adminstratif*) sit on double-height X-shaped steel braces; one block has an aerofoil structure on top. They butt up to a cigar-shaped assembly hall (the *Délibératif*) and are joined by bridges and walkways suspended in atria. Inside the skin of the structure, the spatial relationships are rich and complex. Straightforward use of simple materials – concrete, glass, timber and steel – and utilization of low-cost technologies belie the sophistication of an interior environment conceived on a city scale. The vast entrance floor, for example, has newspaper, tobacco and coffee shops for visitors. A cathedral-like atrium between the two main administration blocks actively moderates the internal climate.

Ecart of Paris collaborated with the architects on carrying key architectural themes – the Mediterranean, symmetry and light – through to the interior design. Ecart's use of oak or mahogany panels, blue enamel, polished metal and mosquito-net blinds reinforces the texture and legibility of Alsop's virtuoso approach. On a difficult site that required the complex to be constructed over an existing metro station, the building has become a local cultural landmark, nicknamed *'Le Grand Bleu'*. Alsop's sheer energy and invention has created a stunning public environment which, for all its seemingly wilful shape-making, is also a rational and comfortable place to be. ●

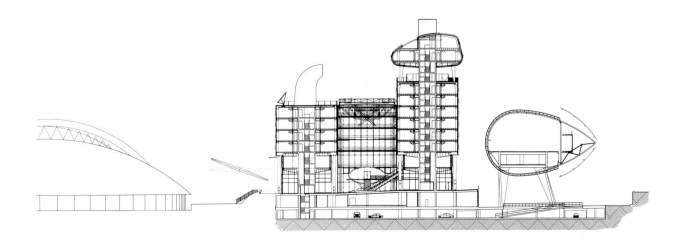

The town hall conceived as a mini-city. The bridges across the large central atrium link the two main administration blocks. The robust double-height X-braces are both an internal and an external motif.

Below: The town hall from the east. The clear blue of the Mediterranean and the white canvas of the deck chair influenced Will Alsop's approach to a landmark public building affectionately nicknamed '*Le Grand Bleu*' by the locals.

Right: Futuristic glass walkways connect the *Administratif* to the *Délibératif* – the cigar-shaped assembly hall – in a scheme of immense imaginative power. The regional authority previously occupied 26 different sites.

Suntory Museum

Osaka, Japan

Architect
Tadao Ando Architect
& Associates

Interior Designer
Tadao Ando Architect
& Associates

Client/Commissioning Body
Suntory Co.

Total Floor Space
13,804 square metres

Number of Floors
10

Date of Completion
October 1994

> Tadao Ando has created a striking seafront museum that symbolizes the tension between culture and nature in the way it reaches literally to the water's edge.

1.3

Inside the main conical drum structure of the museum, the skin of the spherical IMAX theatre can be seen – an autonomous object within the vaulted space.

Aerial view of Tadao Ando's Suntory Museum scheme. The main complex – a conical drum penetrated at different angles by two water-facing rectangular blocks, a restaurant and a gallery – is connected to the sea by a stepped plaza.

View of the sea from a museum that is physically and symbolically anchored to the shore of the waterfront. The monumental pillars on the breakwater echo the line at the water's edge on the plaza.

Built as a result of a pioneering three-way collaboration between the city authority, a private developer and a national body, Osaka's Suntory Museum is defined by its waterfront location and its relationship with the sea. Architect Tadao Ando, a favourite son of Osaka, has used the project as a vehicle to reconnect contemporary life with the waterways, which once played such an important and dynamic role in the affairs of Osaka that the city was known as 'water town'.

Ando has designed his museum as an integrated structure with a stepped plaza, 100 metres long and 40 metres across, descending right down to the water's edge. In Ando's thinking, the steps are seats for an audience and the sea is the stage. Instead of physically distancing the two elements – people and water – with a barrier, he has sought to unite them. Five monumental pillars arranged at the waterfront are repeated by the architect on a breakwater 70 metres from the shore, reinforcing this continuity between plaza and ocean.

There are also uninterrupted views of the sea from the giant inverted conical drum at the heart of the scheme. This houses a circular IMAX theatre, 32 metres in diameter. At the top of the drum, where there is an observation platform, the diameter reaches 48 metres. In Ando's simple plan, this drum-like volume is penetrated by two sea-facing rectangular buildings – one a restaurant, the other a gallery. All three elements of the project are linked by walkways. Ando describes the collision between two rectangles and the inverted cone within a standard planning grid as a physical representation of the clash of energy between culture and nature embodied in this scheme.

But for all the bold geometric form-giving of its steel-and-concrete building elements, the Suntory Museum's spirit resides in front of the complex on the broad seafront plaza where the steps are arranged at one point into a semi-circular amphitheatre. 'At this theatre we enjoy the salt breeze, the motion of the tides, the sun sinking in the ocean, the people who have gathered,' says Ando rhapsodically, reminding us both of Osaka's waterfront traditions and of the formal eloquence of his own concept. ●

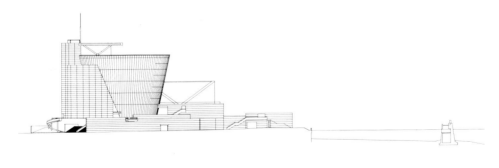

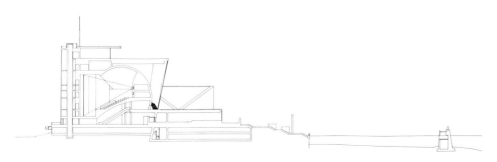

Above left: Elevation. Left: Section through the Suntory Museum showing the circular IMAX theatre within the giant inverted conical drum.

Kunstmuseum

Wolfsburg, Germany

Architect
Architekten Schweger & Partner

Interior Designer
Architekten Schweger & Partner

Client/Commissioning Body
Kunstiftung Volkswagen

Total Floor Space
8,510 square metres

Number of Floors
2

Total Contract Cost
£158.9 million

Date of Completion
May 1994

Wolfsburg, home to the industry of Volkswagen, has a restrained, intelligent new art museum that acts as a southern gateway to the city in its open gallery form.

The art museum as 'urban loggia'. Architects Schweger & Partner have designed the museum as the new southern gateway to the city. The granite of the main foyer extends to the piazza outside. The distinctive overhanging roof is a grate-like steel truss supported by steel columns and reinforced concrete.

Beneath the engineered embrace of the overhanging steel-truss roof, ramps and walkways give the building a machine-like aesthetic, reflecting the industrial patronage of Volkswagen, Wolfsburg's major employer.

The city of Wolfsburg has long been a symbol of the strength of postwar German manufacturing due to its close ties with its major employer, Volkswagen. Fittingly, the city's new Art Museum was commissioned and paid for by Volkswagen, reflecting the company's belief that where there is industry there must also be art. The museum joins an urban centre already distinguished by two outstanding architectural contributions – Alvar Aalto's 1962 cultural centre and Hans Scharoun's 1973 theatre. But the newcomer has an important role to play as a southern gateway to the heart of a city that is in the process of being remodelled with an extended town hall.

Consequently the museum has been conceived, in the words of its architects, 'as a kind of urban loggia', an open gallery that marks the entrance to the city. Its most distinctive feature – a wide, dominating roof structure – spans a range of activities and a composition of simple volumes in a way that immediately commands attention.

This roof, a grate-like steel truss supported by steel columns and reinforced concrete, projects an uncompromising machine-like aesthetic common in many of Germany's newer public and cultural buildings. Internal catwalks, bridges and railings, designed as lightweight steel structures, continue the theme, just as the granite floor of the main foyer is a continuation of the piazza outside.

But the overall severity of the building design is mitigated by the softening influence of a daylighting strategy. This uses multilayer glazing in conjuction with a new sunscreen grid, consisting of plastic surfaces vapour-coated with pure aluminium, to reflect sunlight and minimize glare. Complementary artificial lighting is similarly inventive, especially in illuminating artworks.

The entrance rotunda and lobby areas of Wolfsburg's Art Museum, which has been designed by Professor Peter Schweger with Franz Wöhler, Hartmut H. Reifenstein, Bernhard Kohl and Wolfgang Schneider, are among its most successful spaces. They comprise a flexible, transparent zone opening on to a sculpture court that gives a view of the main top-lit, wooden-floored exhibition hall up and beyond. Spatial flexibility has been a keynote of the scheme, giving the museum curators a wide range of options in staging events. The facilities also include smaller galleries, a café, design studio, workshops, service and storage areas.

This cool, functional, carefully arranged building is dedicated to art, but in form and detail it is more expressive as a model of industry. It may indeed succeed in making a strong statement over the vista of central Wolfsburg as architect and client intended, but the gesture is one of restraint, not celebration. Perhaps given Volkswagen's recent problems and the ending of the German economic miracle at Wolfsburg, that is only appropriate. ●

Left: The main lobby area, which opens on to a sculpture court. The hard interior surfaces are bathed in warm halogen light.

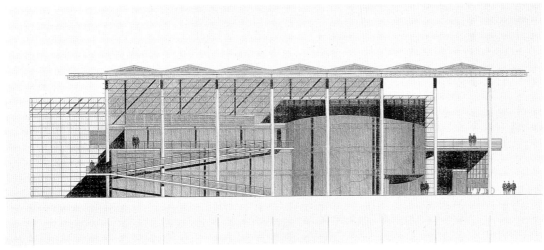

Above: The Kunstmuseum's entrance rotunda, a flexible, transparent zone that is part of a scheme designed to give the museum curators at Wolfsburg maximum flexibility.
Left: The drawing shows a view from the east.

Bibliothèque Nationale de France

Paris, France

Architect
Dominique Perrault

Client/Commissioning Body
Ministry of Culture
Secretariat d'Etat aux Grands Travaux
Bibliothèque Nationale de France

Total Floor Space
8,510 square metres

Number of Floors
20 in each tower

Total Contract Cost
£693 million

Date of Completion
March 1995

Four glass towers shaped like open books surround a sunken garden plaza in Dominique Perrault's audacious and highly controversial new library in the industrial east end of Paris.

Public interiors in the research reading rooms project a warmth and intimacy in finish without losing the vastness of scale on which the library has been built. Much of the lighting and detailing has been custom-designed for the scheme using a limited palette of materials – wood, glass, raw concrete, metallic fabric – in strikingly imaginative ways.

Right: Four giant open books face each other across a vast rectangular garden in Dominique Perrault's controversial scheme, their composition a focal point in the proposed regeneration of the entire 13th arrondissement of Paris. Below: The plan shows the four 'open book' towers at the corners of the rectangle enclosing the garden, which is 28,680 square metres.

While the new British Library in London has been a sorry 30-year saga of muddle and delay, Dominique Perrault's new national library of France reveals the faster track on which Parisian public monuments are built. It took just seven years to complete the building – less time than it took to decide where the British Library should even be located. But speed of action has not made Perrault's *tour de force* any more palatable to its critics.

The Bibliothèque Nationale de France is perhaps the most controversial of Mitterrand's *grands projets*. The competition-winning work of one of France's new generation of architects (Perrault was just 35 when he was chosen) reflects the former president's penchant for the simplistic modernist geometry of object-architecture.

The core idea is of four giant open books facing each other across a vast rectangular garden plaza which is enclosed by their forms. But the sketch-like caricature of this basic premise and the thought of storing the nation's cultural treasures in four 60s-style modern glass towers immediately appalled many academics, who lobbied for the project to be halted and demanded a more sophisticated approach and human scale to the library design.

What appeared to make matters worse was that Perrault's original competition entry specified that the books should be stored underground and his aestheticized glass towers should house administration. But the built scheme partially reverses this layout, and the original idea of developing ultraviolet-resistant glass to filter out sunlight from the towers has also been

dropped. The books in the four giant stacks or silos are now shaded by wooden shutters that make the open-book-form architecture opaque rather than transparent, as first intended.

The architect robustly defends the scheme, arguing that it is a deliberate and human response to its context. Built on a stretch of industrial wasteland on the banks of the Seine in the east end of Paris, the library has been conceived as a rallying point for plans to completely restructure the entire 13th arrondissement. And the monumental impact of the four towers is undeniably softened by those wooden shutters, a wooden esplanade, warm interior tones and, above all, the sunken inlaid garden at the kernel of the project. Planted with 250 trees, this cloisterlike courtyard is surrounded by a number of thematic libraries that are glassed-in on the garden side. These libraries are located on several mezzanine levels within a very tall volumetric space and are serviced from the reading stacks in the towers via a flexible circulation network.

The overall result is a gigantic scheme of technical accomplishment, which has both the simplicity and complexity of an abstract piece of modern art. Significantly, in his interplay between glass, metallic fabric, raw concrete and wood, Perrault acknowledges that the influence of such minimalist artists as Donald Judd is as great as that of modernist architects like Kahn or Corbusier. ●

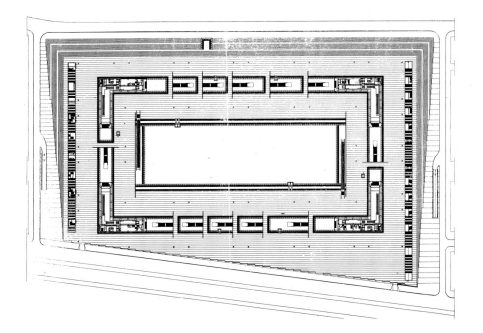

The section shows the formal composition of the scheme. The towers rise 79 metres above the esplanade. Perrault describes his design as creating 'a library for France, a square for Paris'.

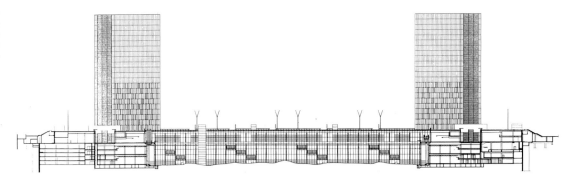

The research library opens out on to the cloister-like garden. Warm interior finishes moderate the more austere external effect of the monumental glass towers.

Right: Minimalist art is as great an influence as modern architecture in Perrault's grand design. Low-tech wooden shutters screen out sunlight, turning the four towers into a complex dialogue between transparency and opacity.

City Theatre De Harmonie

Leeuwarden, The Netherlands

Architect
de Architekten Cie

Client/Commissioning Body
Leeuwarden City Council

Total Floor Space
12,000 square metres

Number of Levels
3

Total Contract Cost
£11.6 million

Date of Completion
1994

A Dutch municipal theatre makes a grand, generous gesture to the surrounding city by presenting its dynamic interior arrangement of three stepped auditoria for public viewing.

The upper-level foyer of the City Theatre De Harmonie; its blue service element provides a buffer within the public space. The project has been designed by architect Frits van Dongen as a 'three-dimensional zoning system'.

The new canal-side municipal theatre for the city of Leeuwarden is described by its architect, Frits van Dongen of de Architekten Cie, as 'an urban decor, a translucent peep show'. That is because its giant frosted-glass façade on one side of the building allows views into and through the theatre. The design reflects the way a theatrical atmosphere has seeped from the three main auditoria into the adjoining public areas.

The theatre was constructed on the site of the old Harmonie building, a gentleman's club built in 1881. Van Dongen won the commission in competition with Pi de Bruijn, a rival architect ironically from the same practice. The original brief called for a 125-year-old plane tree to be preserved on the site, forcing the architects to create complex plans that kept a reverent distance around the old tree. But van Dongen argued successfully for the tree to be removed and he was therefore able to develop a much simpler, more transparent design on the site, with the west elevation (containing the main oval entrance foyer) fronting on to the canal in a very expressive manner. This scheme won him the project.

Along the entire southern length of the building, there is a service strip fronted by a closed orange brick elevation, which includes side stages, offices, artists' foyers, lifts and emergency stairwells. Running adjacent to this along the northern length of the theatre is the broader public zone. This is fronted by the semi-transparent façade, which is perforated in places so that striking elements of the dynamic interior are visible.

The Theatre De Harmonie has three halls, all different in character, with the second suspended four metres above the first and the third stacked four metres above the second. The spaces beneath serve as public foyers. The main hall, an elegant, clean-lined, modern theatre, seats 920. The second hall, designed for all sorts of performances (from pop concerts to chamber music), seats 450 and has standing room for 1,100; its floors and ceiling are clad entirely in steel. The third hall, at the canal end of the building, is a wooden-walled 'black-box' auditorium seating 350.

Frits van Dongen describes his scheme as 'a three-dimensional zoning system': the

An exterior view shows the transparent north and west elevations of the theatre building. The main oval entrance foyer at the corner looks west on to the canal.

vertical stepping of the three auditoria is complemented by the differentiation between the service and public strips along the length of the theatre and the way support functions act as buffers between spaces across its width. Clever in over-arching concept it may be, but the main impression of the Theatre De Harmonie is in its more abstract spatial quality, especially those grand, sweeping vistas through warm, inviting foyers. The real action begins before you even take your seat. ●

Left: Exterior and interior boundaries are dissolved by the use of light, glass and fluent, layered structure in the City Theatre De Harmonie.
Below: The section through the building shows the stacked formation of the three main auditoria.

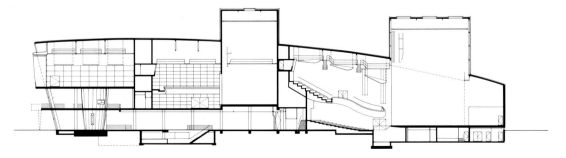

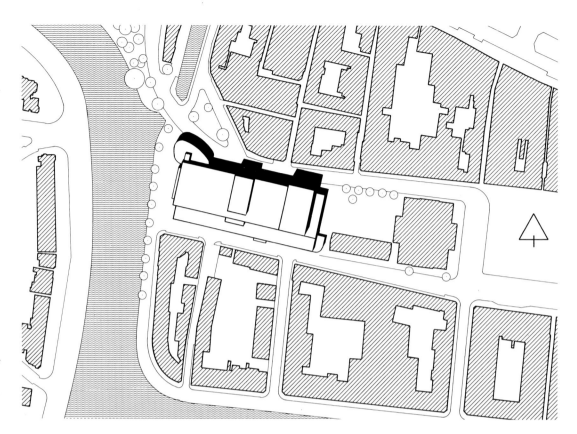

Right: The site plan shows the theatre in its canal-side setting.
Below: In the main auditorium, which seats 920 people, sensual light baffles lend an ethereal air to a curvaceous, clean-lined hall.

Los Angeles Convention Center Expansion

Los Angeles, California, USA

Architect
Pei Cobb Freed
& Partners

Client/Commissioning Body
Los Angeles Convention
& Exhibition Center
Authority

Total Floor Space
2.5 million square feet

Date of Completion
November 1993

James Ingo Freed's skilful extension, marked by two linked, luminous glass towers, at last gives the city of Los Angeles the powerfully articulated public convention centre it deserves.

The dramatic entrance pavilion reintroduces the concept of the grand, soaring, light-filled urban room to the city of Los Angeles.

An aerial view of a new Los Angeles landmark. The twin pavilion towers of the scheme resemble a pair of rocket launch sites at night. Substantial expansion has been achieved without sacrificing a human scale.

Two soaring glass-and-steel towers signal the substantial expansion of the Los Angeles Convention Center, giving the city a notable new landmark that at night presents the compelling image of a pair of luminous NASA launch sites. The towers are the new west and south pavilions of the enlarged complex, which unites the existing west exhibit hall – built in 1971 – with a vast new curved south exhibit hall. The twin towers are connected by a meeting room bridge, 615 feet in length, that serves the critical role of uniting the entire scheme.

Architect James Ingo Freed of Pei Cobb Freed & Partners, who also designed the all-glass Javits Convention Center in New York, has pulled off a spectacular coup on an awkward piano-shaped site hemmed in by streets and freeways, and bisected north to south by a boulevard. The Los Angeles Convention Center's existing facilities, with its piecemeal enlargements, was so inadequate that the city had dropped to 27th in the league table of American convention centres, consequently missing out on millions of dollars of business. But the expansion posed enormous problems. How could the convention centre be enlarged half-a-mile across the 63-acre site, still function as an integrated whole, and remain human in scale?

Freed's answer was to allow the urban context to give the expanded complex its form, and to develop a common architectural language for the old and new elements of the project. The south and west lobby towers open off a five-acre public plaza planted with 40 mature palm trees. The meeting room bridge links these two impressive pavilions and spans that troublesome boulevard on columns. It contains day-lit walkways, a giant 26,500-square foot hall, a business and retail centre, and a series of flexible meeting rooms. The new exhibition hall itself is a vast 347,000-square foot space designed to be flexibly subdivided to accommodate a wide range of large and small events.

What distinguishes the scheme – its giant prefabricated curtain-wall system expressed with simple geometric discipline – is the way it creates a sense of dynamic movement internally and articulates a sense of place externally in an otherwise unremarkable, low-rise, largely unmodulated downtown area of Los Angeles. In particular, the twin towers reintroduce the tradition of the great urban room to the city with their breathtaking, light-filled public welcome. ●

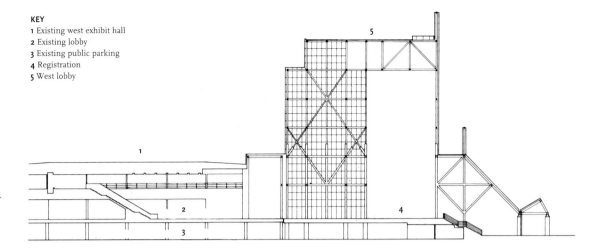

KEY
1 Existing west exhibit hall
2 Existing lobby
3 Existing public parking
4 Registration
5 West lobby

Below: Inside the meeting room bridge. This is the pivotal element of the scheme, linking the south and west pavilions and spanning a boulevard that problematically cuts north to south through the site. Apart from a daylit walkway, the bridge also inventively contains meeting rooms and a business and retail centre. Right: Elevation.

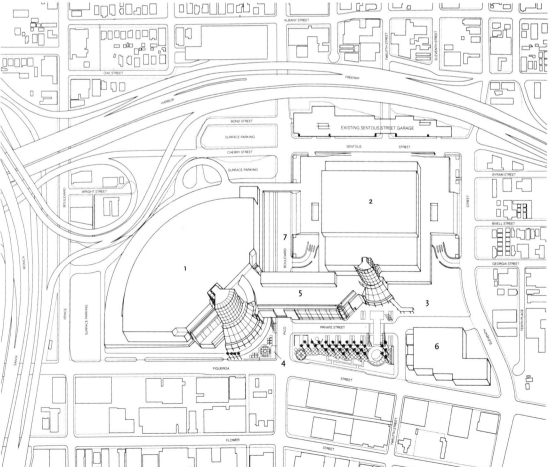

The west pavilion tower, which opens on to a five-acre public plaza planted with mature palm trees. Architect James Ingo Freed has kept the needs and perceptions of users very much in mind.

The site plan shows the south and west lobby towers within the greatly expanded scheme. These two focal points are linked by the meeting room bridge spanning Pico Boulevard, which runs north to south.

KEY
1 New South Exhibit Hall
2 Existing West Exhibit Hall
3 West Lobby
4 South Lobby
5 Meeting Room Bridge
6 Existing North Exhibit Hall
7 Pico Boulevard

1.8 European Court of Human Rights

Strasbourg, France

Architect
Richard Rogers
Partnership

Client/Commissioning Body
Council of Europe

Total Floor Space
28,000 square metres

Number of Levels
6

Total Contract Cost
£61 million

Date of Completion
June 1995

Two steel cylinders at the head of Richard Rogers' expressive scheme for the European Court of Human Rights reflect the 'transparency of justice' on a green river-bank site.

Richard Rogers' European Court of Human Rights avoids the traditional monumentality associated with such buildings by inserting a circular transparent entrance hall between two symbolic, light-steel drums. The Commission Room is on the left, the Court Room on the right.

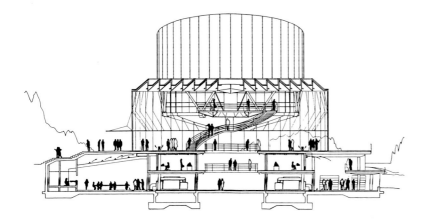

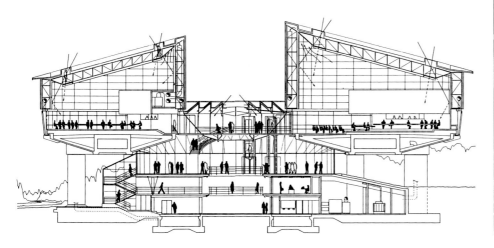

Richard Rogers describes his new European Court of Human Rights complex as 'an open, transparent building that expresses a desire for the transparency of justice'. Its site on the green banks of a majestic curve in the River Ill was a powerful factor in determining the building's form, which was designed in two legible parts to fit its context and requirements.

A large glass-and-stainless steel 'head' containing the building's public functions – the cylindrical court and commission room – is supported by a 'tail' of naturally ventilated administrative offices, which taper away down the site in two curved wings enclosing a courtyard and water cascade. Between the bold expression of the drum-like 'head' and the more serene taper of the double-pronged administrative 'tail', a 'neck' comprising two central chambers completes the plan.

Rogers was determined to avoid the traditional monumentalism associated with *palais de justice*. To make the building more light and accessible, he inserted a circular transparent entrance hall between the two symbolic cylinders at the head of his scheme. These industrial drums, clad in satin-finished stainless steel, were the subject of extensive testing and prototyping to develop a design that optimized the strength of the material while ensuring a low-maintenance uniform satin finish. One can only admire the way Rogers has managed to create a time-honoured sense of the dignity and power of justice in a fragile natural environment without any moderation of his famous commitment to an industrial high-tech language.

The measured response to the landscape is an important factor in this, expressed in the formal cascade between the office wings and the parkland. Rogers talks of the way his expressive cylinders absorb and reflect 'the drama of the environment, sunlight, shadow, rain and wind'. Planting along the river elevation of the office 'tail', in front of opening windows and blinds, enhances this effect. This is also a building designed to meet changing requirements. Even during construction, Rogers extended facilities to accommodate new member countries joining the 34-nation Council of Europe. The result is an essay on structure and nature that gives the institution, and the city of Strasbourg, an important new civic landmark. ●

Left: The approach to the entrance hall at the 'head' of the scheme. Rogers' use of the high-tech vocabulary of glass and satin-finished stainless steel represents his effort to show 'the transparency of justice'.

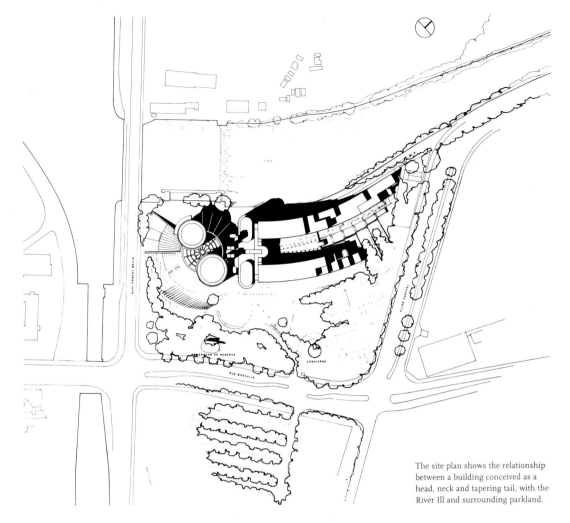

A view of the European Court of Human Rights from the opposite bank of the River Ill shows the grand drum-like head, the bulging neck that comprises the central chambers and the more serene waterside taper of the administrative offices. The entire complex demonstrates a sensitive response to its environment in massing and planting, and is naturally ventilated and cooled.

The site plan shows the relationship between a building conceived as a head, neck and tapering tail, with the River Ill and surrounding parkland.

Light-filled space bespeaks dignity and modernity inside the drum of the main Court Room, which aims to uphold citizens' rights within the new Europe. Vaclav Havel, president of the Czech Republic, officially opened the building.

Left and right: Views of the entrance hall reveal a dialogue in structure and transparency in the building, which took three years to complete.

Tokyo Edo Museum

Tokyo, Japan

Architect
Kiyonori Kikutake

Client/Commissioning Body
Tokyo Metropolitan Government

Total Floor Space
48,000 square metres

Number of Levels
7 storeys, 1-storey penthouse, 1 basement

Total Contract Cost
US $382 million

Date of Completion
March 1993

Hovering above the city on four giant stilts, Kiyonori Kikutake's new museum dedicated to the artefacts of the Tokyo Edo period is a feat of construction on an earthquake-prone site.

The vast main plaza sheltering beneath the giant elevated structure of the Tokyo Edo Museum. A dramatic red escalator pierces the underbelly of the structure.

Kiyonori Kikutake's Tokyo Edo Museum hovers above the urban landscape on four thick legs, its vast form resembling a giant boot over the city or a descending space station. Even in a country increasingly renowned for the audacious scale of its public buildings, this new structure dwarfs all around it. Yet its shape is historic, deriving from the Edo period in Japanese culture, which lasted about 400 years; the museum itself is dedicated to exhibiting artefacts from that period in Tokyo. The milky-pearl external cladding panels even give the impression of Japanese armour.

Built on the east side of the Sumida River in Tokyo next to a sumo theatre, the museum was a feat of construction. Weak soil required strengthened foundations, and the wide span of the distinctive overhanging roof necessitated the use of an iron framework. The external cladding was realized in light cement (with carbon fibres for high durability and ease of maintenance) rather than in metal as originally intended because of the salty climate and the dust and grit thrown up by a neighbouring railway.

The fourth-floor exhibition hall, where the most valuable exhibits are displayed, has been fitted out with stabilizing devices to withstand earthquake tremors. Mindful of the potential for quake damage (the museum is on the site of the 1927 Kanto earthquake in which 70,000 people died), an open atrium on the third floor also doubles as a disaster shelter. This third-floor level – known as Edo Tokyo Hiroba – is sandwiched between the permanent exhibition hall above and a temporary exhibition space, offices and entrance hall below. It is a pivotal area in the scheme, 18,800 square metres in size, and designed to stage a variety of events.

The elevated building sits above a public plaza enlivened by a set of soft-form canopies that glow at night and a red escalator that pierces the underbelly of the museum. The building actually has three entrance points on three sides for vehicles, rail passengers, and people arriving via a planned underground station, but only one exit – at ground floor level where a restaurant, museum shop and rest areas are located.

The architect has ambitious plans to redevelop the area around his new museum, including reinserting historic canals to connect to the river and creating a public park with car parking hidden beneath. But Kiyonori Kikutake's building is already a very significant monument to the Tokyo Edo period – vast in conception, surprisingly deft in touch. ●

One of three side entrances to the museum scheme. The construction of the building on giant stilts takes into account the danger of earthquakes in the locality.

The soft glow of the public canopies in the Edo-Tokyo plaza beneath the museum, which stages a variety of public events.

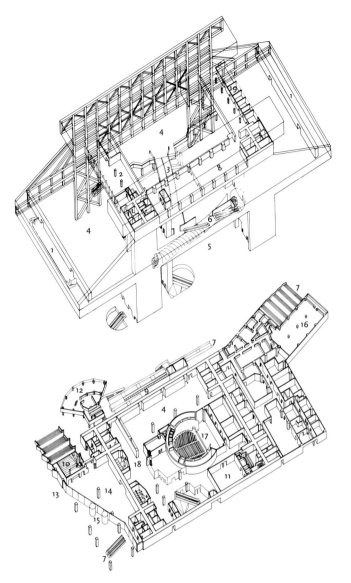

Axonometric

1 Observatory
2 Restaurant
3 Nihonbashi, the surrounding town
4 Exhibition room
5 Edo-Tokyo Plaza
6 Entry escalator
7 Entrance
8 Information library
9 Museum shop
10 Video hall
11 Small exhibition hall
12 Restaurant
13 Porch
14 Entrance hall
15 Main entrance
16 Office
17 Grand hall
18 Exhibition lobby
19 Meeting room

An aerial view from the south shows the massive scale of the Tokyo Edo Museum in relation to the rest of the city. It resembles a giant boot hovering over the urban landscape, yet its shape is historic and its milky-pearl exterior cladding evokes ancient Japanese armour.

1.10

Museum of the History of the Federal Republic of Germany

Bonn, Germany

Architect
Architekten BDA
Hartmut and Ingeborg
Rüdiger

Interior Designer
Architekten BDA
Hartmut and Ingeborg
Rüdiger

Client/Commissioning Body
Federal Republic of
Germany

Total Floor Space
22,200 square metres

Number of Levels
5

Total Contract Cost
£52.6 million

Date of Completion
June 1994

In a museum dedicated to the history of the Federal Republic of Germany the architects avoid making a grandiose statement by opening the building out to the street beneath three innovative glass vaults.

The façade is clad in beige granite. Monumental massing in the museum, which is dedicated to the history of the Federal Republic of Germany, is avoided by the use of large glazed areas and three innovative glass roof vaults.

A view of the vaulted glass roof, which uses a new laminated glass plate specially developed for the museum to maximize the benefits of natural lighting and eliminate the harmful effects of the sun on exhibits.

Architectural couple Hartmut and Ingeborg Rüdiger have pulled off a notable coup with their first major project. This 'House of History' commission from the Federal Republic of Germany has a symbolic significance usually reserved for architects with far greater experience. However, there is virtue in the freshly minted approach of the Rüdigers, who were winners of an open competition. They have avoided anything that would make the museum, which is dedicated to the history of the Federal Republic, solemn or monumental. Instead, beneath three innovative vaulted glass roofs, they have sought to create an environment that attracts rather than intimidates.

An expansive glass façade along the front of the building encourages passers-by to step inside the curved foyer area, which features a giant video screen and is conceived as part of an urban thoroughfare so that exterior and interior separations are dissolved. Paths through five large, day-lit museum exhibition halls are an extension of this public space.

An emphasis throughout on daylighting, developed with the Austrian lighting designer Christian Bartenbach, supports this open strategy. A special technological solution in the form of a new laminated glass plate was developed for the museum's extensive glazing to maximize the benefits of natural lighting and eliminate the harmful effects of rays on museum exhibits. Careful choice of materials was also influential. Natural concrete is used for the foyer, as well as for ramps, walkways and bridges that connect the different levels of the building; walls are clad in beige granite.

The Germans bestow a special onus on their museums, investing in them the responsibility for defining the image and expressing the values of their cities and regions. Bonn's new Museum of History does not shirk this challenge, although its response is much lighter and less dogmatic than those of some of its predecessors. Interestingly, the building sits just a few hundred metres away from the Bonn Art Museum and Exhibition Hall complex, which has a very different architectural language. The contrast is instructive. ●

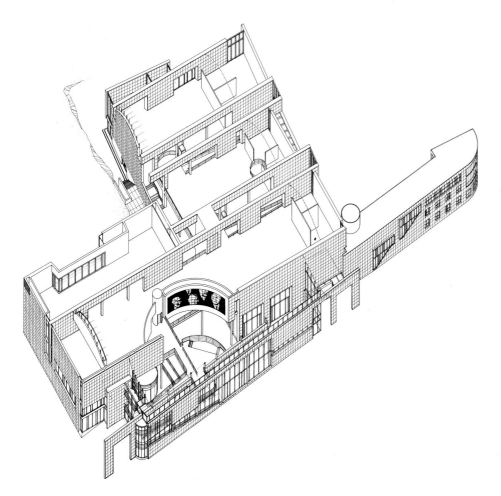

The axonometric reveals the expansive glass façade at the front of the building, opening into a curved foyer area. From there, paths through five large exhibition spaces create a gradual progression in Hartmut and Ingeborg Rüdiger's competition-winning design.

Left: The main foyer area, with its giant video screen and predominant use of untreated concrete finish. The architects have managed to avoid solemn or intimidating gestures without trivializing the museum's subject matter.

The perspective of the foyer areas reveals the openness of the interior plan.

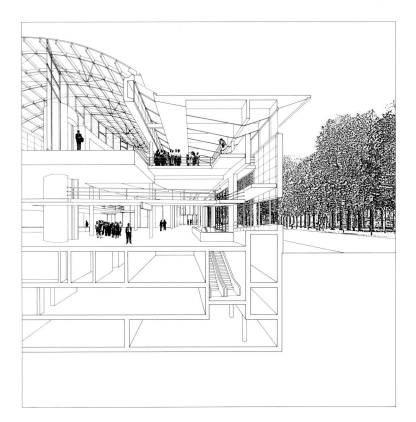

Above: The three vaulted glass roofs of the Museum of History signal its undogmatic presence on the Bonn skyline. Its expressive form sits near the distinctive cones of the Bonn Art Museum complex, at right.

1.11

East Wing of the Cité de la Musique

Parc de la Villette, Paris, France

Architect
Christian de Portzamparc

Interior Designer
Christian de Portzamparc

Client/Commissioning Body
Etablissement Public du Parc de la Villette

Total Floor Space
45,000 square metres

Total Contract Cost
£68.3 million

Date of Completion
1995

The new East Wing of a unique national complex devoted to music and dance is conceived as a miniature French city with an unfolding sequence of streets and spaces.

The main entrance to the East Wing of the Cité de la Musique. A grand, sweeping gesture in a scheme envisaged by architect Christian de Portzamparc as a 'mini-city' dedicated to music and dance through which the visitor makes a narrative journey.

View of the East Wing on its Parc de la Villette site in Paris. At its core is the ellipse-shaped concert hall. This is connected to other spaces in the scheme by a horn-shaped glass-covered foyer section that wraps around it.

At the vast southern entrance to Parc de la Villette in Paris, Christian de Portzamparc's west wing of the Cité de la Musique – completed in 1990, with its great white wave-form façade on avenue Jean Jaures – today has a worthy counterpart to the east, designed by the same architect. The new east wing of this unique national complex devoted to music and dance contains all the areas open to the public – concert halls, practice rooms and a museum of instruments – whereas the west wing is reserved for teaching and performance spaces.

The two wings are deliberately very different in character. The west wing tightly borders an avenue; the east wing opens on to the park with a freer, geometric design. Between them is the Grand Hall, but the dynamic asymmetric axis between the two wings avoids making this too emphatically the focus of attention. The west wing houses a single institution, the National Conservatory of Music and Dance, but the newer east wing comprises a series of diverse facilities, including a magnificent amphitheatre, rehearsal rooms, music shops, a teaching institute and student residences. These, explains the architect, are 'unified in a miniature city composed of varied spaces through which one can stroll'.

The main concert hall of the east wing seats up to 1,200 people and is in the shape of an ellipse inscribed within the overall triangular plan of the new development. From its coiled spiral form emerges a long glass-covered 'horn'-shaped foyer section, which connects to the museum of instruments and enables a number of associated spaces to unfold concentrically around it. The entire length of the east wing can be traversed along a metal-beamed promenade that gives access to a museum of music and reinforces the architect's core idea of creating a real living city with buildings and streets within the envelope of the complex. Interior spaces are articulated to frame a series of unexpected vistas, with meeting and circulation spaces either encased in glass or open to the skies.

In harmonic counterpoint to its elder cousin to the west, the new Cité East reflects de Portzamparc's interest in building a narrative journey through architectural space – complete with sequences, ruptures and discoveries – that is similar to a piece of music with its own narrative intention and duration. ●

The site plan shows the relationship between the East and West Wings of the Cité de la Musique, both designed by de Portzamparc, at the southern entrance to Parc de la Villette. The new, freer-flowing, triangular-shaped East Wing sits at an angle to the earlier West Wing, which tightly borders an avenue. A Grand Hall sits between them.

Concert hall interior. The magnificent alcove lighting strategy enhances the general theme of landmark 'mini-city' elements within the overall building envelope.

The exploded axonometric shows how the scheme fits together. The complex is traversed by a long, metal-beamed promenade that unites the many varied spaces to create a coherent whole for the visitor to pass through. Some areas are encased in glass, others are open to the skies.

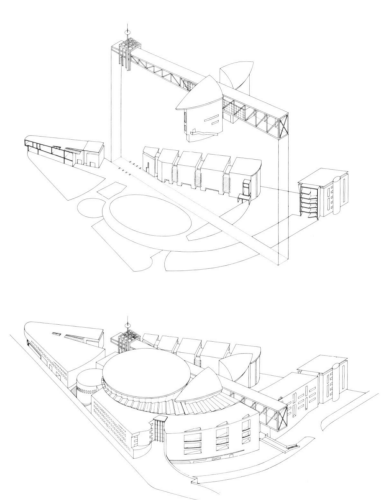

Internal street in the East Wing of the Cité de la Musique – a generous skylit foyer passage that unfolds in a spiral around the main concert hall and links to other spaces.

Tokyo Tatsumi International Swimming Centre

Tokyo, Japan

Architect
Mitsuru Man Senda &
Environment Design
Institute

Interior Designer
Mitsuru Man Senda &
Environment Design
Institute

**Client/Commissioning
Body**
Tokyo Metropolitan
Government

Total Floor Space
22,319 square metres

Number of Floors
5 (including 2
underground)

Total Contract Cost
US $187 million

Date of Completion
March 1993

Conceived as a water fowl flapping its wings on the Tokyo seafront, this grand swimming centre combines technology and theatre to create a memorable experience for visitors.

The municipal swimming baths redefined. This international swimming centre combines the application of science with a sense of theatre. Even the water-treatment system has been redesigned to minimize the odour and colour of chlorine.

The exterior view of the swiming centre's truss-structure roofline suggests a giant seabird at the water's edge about to take flight. The architects deliberately conceived the building as a local landmark that is highly visible from the road and rail routes that traverse the site.

Built along the Tokyo waterfront close to Tatsumi Park on the reclaimed land of Fukagawa, where the city's timber dealers once gathered, this vast swimming centre takes the image of a giant seabird flapping its wings at the water's edge, about soar into flight. The site is bordered to the south by a highway and to the east by an elevated railway, but the exterior form of the complex is quite unrestrained in expression. The architect deliberately set out to make the building a local landmark to orient drivers on the highway, and as transparent as possible so that its activities would be visible at night to rail travellers.

A particular condition of the brief was that the centre should be enjoyable and pleasant for children, but it also needed to host international competitions. Beneath overlapping vaulted roofs sitting on a three-dimensional truss structure, the complex is laid out in a way designed to make rotational circulation as safe and as interesting as possible. Next to the main pool, a sub-pool at a lower level offers an open space with a wooden deck in a sun trap for families to splash about. The lighting programme especially addresses the issues of warmth, colour and gentleness in an environment largely populated by semi-naked people.

This is a most high-tech facility, which combines the application of science with more than a dash of theatre. Wide-screen television has been installed in the main events auditorium which seats 3,500 people. The main pool has an adjustable bottom so that the depth can vary from 1.4 to 2 metres. High-speed, ceiling-mounted video cameras and a moving monorail camera assist competition judges. The complex is heated by energy from a local waste incinerator. Even the water treatment system is innovative, reducing the smell and colour of chlorine.

The architects describe their approach as 'environmental architecture', and one can see their point. External symbolism and interior functions have been married in this swimming centre in a way that is exceptional in clarity, invention and appeal. ●

Section
1 Main pool
2 Machine room
3 Wide video screen
4 Spectators' seats
5 Small swimming pool
6 Gymnasium

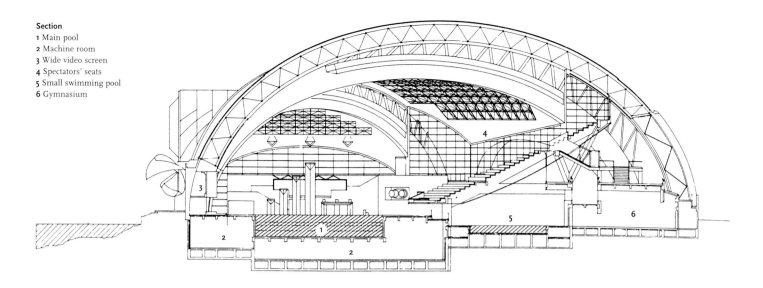

View of the main pool area,
showing the scale of the scheme.
The depth of the pool is adjustable
from 1.4 to 2 metres.

Above: The wide-screen television shows the competitors in action in the main events auditorium.

The froglike south elevation reveals the organic nature of the overlapping roof structure.

The Spirit of Learning

SECTION 2

Opposite:
Exhibition interior of the Nieuw Land
Poldermuseum at Lelystad in The
Netherlands, designed by architects
Benthem Crouwel: a symbolic
approach to teaching people about the
Dutch struggle against the sea.

With education and training officially pronounced Europe's largest industry, and most of the world's economies looking afresh at strategies in teaching and learning, it is no surprise that the architecture of schools, libraries, university faculties, and educative museums and exhibits should be undergoing transformation.

Architects and designers are leading a high-profile quest for new solutions, reflecting the fact that the plan and detail of environment, space and structure can have an enormous impact on the education process and even engender a new spirit among the users of such public facilities – teachers, students and visitors alike.

As architect Alistair Sunderland, who led the Austin-Smith:Lord design team on the development of a new multimedia learning centre at Liverpool John Moores University, explains: 'Through the design of the building and the way the facilities are organized, we are encouraging a new way of learning.'

The Liverpool project is just one of a trio of innovative British university buildings included in this selection, its high-tech cube form aptly describing the computerization of traditional library services. The others – Rick Mather's Constable Terrace at the University of East Anglia and the Queens Building, De Montfort University, Leicester, designed by Short Ford & Associates – share an interest in low-energy strategies, but little else.

Mather's sensuous modernism simultaneously extends and softens the language of the urban concrete landscape first developed on the UEA campus by Sir Denys Lasdun in the 1960s. The eclectic Leicester building, meanwhile, revives an earlier tradition – the Gothic red-brick vernacular of the prewar inner city. It is interesting to note here that the Queens engineering block has itself been developed as a giant learning aid for young engineers to study about green, energy-conscious architecture.

Many of the schemes in this selection make compelling architectural gestures about the nature of the subject matter, when there is an opportunity to do so. The two museum projects shown here do so most overtly: Massimiliano Fuksas' steel skeletal entrance to the cave-painting grotto at Niaux evokes a giant prehistoric creature; Benthem Crouwel's Poldermuseum is an elaborate metaphor for the Dutch struggle against the sea. But others, too, are sensitive to and symbolize content.

Thus, Zimmer Gunsul Frasca Partnership's Bellevue Regional Library expresses the continuity of the monumental civic library through a sweeping new structure that imposes its own authority over a car-congested context. And Dubus and Lott's ESIEE Engineering College in Amiens, France, arranges its many elements in an abstract jigsaw around the focal point of a vast white futuristic amphitheatre building, an upturned concrete bowl that symbolically suggests what education is really all about – the future.

Indeed many of the facilities shown play in some way with the educational idea of investment in potential, from Mecanoo's Dutch secondary school skilfully crafted into a curved riverside site, to Gwathmey Siegel's gatehouse-like Broad Center at Pitzer College, which uses a Cubist language to set the tenor for interaction on campus. When Goethe visited the Göttingen University Library in 1801, he declared: 'It is like having access to a huge sum of capital which soundlessly pays incalculable amounts of interest.' Today that library, one of Germany's largest, has been housed in a gleaming new industrial building on a geometric scale of which Goethe could only have dreamed. ●

Aldham Robarts Learning Resource Centre

Liverpool, UK

A multimedia learning centre at the Liverpool John Moores University uses the high-tech language of the modernist project to express a seamless unity of library and computer and media facilities.

Architect
Austin-Smith:Lord

Interior Designer
Austin-Smith:Lord

Client/Commissioning Body
Liverpool John Moores University

Total Floor Space
5,500 square metres

Number of Floors
4

Total Contract Cost
£4.8 million

Date of Completion
Summer 1994

The new multimedia library has been delicately inserted into a crowded conservation area close to Liverpool city centre. The internal streets that bisect its cube form are aligned to such local landmarks as the Anglican Cathedral and the Liver Building on the skyline.

An axonometric of the building reveals a strict linear geometry broken at one corner where a sensuous full-height glazed element opens on to an informal garden. The design makes no contextual concessions to its surroundings.

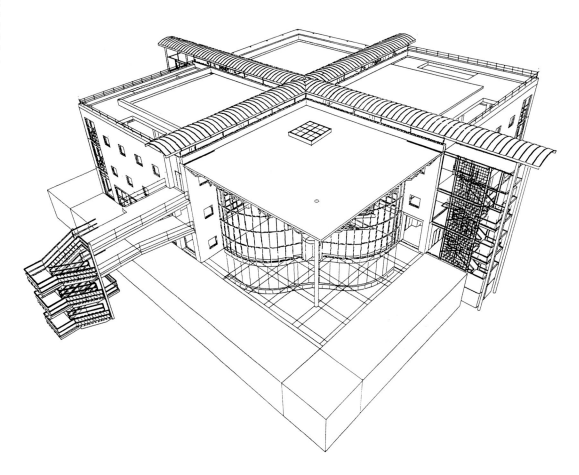

After being housed for centuries in cloistered stone halls displaying antiquarian books amid shadow and dust, the British university library is in light, bright, high-tech transition. The new multimedia learning resource centre at the Liverpool John Moores University, one of Britain's new universities, offers a powerful vision of what a new university library should look like, how it should perform and how it should be perceived.

Architects Austin-Smith:Lord have expressed the seamless unity of library, computer and media services in a building named in honour of its main sponsor, Canadian newspaper magnate Aldham Robarts, by using the modernist vocabulary of glass, steel, concrete and white plaster in an especially legible and intelligent way.

The building has been conceived as a large, simple, white cube deftly and delicately inserted into a crowded conservation area on the university's Mount Pleasant campus close to the city centre. The cube, which sits among

Georgian terraces behind a derelict nineteenth-century church, is bisected by a series of internal streets, each aligned to local landmarks including the Liverpool Anglican Cathedral. Its strict linear geometry is broken only at one corner where a sensuously curved full-height glazing defines an entrance surrounded by an informal garden.

Designed to service the needs of 7,000 students from seven schools within the university and to handle the traffic of 3,500 people a day, the centre has been organized with the accent on ease of access, quality of daylight and freedom of information. Each of the upper floors, connected by lightweight steel staircases, is subject-specific and fully equipped so that students are not forced to go to a different floor to use a computer after reading a book or journal. An art and design library housed in an annexe (a converted convent) can be reached from the main centre via a futuristic walkway. A double-height basement area, with light spilling down from a skylight above, includes a coffee shop and bookshop.

The usual 2:1 ratio of book storage to study area was reversed on this library project, and the overall feeling for users is of space and light. The building enhances a city of great cultural vitality undimmed by an entire generation of industrial decline and currently trying to reinvent itself. But while it makes a positive contribution to a new image for Liverpool, perhaps the real lessons of this learning resource centre are to do with the way it seeks to reshape the education process. ●

Modernist façade of the Aldham Robarts Learning Resource Centre at Liverpool John Moores University, tucked into the Mountain Pleasant area of the city amongst Georgian terraces. It sits behind a derelict nineteenth-century church into which it may one day expand.

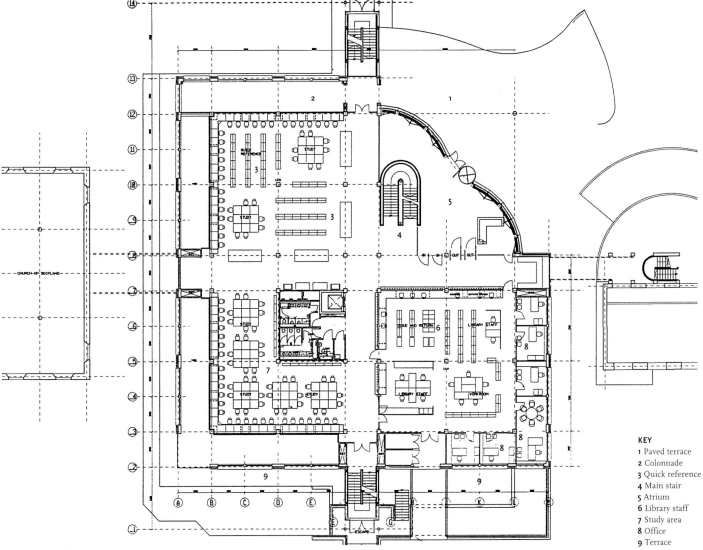

Ground-floor plan of the multimedia library. With its glass-wall entrance atrium space, bespoke perimeter benches and quick-reference areas, this is the only floor in the facility that is not subject specific.

KEY
1 Paved terrace
2 Colonnade
3 Quick reference
4 Main stair
5 Atrium
6 Library staff
7 Study area
8 Office
9 Terrace

A generous circulation corridor in a building designed to accommodate the learning needs of 7,000 students from seven schools within the university. Library use during the academic year is heavy, estimated at 3,500 people a day. The overall impression is of space and light.

Musée des Graffiti – Entrance to Cave Painting Museum

Niaux, France

Architect
Massimiliano Fuksas,
with Jean-Louis Fulcrand,
Jean Capia and Gui
Jourdan

**Client/Commissioning
Body**
Conseil Général de
l'Ariège

Number of Levels
1

Total Contract Cost
US $13,550

Date of Completion
July 1993

A spectacular reception point for visitors to the prehistoric cave painting grotto at Niaux provides a walkway in the form of a giant creature reaching out across the landscape in welcome.

Prehistoric graffiti in the caves at Niaux: a magnet for visitors from all over the world who want to learn about prehistoric art and culture.

High up on a rocky ledge, the suggestion of articulated scales in the form of the broken lateral screens reinforces the image of a giant prehistoric creature in the landscape.

The overall function, which is to define an accessible pathway from the car-park level and protect a formal entrance to the grotto, is not compromised by this form.

Entrance gates 28 metres high, clad in sheet Cor-ten steel: a dramatic focal point on a unique architectural site, designed by Fuksas following an unusual architectural competition organized by the local authority.

This small-scale project provides a heroic solution to a potentially contentious architectural problem. The caves of Niaux sit 650 metres high on a rocky ledge. One of them is home to cave paintings dating from 11,000 BC and is a magnet for numerous visitors seeking to learn about prehistoric art and culture. The task was to create a structure that would not only provide a practical visitor entrance to the hidden caves, but also celebrate this unique archaeological site.

The context, far removed from the usual time frame in which such issues are considered, demanded a bold response. Paris-based architect Massimiliano Fuksas complied, with a structure as simple as it is spectacular. In addition to evoking a giant prehistoric creature, the entrance dramatizes the idea of a fissure in the landscape whilst creating an artificial pathway from which visitors are able to view the surrounding scenery, part of which they are about to enter.

Despite its sense of theatre, the entrance deliberately blurs notions of 'inside' and 'outside', creating an ambiguous open/closed introduction to the grotto and prompting its architect to observe that 'architecture can be transformed into landscape, and vice versa'.

This study in immateriality, by a designer who spent part of his youth in the studio of the Surrealistic painter Giorgio de Chirico, was achieved via an unusual competition that took place on site. In 1988, five architects were invited by the local administrative body, the Conseil Général de l'Ariège, to explore the caves before sketching ideas spontaneously in a local workshop. The resulting scheme is a rich reward for such a daring approach to architectural competition.

Fuksas has used sheet Cor-ten steel to clad the tall (28 metres high), skeletal entrance because the surface of the material will assume new colour tones and different patinas over time – so echoing the natural weathering of the live landscape in which it sits. The walkway flooring is a combination of timber and galvanized metal grilles supported on pilotis that equalize the irregular nature of the terrain on which the structure lies. The tunnel-like footpath twists and turns before opening dramatically on to the heart of the scheme – a 30-metre-high vault covered completely in cave paintings. ●

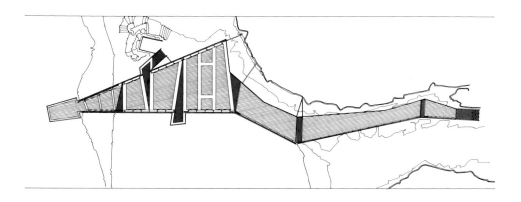

The plan shows the sinuous nature of the walkway deck, an artificial intervention in the landscape made of materials that will weather like the surroundings.

Bellevue Regional Library

Bellevue, Washington, USA

Architect
Zimmer Gunsul
Frasca Partnership

Interior Designer
ZGF Interiors

Client/Commissioning Body
King County Library System

Total Floor Space
80,000 square feet

Number of Floors
3

Total Contract Cost
US $11.8 million

Date of Completion
June 1993

The new Bellevue Regional Library provides an exceptional public facility in the tradition of the monumental civic library that also signals a welcome shift in the city's planning policies.

View through a section of the library's 10,000-square foot children's area. Generous spaces and thoughtful detail are keynotes of a scheme that reinterprets the come-hither American city library tradition for a new generation.

The south-facing façade of Zimmer Gunsul Frasca's Bellevue Regional Library reflects the subtle contemporary-Gothic styling which creates an elegant new civic monument on a Seattle 'edge-city' site.

The Regional Library, commissioned by the city of Bellevue in King County, Washington State, from Oregon-based partnership Zimmer Gunsul Frasca, is the focal point of a new pedestrian area being created at the edge of the city's commercial zone. If this downtown library impresses with its generous spaces (including a 10,000-square foot children's area), contemporary Gothic styling, use of light and ease of orientation, one should appreciate that its apparently smooth effects were achieved in the face of many zoning constraints and some curiously inconsistent planning restrictions.

The city's laudable instruction to encourage pedestrian use of the building, for example, was rather compromised by its simultaneous decision to widen the approaching cross-streets from two lanes to five. Despite this difficulty, Zimmer Gunsul Frasca not only solved most of the problems of the site, they also created a building whose exterior and interior combine to create a thoughtful public space at the perimeter of a busy car-oriented conurbation.

A high entry gallery provides the 'official' introduction to the building, running right through it and separating the library proper from public meeting rooms. At the opposite side a less imposing entrance leads from the car park, which few visitors were supposed to use but which most do. Inside, these two entry points – and a third from an underground car park for 115 cars – are united in the 12-metre high gallery which provides a genuine sense of drama throughout. To one side, the main reading room is illuminated during daylight hours by a curving glass wall facing a proposed

'town square', as yet unrealized. To the other, the public meeting rooms overlook the street, and above them two north-facing clerestories admit additional light and give the roof a saw-tooth finish.

There is something of a raw industrial feel to the interior, with fir ceilings and exposed trusswork, but the dominant impression remains one of generous

spaces and well-handled light. Irony surrounds the Bellevue Regional Library project in that it stems from a tradition in which public buildings were meant to reflect civic values, not define them. Here, however, a well-considered public building has been necessarily shoe-horned into an uncomfortable urban present, and yet its civilized scale and mood survive intact. ●

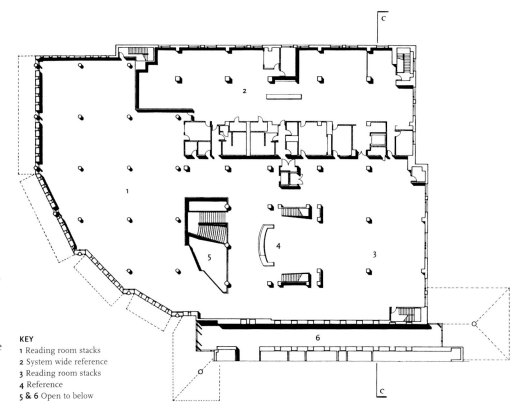

KEY
1 Reading room stacks
2 System wide reference
3 Reading room stacks
4 Reference
5 & 6 Open to below

Second-level floor plan shows open reading rooms serviced by administrative offices to the north.

The library's steel entrance canopy is sheathed in fir and supported by a tree-like concrete structure in a conscious echo of the library buildings of Alvar Aalto. The architects claim that the Pacific Northwest of America has an affinity with the Finnish landscape and climate.

Below: South-north section. The functional character of the rear façade to the north is offset by the elegant drama of the canopies facing to the south. The saw-tooth roofline admits daylight to second-floor reading rooms through north-facing clerestories.

Opposite: A slate-floored gallery extends between the front and rear entrances in a building of spatial quality. Square openings in the wall provide views into this gallery from second-floor reading areas.

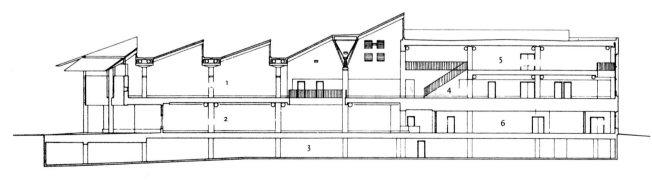

1 & 2 Reading room stacks
3 Parking
4 Reference
5 Reading room stacks
6 Administration

2.4

ESIEE Engineering College

Amiens, France

Architect
Jean Dubus and
Jean-Pierre Lott

Interior Designer
Jean Dubus and
Jean-Pierre Lott

Client/Commissioning Body
City of Amiens

Total Floor Space
12,000 square metres

Number of Floors
3

Total Contract Cost
US $14 million

Date of Completion
1993

An abstract study in white, interlocking concrete shapes, the new engineering faculty at Amiens allows function to dictate individual elements but still manages to create a satisfying whole.

A light-well crowns an inverted conical column in just one of the scheme's many expressive interiors that demonstrate the plasticity of concrete.

The keynote of the engineering college at Amiens designed by Jean Dubus and Jean-Pierre Lott is a giant white bowl, 50 metres in diameter at its top, which accommodates three lecture halls within its shell. A restaurant, library and main entrance to the left of the bowl share its waterfront location.

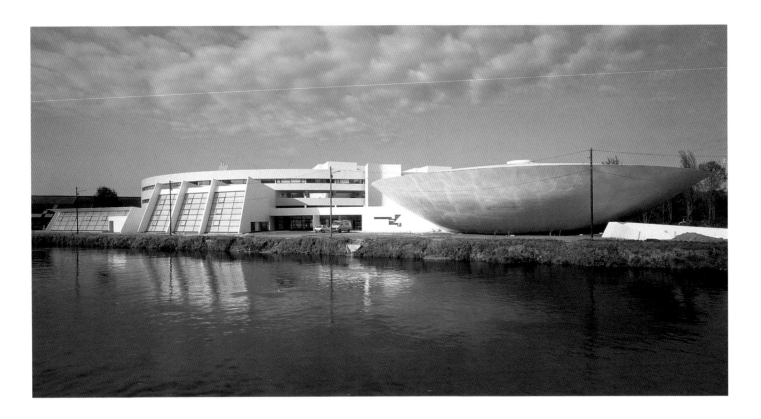

Dubus and Lott's university building for electrical and electronic engineering at Amiens in northern France is a complex composition of white abstract forms in reinforced concrete. It pays conscious homage to the modernism of Le Corbusier and Niemeyer but, at the same time, strikes a wholly contemporary chord within the university district, heart of the city's ambitious urban redevelopment plans.

The focal point for the entire riverside scheme is a vast white bowl – the lecture amphitheatre building – which accommodates three lecture halls of 350, 250 and 150 seats in an upturned shell of prestressed concrete. Snaked round its circular form is a three-storey S-shaped administrative and classroom block. Viewed from the river, this block is preceded by the sloping glass façades of a restaurant and library and by a low-level main entrance hall that provides access up a gently raked floor of grey ceramic tiles.

At the bend of the S-shape, the plan shows three laboratories set at a north-easterly angle to this administrative block, which are supported on piles, beneath which is parking space. One of the three laboratories has yet to be built.

This is a scheme in which the parts – library, restaurant, offices, laboratories, lecture theatres and so on – have been designed on their own terms and dictate the form of the whole. Yet there is a satisfying clarity in the interrelationship of the various elements. As Jean Dubus explains: 'The idea was to give a special shape to each part according to its specification. It's a complex building. It creates its own landscape.'

External diversity, however, gives way to interior harmony as the architects develop a consistent internal theme of curved and angled walls, deep wells of natural light and carefully framed views of the exterior as you proceed through the different spaces. The awareness of the enormous amount of technical concrete calculation that must have gone into the cone-shaped pillars, convex partitions and curving façades – especially in the laboratories – dissolves in an effortless form-giving exercise.

ESIEE stands for Ecole Supérieure d'Ingenieurs en Electrique et Electrotechnique, but it symbolizes much more besides. The richness of the scheme not only demonstrates the plasticity of concrete when shaped by the right hands, but – reflected in the giant white amphitheatre bowl, cast as a single piece of concrete 50 metres in diameter at the top and 16 metres at the base – it shows the enduring legacy of pure modernist ideals used to express the future. ●

A cross-section reveals, from left to right, the view through the three-storey administrative and classroom block and the amphitheatre bowl.

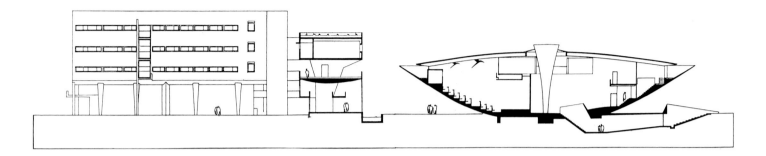

The S-shaped block, which unifies the elements on the site, is conceived in a style of architecture that pays conscious homage to the heroic gestures of Le Corbusier and Niemeyer.

Cool, perfectly-composed public areas
created by the architects' curvaceous,
form-giving scheme and enhanced by
sensitive lighting.

The site plan shows the
interrelationship between building
forms that were conceived
independently in response to function
but fit together with satisfying clarity.
An S-shaped block snakes between
the circular amphitheatre bowl on the
waterfront and a trio of northwest-
facing laboratories.

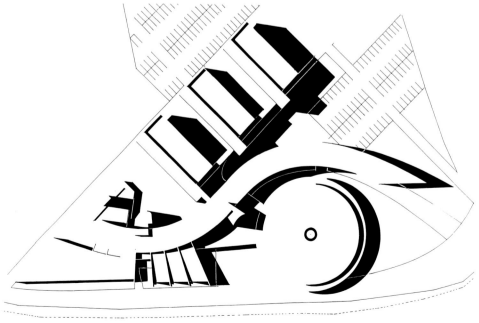

Nieuw Land Poldermuseum

Lelystad, The Netherlands

Architect
Benthem Crouwel
Architekten

Exhibition Designer
Donald Janssen
Onterwerpers

Client/Commissioning Body
Stichting Initiatiefgroep
Nieuw Land

Total Floor Space
1,940 square metres

Number of Floors
3

Total Contract Cost
US $2.5 million

Date of Completion
March 1994

The Nieuw Land Poldermuseum is an object building that celebrates the ambiguous relationship the Dutch people have with the sea, and invites an emotional response through deliberately rhetorical flourishes.

The Poldermuseum's timber-propped, flattened tube form is a visual metaphor for the cannons that were once fired across the Dutch countryside to announce the imminent arrival of high spring tides.

The Poldermuseum sits, appropriately enough, on reclaimed land four metres below sea level. The setting provides the context for the museum's rhetorical appearance.

In one of history's little ironies, the only museum in The Netherlands dedicated to that nation's endless struggle against the sea was destroyed by fire in 1988. A new museum was subsequently proposed by the Stichting Initiatiefgroep Nieuw Land and designated to be built on the same site. That site is on a polder – a piece of low-lying land reclaimed from the sea – four metres below sea level, and therefore an appropriate scene for a dramatic architectural gesture.

The museum is composed of two basic elements: a lower glazed pavilion representing a section through a dike, and a long, flattened cylinder on top, symbolic of the cannons that were once fired to announce imminent high spring tides. The representational approach of the exterior is also carried through to the interior. The glazed pavilion houses both public and private spaces and incorporates an entrance that mimics rippling waves and is in the form of a cross-section of a dam. Inside, the pavilion extends upwards to offer an introduction to the 60-metre long tube that houses the exhibition. Timber-propped, this tube reveals itself to be a stratified structure, marked by physical references to the relative heights of the ground- and water-level.

When you arrive from the entrance building, whether by lift or narrow stairway, you are guided between glass banisters past display cases and symbolic masses calculated to dramatize the achievement of a nation accustomed to living below sea level. Little is left to the imagination in this stylized re-creation of the natural elements and the mechanical solutions upon which the very existence of The Netherlands depends. The building's lightweight industrial-metal interior recalls the inner-workings of a pumping machine. On leaving the guided tour the visitor descends again into the dike pavilion, passing an archaeological section en route.

Unavoidable similarities between this project and Will Alsop's Cardiff Bay Visitor's Centre in Wales prove, on closer examination, to be quite superficial. Both tubular structures offer a 'controlled' view of a seascape, but the power of Benthem Crouwel's technologically unremarkable building – its cylinder trussed with hot-rolled steel tubes – derives from the strength of its imagery and the way it communicates and celebrates an engineering ingenuity that is the key to national survival. ●

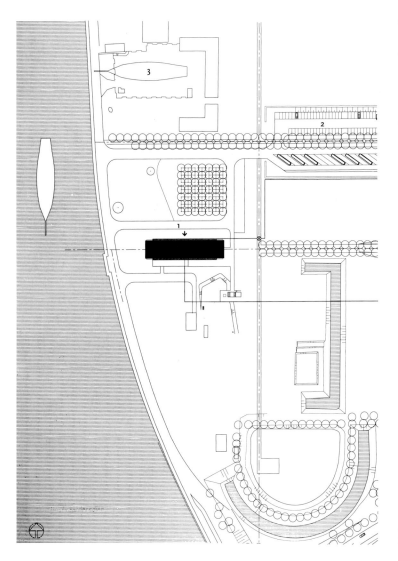

The site plan shows the museum's command of views over land and water. The polder was only reclaimed from the sea in 1970 and the site forms part of a master plan – not yet fully realized – which includes a reconstructed seventh-century sailing ship called *The Batavia* in a dry dock to the north of Benthem Crouwel's building.

KEY
1 Entrance to Nieuw Land
2 Parking
3 *The Batavia*

The entrance façade reflects the idea of cascading waves, also the cross-section of a dam, in an elaborate metaphor for the Dutch struggle for survival against the sea.

The main museum exhibition is housed inside the industrial-metal tube, its acoustic and spatial properties evoking the inner-workings of a pumping machine.

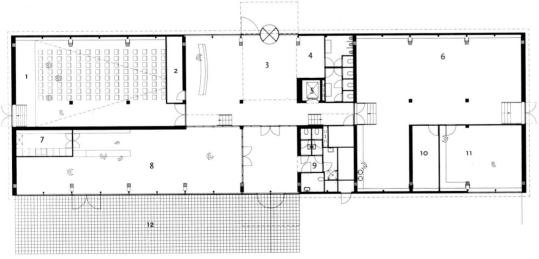

1 Auditorium
2 Projection
3 Entrance
4 Toilets
5 Lift
6 Archaeological depot
7 Kitchen
8 Coffee corner
9 Toilets
10 Storage
11 Office
12 Terrace

The ground-floor plan shows the layout of the glazed entrance pavilion facilities, including an office, coffee corner and auditorium. Visitors pass upstairs to the main exhibition area, then return to this level to visit an archaeological exhibit.

Constable Terrace, University of East Anglia

Norwich, UK

Architect
Rick Mather Architects

Interior Designer
Rick Mather Architects

Client/Commissioning Body
University of East Anglia

Total Floor Space
3,300 square metres

Number of Floors
3

Total Contract Cost
£6.2 million

Date of Completion
September 1993

The modern tradition of the UEA campus is skilfully and undogmatically updated by master-planner Rick Mather's low-energy student block, which defines a sensuous new aesthetic for the site.

Communal space for students at Constable Terrace: robust materials and finishes belie the rather fragile and delicate aesthetic.

The curved Constable Terrace development not only provides high-quality student accommodation, it updates the modern tradition of the UEA campus with a sensuous new signature.

The campus of the University of East Anglia has a special place in postwar modern architecture in Britain. Designed in the early 1960s by Sir Denys Lasdun as one unbroken continuum of teaching and living spaces to house 6,000 students, the university's entire accommodation comprised a single concrete structure snaking across a meadow between a lake and the encroaching suburbs of Norwich. Lasdun introduced the language of the urban landscape to the rural university campus, and successive master plans for the site have sought to reflect the spirit that built Europe's longest university building.

Current master-planner for the University of East Anglia is architect Rick Mather, whose curved Constable Terrace development not only provides new residential accommodation for 400 students but symbolizes the skilful, undogmatic updating of a modern tradition at UEA. Mather first became involved in the site in the 1980s through a recommendation from Sir Norman Foster, whose much-acclaimed Sainsbury Centre now faces the Constable Terrace.

Lasdun's unitary concept for UEA meant that, in theory at least, his original structure was infinitely extendible. However, Constable Terrace is a new stand-alone building, as are others by Mather and associated architects on the campus. What distinguishes Constable Terrace is the way it blends into the whole while retaining a sensuous personality of its own. It arranges accommodation in groups of up to ten – all with en-suite toilet/shower facilities – not down long corridors but in the manner of a three-storey terraced house with its own individual front door.

If Lasdun originally defined an abstract notion of community through architecture, then Mather breaks that idea down into smaller family units – and low-energy ones at that. The skin of the building is sealed tight, there is mechanical interior ventilation, and larger rooms have south-facing windows to benefit deliberately from winter solar energy.

Robust detailing, industrial-chic interior fitments and challenging circulation towers lend a confidently modern flourish to a block with a snakelike footprint, which at one end nestles against both a 1960s Lasdun teaching wall and John Miller and Partners' excellent new 1994 School of Occupational Therapy and Physiotherapy. This John Miller building, with its courtyard and rotunda, and indeed the same practice's 1995 Elizabeth Fry building, capture the kind of formal, flowing aesthetic qualities that Mather as master-planner has been trying to encourage at UEA and which are exemplified in Constable Terrace. ●

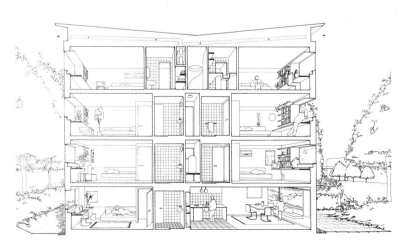

A section reveals how housing is organized communally as a series of three-storey terraced houses – each accommodates ten people and has its own front door – rather than in the more conventional model with student rooms off rows of long anonymous corridors. The top storey has two-person flats.

A circulation tower shows the combination of function and artistry in Mather's architecture. He confronts the utilitarian spirit of the university residence and achieves a striking exterior feature.

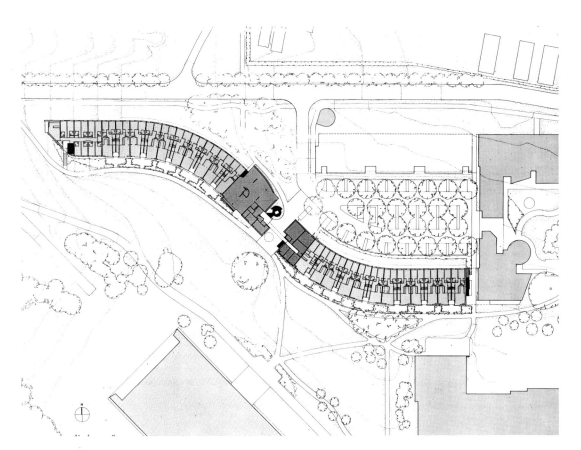

The site plan shows how Constable Terrace connects old and new at its east point, nestling against Denys Lasdun's original architecture as well as the courtyard and rotunda of John Miller's new School of Occupational Therapy and Physiotherapy.

Below: A confident flourish to the Constable Terrace façade gives the building an expressive identity in its own terms, yet it fits into the whole 'urban landscape', as conceived by Lasdun, with consummate ease.

Isala College

Silvolde, The Netherlands

Architect
Mecanoo Architekten

Interior Designer
Mecanoo Architekten

Client/Commissioning Body
Katholieke Stichting Voor Voortgezet Onderwijs, Regio Oude Ijssel

Total Floor Space
6,500 square metres

Number of Floors
3

Total Contract Cost
£4.8 million

Date of Completion
January 1995

A thoughtful secondary school follows the curves of the river in a rural Dutch landscape and pivots two contrasting wings from an assembly hall at the heart of the scheme.

The wooden panelling on the classrooms on the southern façade of the Isala College in Silvolde, Holland, responds to the leafy riverside landscape in which this private secondary school sits.

The axonometric shows the two main elements of the scheme. A sports and administration block is connected by an assembly hall, the pivotal 'hinge' point, to the main crescent-shaped building which echoes the shape of the river it overlooks.

The school as architectural raw material has long been tempting to architects who believe that changes in the designed environment can make teachers less stressed and pupils more motivated. Unfortunately this tradition has sometimes encouraged architects to do as they please with schools, engaging in social engineering without social responsibility. However, this scheme by architects Mecanoo for a private Catholic secondary school in the small town of Silvolde near the Dutch-German border stands as an exemplary facility – practical, honest and very much in tune with its surroundings.

Isala College caters to about 800 pupils and 50 staff. Its temporary facilities, expanded in an unconsidered way since the 1970s, meant inconvenient walking distances between blocks and the loss of a charming view of a river landscape. To create a more compact facility oriented more closely to the green surroundings, Mecanoo proposed a long, curved building to echo the shape of the river it overlooks.

A bright, wide central corridor runs the length of the crescent-shaped building, separating the classrooms on the south from the science laboratories and directors' offices on the north. The southern façade is finished in wooden panelling to blend in with the surroundings, and an awning is supported by slim posts.

All administrative areas are housed in a second block which is set at an angle to the curved building. There is a sense of tension at the point of contact but also a feeling of lightness: this is no monolithic shed, but a pleasantly articulated combination of elements that never forget their context. An assembly hall is located at the pivotal 'hinge' point between the two wings of the scheme, forming the heart of the building and providing access to a subdivided gymnasium with changing rooms sunk below ground level. Some remaining classrooms are situated above the administration offices while cloakrooms and a caretaker's office are arranged beneath the assembly hall.

Freedom of circulation, large hallways and staircases, and a calculated contrast between plain and luxury materials characterize the interior. Heating ducts laid on plaster or concrete, and hand-operated ventilation flaps may suggest spartan minimalism, but sometimes they can look very good indeed. The budget may have been modest, but real value is delivered in the generous quality of space and light and in the happy rediscovery of surroundings that were there all the time. This, then, is a study in reconnection, creating a better place to teach and learn. ●

Slim poles punctuate the pleasing articulation of the river-facing south façade of Isala College: the new school has 'rediscovered its surroundings'.

Right: A calculated contrast between plain and luxury materials adds distinction to interior spaces in a scheme that provides a more open and conducive learning environment for 800 Dutch pupils.

Clad in zinc sheet, the gymnasium block is sunk half a storey into the ground and deliberately provides a difference in height at the point where it collides with the crescent structure.

Large hallways and staircases are a keynote of a generous scheme in which organic forms and materials echo the rural surroundings.

The State and University Library, Göttingen

Göttingen, Germany

Architect
Prof. Eckhard Gerber
& Partner

Interior Designer
Prof. Eckhard Gerber
& Partner

Client/Commissioning Body
Land Niedersachsen

Total Floor Space
47,059 square metres

Number of Floors
4

Total Contract Cost
US $88 million

Date of Completion
1993

Göttingen's library played host to Goethe. Today it has been reinvented as an industrial learning centre in an innovative form that points a handful of giant architectural fingers towards the city.

Separate fingers of Göttingen's new library on the university campus point towards the city through a botanical garden.

Entrance hall to the library, from which reading rooms, cafeteria and lending desks are accessed. This space also doubles as an exhibition area.

Acting as a link between the university and Göttingen city centre, this new library is nothing if not carefully considered. It was originally proposed 30 years ago and begun in earnest in 1984 when an architectural competition was held involving 80 practices. A scheme by Prof. Gerber & Partner was chosen and work began on site the following year.

The building is situated in the southern part of the university's humanities faculty and joins existing central facilities in this area, including a dining hall, auditorium and administration. Meanwhile the city-facing side is defined by a green embankment and botanical garden. So the new library responds to both with a plan that resembles a human hand, with the solid portion relating to the university complex and the separate fingers pointing out towards the city.

The design of the building is largely based on a reinforced concrete skeleton. A rotunda – a system of interlinked steel and glass cylinders – provides an introduction to the user's area via a grand entrance hall that extends through all four floors. Here the building's most important functions 'open up' for the visitor like the pages of a book. From this point there is access to upper areas and to the isolated 'finger' sections.

Despite the vast scale involved and the sophistication of the building's geometry, its interior spaces are simply conceived with choice of material influenced by their natural colouring. Pillars, girders and beams are visibly concrete, loadbearing steel members are covered with metallic paint, ceilings and bulkheads were kept plain white. Light grey floors echo the

natural stone exterior, while fitted and freestanding furniture is in a complementary light beechwood.

Muted functional finishes, transparent vistas, custom lighting solutions and the thoughtful disposition of volumes do much to soften an industrial-looking – not to mention futuristic – building that initially came as a shock to some people rooted in a venerable academic tradition: Goethe, after all, studied at Göttingen. However, the new university library has already started to prove itself an appropriate contemporary facility for such a distinguished institution which has one of the five largest library collections in Germany. ●

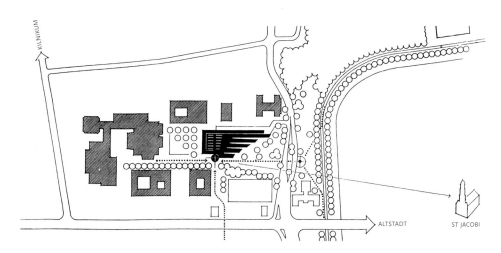

The site plan shows the library's pivotal position acting as a link between the university's humanities faculty, where it completes facilities, and the city beyond. The sightlines of the building's five 'fingers' fix on St Jacobi church in the distance.

Left: Library users read under an open structure of glass and steel, with unobstructed views from the upper levels into lower or neighbouring areas. Simple geometries and natural colours predominate.

Göttingen's industrial aesthetic: the rotunda, with connected fire escape, has a system of sheet-metal sun shields that respond to the position of the sun.

An upper-level floor plan reveals how isolated 'finger' reading-room sections relate to the cafeteria in the rotunda and to the service core.

Queens Building, De Montfort University

Leicester, UK

Architect
Short Ford & Associates

Interior Designer
Short Ford & Associates

Client/Commissioning Body
De Montfort University

Total Floor Space
10,140 square metres

Number of Floors
4 and 2 variously

Total Contract Cost
£11.1 million

Date of Completion
August 1993

The new low-energy School of Engineering and Manufacture is an advanced 'green' building clothed in the garb of the inner city's red-brick Gothic vernacular architecture.

The south-facing façade of the Queens Building reveals the complexity of a building that combines solar stack chimneys with the local red-brick Gothic style.

Second-floor plan
1 Auditorium 1
2 Auditorium 2
3 Staff accommodation
4 Heads of schools and departments
5 Heads of schools and departments
6 Network and communications lab.
7 Electronic computer aided design
8 Staff accommodation
9 Computer node mezzanine

The new School of Engineering and Manufacture at De Montfort University in Leicester unites the inner-city campus of Europe's fastest growing university around a highly innovative and individual flagship building that looks back and forward simultaneously. The Queens Building revives a red-brick Gothic ethos in tandem with an advanced low-energy approach, using form and fabric to eliminate mechanical cooling and artificial light.

This reconciling of such opposites – juxtaposing green building ideas with a traditional vernacular architecture that can be traced back to Ruskin and Pugin – may appear improbable to some. But architects Alan Short and Brian Ford have managed to create a showpiece structure that can itself be used as a learning aid for engineering courses with an environmental bent, while at the same time redefining part of the

campus landscape that has been ravaged since the 1960s by urban blight.

A complex plan provides a range of facilities, including two auditoria for 160 people each, seminar rooms, laboratories, a computer library, social facilities, and offices for 90 staff in the departments of Mechanical Engineering, Electronics and Computing, whose integration the Queens Building is intended to encourage.

Unusually for a modern building, the construction is unframed and the masonry is loadbearing. The feature of the pointed arch therefore has a functional presence in that it supports up to four floors of masonry. Though the dominant architectural language is Gothic, the architects have drawn on much else besides, giving the project what they describe as a 'chameleon-like quality to closely fit the locality'. Externally, mortar and brick colour-matched to create modern

planes of red, cedar cladding and tall brick buttresses all draw the eye for different reasons; internally, elaborate metalwork and glass block walkways spanning shallow, naturally lit space give the idea of the 'inner-street' – evident in the architecture of Herman Hertzberger or Niels Torp – a post-Modern concept.

It is the sheer eclecticism of the Queens Building that perhaps makes it so controversial – and so compelling. It demonstrates what can be achieved when architects, environmental and structural engineers, quantity surveyors and research physicists all work together towards a common goal. But above all, despite a deliberately low-key main entrance, it exudes a civic confidence, an unusual glamour, in the age of the all-too-self-effacing educational building.

The heavily detailed central concourse of the building gives a post-Modern reading to the idea of the inner-street. Natural light and ventilation are integral to the scheme.

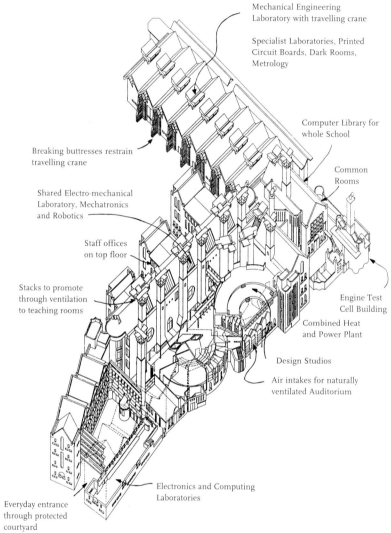

Mechanical Engineering Laboratory with travelling crane

Specialist Laboratories, Printed Circuit Boards, Dark Rooms, Metrology

Computer Library for whole School

Common Rooms

Breaking buttresses restrain travelling crane

Shared Electro-mechanical Laboratory, Mechatronics and Robotics

Staff offices on top floor

Engine Test Cell Building

Combined Heat and Power Plant

Stacks to promote through ventilation to teaching rooms

Design Studios

Air intakes for naturally ventilated Auditorium

Electronics and Computing Laboratories

Everyday entrance through protected courtyard

The street façade introduces a 'chameleon-like' flavour to the De Montfort University campus. The masonry of the Queens Building is loadbearing, which is unusual for a modern building. The pointed arch, therefore, has a structural significance.

Broad Center
Pitzer College

Claremont, California, USA

The new gateway to an artfully arranged California campus not only sets the architectural mood in its assembly of Cubist forms, but defines the ethos of cultural interaction for the college.

Architect
Gwathmey Siegel & Associates Architects

Interior Designer
Gwathmey Siegel & Associates Architects

Client/Commissioning Body
Pitzer College

Total Floor Space
12,960 square feet

Number of Floors
2

Date of Completion
October 1994

A section of the south façade of the Broad Center, Pitzer College: a 'Cubist' colour palette enriches the simple volumes of the building and reinforces the themes of dialogue and diversity.

The main entrance to the Broad Center from the west: an invitation to interact with the university.

he Edythe and Eli Broad Center is an important new element in Gwathmey Siegel's master plan for the Pitzer College campus in California. It provides a new gateway to the campus and, in doing so, sets the initial architectural image for visitors and new students as they enter the college.

The new building sits at the intersection of Twelfth Street, the approach road to the campus, and Mills Avenue, on axis with the existing Brandt Tower and shielding the college's carefully landscaped lawns from the outside eye.

It is said that although the architectural profession tends to discuss college buildings as a single building type, these are in experience as diverse as their owners will allow their architects to make them. In the case of the Broad Center, a composition of geometric forms – further animated by a 'Cubist' colour palette – reinforces the themes of diversity, dialogue and interaction

that Gwathmey Siegel has been developing throughout the Pitzer College campus.

The Broad Center includes an art gallery, a musical performance and lecture space, classrooms and seminar rooms, admissions and faculty offices, and the president's office. A two-storey entry space

provides public orientation beneath a glass block ceiling and conical skylight. Indeed, the glass block and the glass grid are recurring interior motifs as the spaces unfold with almost creamy precision, the simple elegant punctuation of the cube broken at intervals by the graceful curvilinear forms of grey columns and circular ceiling cutaways. Exterior stucco walls and aluminium doors and windows reveal spaces floored with wood block, carpet and vinyl tile.

The Broad Center reaffirms Gwathmey Siegel's skill in developing appropriate metaphors for American academic buildings. The practice has recently completed accomplished schemes at Duke University in North Carolina and at Cornell University in Ithaca, New York, as well as a double building for fine arts and theatre arts at the State University of New York at Buffalo. But the Broad Center goes further: it not only creates a focal gateway to the campus, but in its role as a place of information exchange and cultural interaction between faculty, students and visitors, it defines the ethos of the campus as a whole. ●

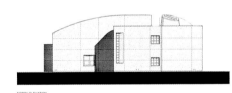

NORTH ELEVATION

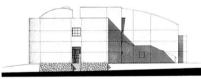

SOUTH ELEVATION

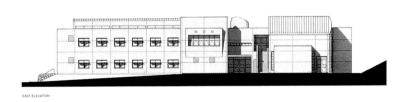

EAST ELEVATION

WEST ELEVATION

North, south, east and west elevations reveal the subtle composition of Gwathmey Siegel's focal gateway building on the Pitzer College campus.

Left: A section of the east façade showing how the composition of geometric forms animates the building.

A conical skylight sits above a spacious two-storey entrance area. The glass block and the glass grid are recurring interior themes.

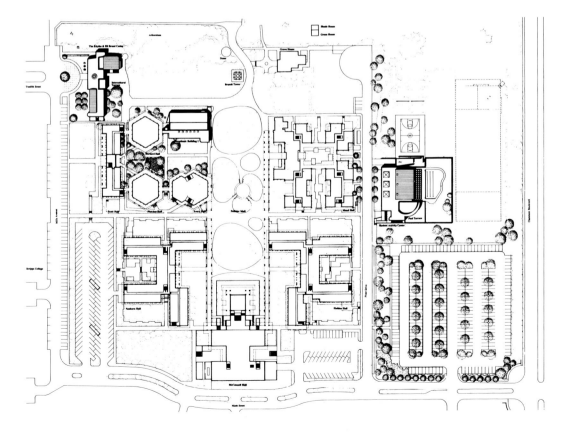

The site plan shows the Broad Center, top left, as the new entrance signature of the Pitzer College campus, as approached from Twelfth Street in Gwathmey Siegel's master plan. The building shields the college's landscaped lawns and provides the defining image for new students and visitors.

3

Dramatic Interventions

The dramatic intervention as a theme of new public architecture owes its growing prevalence, like the grand statement, to increasing competition between cities, regions and prefectures for commercial investment and cultural prestige.

Whether it is a new art museum for Tokyo to rival the Louvre in Paris, or a new Stadthaus for Ulm to unify its city centre and complement its famous cathedral, getting noticed is what matters. And often the more thrusting and contentious design solutions are those that attract the most interest. As this section suggests, libraries, museums, embassies, assembly halls and civic centres have become the dealing chips in a game where the stakes are getting higher all the time.

The dramatic intervention adopts many different forms, although its symbolic definition of local, regional and national aspirations – social, political and economic – remains common to all the projects shown here. The term can include interior architecture that creates an independent presence within the shell of an existing building and avoids physical or conceptual contact with its host. Ron Arad's richly inventive interior foyer spaces for the sober new Tel Aviv Opera House, designed by Yacov Rechter, express this idea most clearly. Arad describes his work as 'all about making spaces with autonomous objects'.

Or a dramatic intervention can mean the insertion of new modern elements into an old structure, as in the case of Dominique Perrault's scheme for the mayoral authority at Bar-le-Duc in northeastern France, where a classic nineteenth-century building has been renovated and extended with the addition of a network of futuristic walkways leading to a glass-domed auditorium.

More usually, however, the dramatic intervention refers to the way a new public building responds to its urban, suburban or rural context – whether mediating on a site of natural beauty or cutting a swath through a dense, historic urban district. Sometimes this intervention can be in the form of a single public building – as in Gunnar Birkerts' sculptural, multi-space museum in Kansas City, Missouri, or Antoine Predock's Civic Arts Plaza in Thousand Oaks, California, which addresses two very different contexts – freeway and meadow – with one integrated structure. The building can also be bifurcated, as with the new double-wing Münster library, which straddles either side of a narrow pedestrian street. A structure might even be broken down into several geometric fragments and scattered at the foot of the mountains to avoid monumental massing, as in Kisho Kurokawa's exceptional Ehime Science Museum.

Richard Meier's dramatic intervention achieves a striking counterpoint to its surroundings: his cool white, modern Ulm Stadthaus lands as if from another planet in the city's *Münsterplatz;* while Alessandro Mendini gives the sedate ancient city of Groningen a loud awakening with his crazy, colourful, canal-sited montage-museum. Yet some of these buildings seek visual continuity with the locality. The glazed sections of the giant new Tokyo Museum of Contemporary Art, for example, show a sensitivity to the municipal parkland in which the new complex sits. On a much smaller scale, the Finnish embassy in Washington, D. C. dramatically reaches out to embrace its tree-filled site by means of a white canvas canopy extending from a landing stage – a small symbolic gesture reflecting the way new public architecture of towns, cities, regions and nations must reach out to make a difference in perception to users, visitors and potential investors. ●

Groninger City Museum

Groningen, The Netherlands

Architect
Alessandro Mendini,
Atelier Mendini
Guest Architects
Philippe Starck
Coop Himmelblau
Michele de Lucchi

Client/Commissioning Body
Foundation for the Construction of the New Groninger Museum

Total Floor Space
9,000 square metres

Total Contract Cost
US $19.7 million

Date of Completion
October 1994

Alessandro Mendini's audacious assembly of different architectural styles has crash-landed on a prime canal site in the centre of Groningen to give the city a controversial new museum.

View of Coop Himmelblau's deconstructivist-style East Pavilion of the Groninger City Museum, which houses works of art dating from the sixteenth century in a shiplike construction of welded-steel plates decorated with tar. The architects' rationale is that the metal structure will rust away in 100 years, leaving only the marks of the tar as evidence of the scheme.

Alessandro Mendini, architect-in-chief of the new Groninger Museum, has mixed his metaphors in the most dramatic way possible to create one of the most extrovert and outspoken examples of the new wave of public architecture in Holland.

The museum sits on a narrow strip of land in the middle of a canal at a key axis point between the main railway station and the ancient town centre of Groningen. Mendini, *agent provocateur* of the Italian avant-garde, has welded together a montage of various architectural styles that turns the building into a kind of floating academic discourse on the nature of art and architecture, tension and structure, form and detail. The museum is its own principal exhibit.

At one end of this showy supertanker of design, Austrian architects Coop Himmelblau have created an East Pavilion in overt deconstructivist fashion to house art dating from the sixteenth century. Shiplike in its welded steel-plate construction, this geometric study of chaos sends shards and fragments flying in every direction. It would resemble a crash site even if it were not incongruously attached to Mendini's own yellow mast of a post-Modern box-tower at the heart of the scheme and Philippe Starck's Deco-flavoured circular drum, which houses the ceramic collection. A fourth collaborator, Michele de Lucchi, contributed a square brick pavilion devoted to the city's history and archaeology.

Mendini's approach has been to eschew the 'traditional idea of the synthesis of the arts'. Instead, he says, he has aimed for a 'narrative complexity' in which the 'building will itself be a system of museum works, while the exhibits integrate with and interpenetrate the architecture that receives and expresses them'. The colour palette – gold, silver, black, ochre, pink, pale blue – is deliberately diverse, while the range of materials and finishes is correspondingly enormous. Laminate panels clad Mendini's block, while vacuum-shaped aluminium

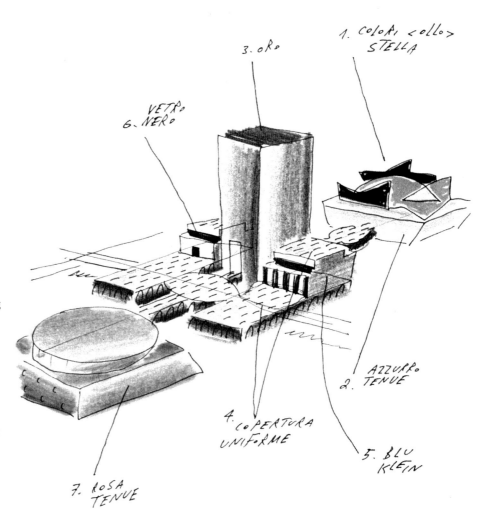

panels – with replicated moulds of an urn – adorn Starck's drum. Coop Himmelblau's steel plates are decorated with tar. Silkscreened, cement, brick, ceramic, wood, iron and bronze elements add to the dazzling mosaic of impressions.

Everywhere you look in this extraordinary complex, a host of contrasting design features strain for effect. Critics have described Mendini's plan as a cynical and over-bearing exercise in arbitrary dissonance in which the museum exhibits themselves will struggle for status. But the Groninger Museum is also an expression of Holland's liberal cultural values, and Groningen's fortuitous position sitting on a vast gas field – the national gas company stumped up much of the money for the project. ●

The exploded diagram reveals the juxtaposition of different elements, involving four different architectural collaborators. Architect-in-chief Alessandro Mendini's yellow tower sits at the heart of the scheme.

A showy supertanker of design, the Groninger City Museum sits in the middle of a canal, a startling new addition to the sober ancient town of Groningen. Philippe Starck's Deco-flavoured drum building on the left is decorated with moulded urn-shaped reliefs in the aluminium panels.

...THOUGHT...

...MADNESS...

...MELANCOLY...

Mendini's initial sketches for the museum extend from the themes of melancholy to madness.

Right: A delicate mosaic stairwell designed by Atelier Mendini, one of many jewels in a rich interior scheme. The architect-in-chief has revelled in a diversity of materials and finishes.

Above: The project has been conceived as a series of domestic objects in the landscape.

The different faces of the Groninger City Museum. Left: The utilitarian interior of Coop Himmelblau's East Pavilion is based on the idea of the unfolding of positive and negative spaces, according to the architects. A computer model developed the interior 'skin' of a scheme intended to establish different levels on which to experience art. Above: Warm, domestic-looking entrance hall by Atelier Mendini. Colour and form engage the visitor. Neon arcs overhead illuminate the mosaic desk.

Stadthaus

Ulm, Germany

Architect
Richard Meier & Partners

Interior Designer
Richard Meier

Client/Commissioning Body
City of Ulm – Building Department

Total Floor Space
10,000 square feet

Number of Levels
5

Total Contract Cost
£14.6 million

Date of Completion
November 1993

The white geometry of Richard Meier's new assembly building complements the tallest Gothic cathedral spire in the world in a way that the citizens of Ulm would never have believed.

The glazed open form of Richard Meier's modern, white Stadthaus gives the impression of an alien spacecraft landing in the square opposite Ulm Cathedral. Yet it is also a masterful response to a sensitive city site that has defied planning efforts for a century.

Below: The elevations show the
scheme's effort to fit into its sensitive
city-square context.

Meier's interior configurations frame
oblique views of the cathedral – the
tallest Gothic spire in the world.

Richard Meier's white geometric spacecraft of an assembly building has landed in the Ulm *Münsterplatz* in front of the largest gothic cathedral spire in the world, at last colonizing a pedestrian square that has defied planners and failed to inspire competition winners for a century. But far from being an alien invader, this masterful modern structure – based on Meier's familiar interplay of circle and square – is a worthy complement to Ulm Cathedral and a generator of a renewed sense of place in the city centre.

Ulm Cathedral miraculously survived war-time bombing of the city when all around it fell, but Meier's new companion piece – the winner of a 1986 design competition – nearly didn't survive a public referendum. That the architect has managed to get his scheme built at all is a tribute to the measured way in which the building responds to its historic context.

There is also a careful balance between substance and transparency achieved by cutaways in the reinforced concrete structure and expansive glazing on each floor.

The open form of the building, placed at the southwest corner of the *Münsterplatz* and glowing from within, invites access to the parvis. Its tripartite glazed roofs relate to the forms of the gable of facing commercial shops, while its use of white stucco reflects local building traditions. (The whiteness of Meier's buildings are more usually due to reflective metal panels.)

A public area within the Stadthaus itself extends the plaza and encourages visitors to explore a generous plan, flooded with natural light, in which a number of spaces frame oblique views of the neighbouring cathedral. Ticket and tourist offices in the foyer lead to a main elevator going up to the assembly room on the first floor. Two

successive levels of exhibition galleries can be found above. A covered bridge links the entrance foyer to a ground-floor restaurant.

The overall design is complemented by a new paving grid for the *Münsterplatz*, with dimensions derived from the cathedral, and an open square deliberately kept free of furniture. Both serve to accentuate the sheer quality of Meier's intervention at Ulm. ●

Right: Under the glazed roofing, a generous upper-floor exhibition area also puts Ulm Cathedral on display.

The southeast-facing elevation of the Stadthaus reveals the cutaways that break up the geometric whiteness of the building's volumes. The use of white stucco reflects a concern to observe local building traditions.

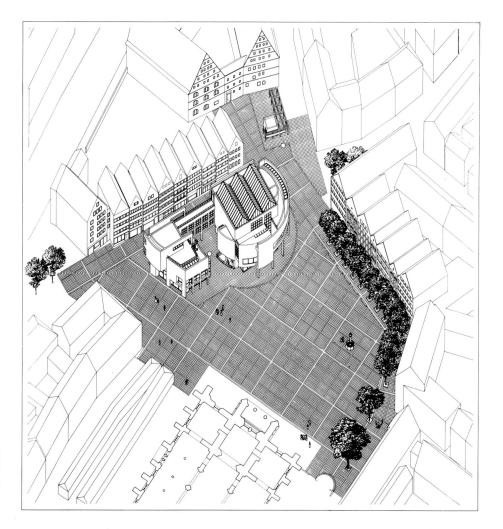

The site plan shows the new building in its context at the southwest corner of the cathedral square, set at an angle to the cathedral. Its tripartite glazed roofs echo adjacent shop-fronts.

The Civic Arts Plaza

Thousand Oaks, California, USA

Architect
Antoine Predock
(in association with
executive architect,
Dworsky Associates)

**Client/Commissioning
Body**
The City of Thousand
Oaks

Total Floor Space
182,000 square feet

Number of Levels
3 (each section: offices,
theatre, auditorium)

Total Contract Cost
US $53 million

Date of Completion
1994

Inserted between busy freeway and rolling meadow, Antoine Predock's Civic Arts Plaza in Southern California addresses the man-made and the natural in one comprehensive solution.

Main auditorium building of the Civic Arts Plaza in Thousand Oaks, California. Using neon tubes embedded in the façade, the Pictograph Wall makes a stylized reference to the art of the original native inhabitants of the Coneyo Valley.

The city of Thousand Oaks is a typical linear urban development north of Los Angeles. Defined and dominated by freeways but also with unexpected stretches of meadowland, the city lacked any real sense of urban focus. This is what Antoine Predock's Civic Arts Plaza set out to remedy in making a dramatic intervention alongside the city's Ventura Freeway.

The primary challenge was clearly the awkwardness of the site, with a steep change of grade from the freeway to its adjacent meadowland. Predock dealt with this contrast of elevation and character by building a monolithic façade that addresses the freeway, and creating a plaza that opens out more informally towards the meadowland and the Coneyo Valley beyond. As he explains, 'This building confronts the fantastic duality of Southern California – the man-made realm and the landscape.'

The largest elements of the complex – a 1,800-seat auditorium and parking facilities for 850 cars – are located closest to the freeway where their bulk helps to reduce the amount of traffic noise filtering through to the spaces beyond. The rear of the auditorium's fly tower, its planar surface covered with a tapestry of copper panels, confronts oncoming traffic like a giant billboard, providing a focal point for a cultural monument advertised as being 'impossible to miss at 70 mph'.

The complex is accessed by car from Thousand Oaks Boulevard to the north. A covered pedestrian walkway then introduces visitors to the building itself. The first encounter with the auditorium is its external Pictograph Wall – a stylized reference to the art of the native inhabitants of the Coneyo Valley. An entry tower then gives access to the plaza beyond; this effectively forms the fulcrum of a scheme that positions the civic

View of Antoine Predock's building from the Ventura Freeway. A tapestry of copper panels on the rear side of the auditorium fly tower confronts oncoming motorists, blocking noise from the more enclosed spaces beyond.

auditorium above and local government offices below. These city administration work spaces are in turn related to a seven-acre community park that surrounds the plaza and its reflecting pool. A dual purpose, 398-seat council chamber/community theatre sits astride the main mid-level plaza, symbolizing the twin purpose of the whole project.

Despite its considerable mass, the Civic Arts Plaza succeeds in keeping its scale accessible. Light slices the building in public zones, and circulation flows up and over the building to rooftop terraces. The result is a much-needed community centre for a city whose cultural heart previously only existed in the cars on the freeway outside. ●

Interior detailing reflects Predock's play with light and structure, a scheme that revels in the dichotomy between the natural and the man-made.

Section
1 Civic plaza
2 Reflecting pool
3 Civic auditorium
4 City office
5 Light court

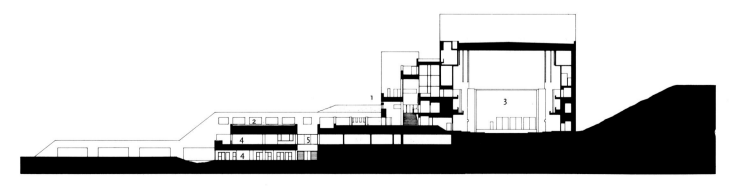

Above: The site plan reveals the way the building mediates between the freeway and the rolling meadow, negotiating a steep change of grade between the two levels. Government offices, which are part of the civic centre, point north into the meadowland.

Right: Predock's building cascades down in layers of administrative offices to the meadow park below.

The Foyer of the New Israeli Opera House

Tel Aviv, Israel

Architect
Ron Arad and
Alison Brooks,
Ron Arad Associates

Client/Commissioning Body
Tel Aviv Performing Arts Centre

Total Floor Space
2,450 square metres

Number of Floors
4

Total Contract Cost
£1.5 million

Date of Completion
October 1994

Ron Arad Associates has inserted a creative, curvaceous interior architecture to work autonomously within the respectable shell of Yacov Rechter's new Tel Aviv Opera House.

View of a waiting area beneath the cantilevered auditorium volume, which shows the sculptural quality of Arad and Brooks' interior scheme for the new Opera House in Tel Aviv.

A view of 'Chinese eyes' in the black
auditorium volume, with the bronze
wall below and 'spiral island' in the
background. Arad and Brooks have
used autonomous objects to create a
series of beguiling public spaces.

The sculptural interior foyer spaces of the new Opera House in Tel Aviv, which were designed by Ron Arad and his Canadian partner, Alison Brooks, represent the dramatic insertion of an architecture within an architecture. The building itself was designed by Yacov Rechter, one of Israel's most experienced and respected architects, as part of a far larger complex – the Tel Aviv Performing Arts Centre. This complex by Rechter incorporates a concert hall, theatre, housing and office accommodation as well as the new opera house.

Working on such a vast development, Rechter wanted to enrich aspects of his scheme by bringing in other designers to work alongside him. He recommended Arad, who had worked in his office as a student and whose furniture he admired, to the opera house management as a designer capable of providing a theatrical sense of occasion within the building shell. This was especially important given an unpromising external context: the opera house piazza is flanked by two matching commercial office buildings that comprise the Tel Aviv Performing Arts complex.

From the start of the scheme in 1988, there was a mutual 'hands-off' policy between two contrasting architectural approaches. Within the sober, logical geometries of Rechter's building, Arad and Brooks have worked autonomously in negotiated areas to create an energetic, curvaceous interior architecture, ensuring a minimum of contact – either physical or conceptual – with Rechter's design.

There are four main elements to a scheme that embraces all the public spaces within the new opera house, from the outer envelope to the auditorium: an 'Island', 'Bronze Wall', 'Drum' and 'Crush Bars'. The 'Island', which has the scale of a small four-storey building, wraps the auditorium in a curved ribbon of steel and concrete of constantly changing thickness and extraordinary plasticity. Punctured in places to allow views through it, this structure enfolds box office, restaurant and mezzanine slab.

The 'Bronze Wall', comprising thousands of stacked and soldered 15 mm bronze rods, is a sinuous invention which begins as a screen, folds into a bench, swells and turns back on itself near the foyer entrance to make an enclosure for a bookshop. The 'Drum' is a skin in concrete that turns the auditorium itself into a giant object in a boulder-strewn interior landscape, while the 'Crush Bars' are made of skeletal frames of aluminium castings with woven translucent stainless steel fronts.

Arad's customarily iconic furniture for the scheme relates in form and scale to the larger ideas of his interior architecture, and there are further enhancements with a little help from his friends – Neville Brody, who designed the signage, and Ingo Maurer, who contributed sensitive lighting fixtures on gilded aluminium. Overall, the maverick intervention of Arad and Brooks in Rechter's building is one of calculated risk, creating foyers of undeniable richness and fascination. ●

Above: A view of the café area from an opening in the spiral wall. This interior architecture has no physical or conceptual contact with architect Yacov Rechter's host building shell.
Right: The plan of the scheme reflects Arad's concern to inject a sensual theatricality into a sober building.

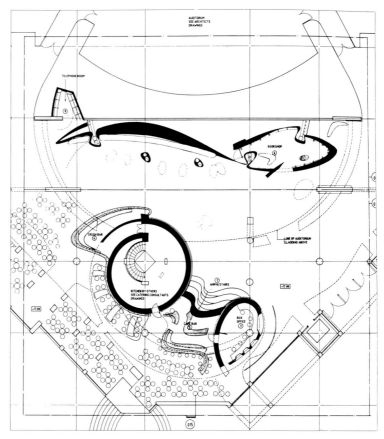

Right: The upper-level bar, with spiral wall beyond. Below: The foyer bookshop, comprising thousands of bronze rods, is part of an elaborate and sinuous interior structure.

Museum of Contemporary Art

Tokyo, Japan

Architect
Takahiko Yanagisawa
and TAK Associated
Architects Inc.

Client/Commissioning Body
City of Tokyo

Total Floor Space
36,075 square feet

Number of Levels
6 (including 3 below ground)

Total Contract Cost
US $403 million

Date of Completion
March 1995

Japan's largest art museum, spanned by a dramatic glazed entrance plaza, sacrifices monumental scale to achieve visual and spatial continuity with its Tokyo park site.

Aerial view of the Tokyo Museum of Contemporary Art which faces Kiba Municipal Park to the south. Running along the southern length of the scheme is a glazed 140-metre-long entrance lobby.

The defining image of the scheme. The V-shaped trusses of the elongated entrance lobby give the Tokyo Museum of Contemporary Art a recognizable visual symbol to compete with the glass pyramid of the Louvre.

Below: The section gives an idea of the sheer volume of the building, which has been moderated by its artful placement in the landscape.

Tokyo's new Museum of Contemporary Art, located on the northeastern edge of Kiba Municipal Park, has the distinction of being Japan's largest art museum. This, in a country of increasingly expansive cultural amenities, is no mean feat. Its large scale encompasses permanent and temporary exhibition spaces, an art library and art information centre within six levels – three of which are below ground; its giant-sized ambition is to create an artistic symbol for Tokyo on a par with the Louvre in Paris or the Metropolitan in New York.

But, despite all the civic expectation invested in the building, this is no grand monument or behemoth looking down on the city from lofty heights. Instead it goes to extraordinary lengths to achieve both visual and spatial continuity with the public park in which it sits, primarily through the use of large glazed surfaces that provide transparency, and generous external exhibition spaces that enhance the surrounding green areas.

Facing the park on the south side of the site is a long, fully glazed entrance lobby that runs along the entire length of the scheme and is its outstanding feature. 140 metres long and 10 metres wide, this entrance hall has a truss structure that spans across a water garden, and V-shaped structural members infilled with metal panels. Into these panels are punched a series of small holes, some containing glass lenses, that scatter speckled patterns of light through the lobby.

Between this elongated public lobby to the south and a parallel administrative block to the north, the permanent and temporary exhibition galleries and art information centre are arranged as three distinct and easily comprehended volumes. Clarity of form and function was a central objective, according to the architects.

The permanent exhibition galleries are designed as 'white cubes' with natural light filtering through toplights into a two-storey atrium to give a sense of movement and expansiveness. The temporary exhibition spaces adopt a similar strategy, split over three floors and wrapped around a 19-metre high atrium that adjoins a sunken garden used for external exhibitions.

The art information centre is circular and incorporates a range of state-of-the-art facilities, including an audio-visual gallery, beneath which can be found a large arts library with a floor area of 780 square metres. The museum also includes a public plaza, education department, storage areas, restaurant and cafeteria – each facility and space related to the next with a calm logic. The result is a very large museum, skilfully erected on reclaimed land despite poor loadbearing properties, which is not an extrovert landmark for the city to assimilate but a genuinely intelligent response to a municipal park site. And in those V-shaped trusses of the glazed entrance plaza, there is even the memorable artistic symbol that Tokyo craves to make its mark on world culture. ●

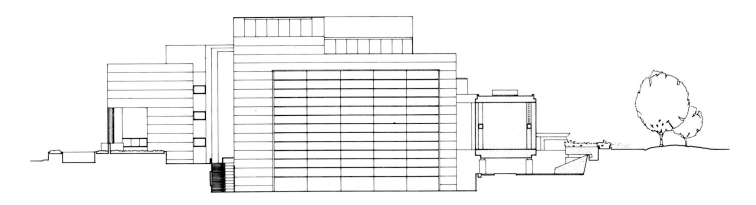

Artwork stands in splendid isolation in a double-height exhibition space, daylit from above. The main galleries were conceived as 'white cubes' to provide a sense of expansiveness.

Right: Inside the glazed entrance lobby. The metal panels that fill the V-shaped structural members are punched with small holes, some containing glass lenses, which spread speckled patterns of light through the lobby.

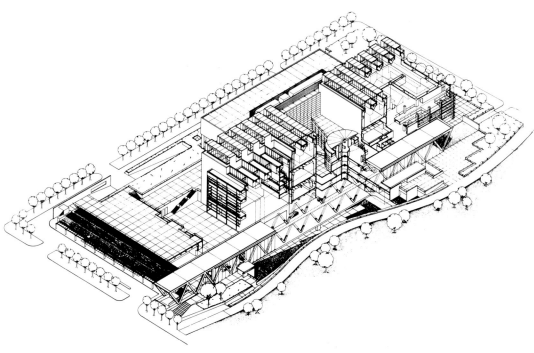

The axonometric shows the two main exhibition halls and the circular art information centre wedged between two elongated elements – the glazed lobby to the south, and the administration block to the north. The volumes of Japan's largest art museum are designed to be readily comprehensible.

3.6 Finnish Embassy

Washington, D.C., USA

Architect
Heikkinen – Komonen Architects

Interior Designer
Heikkinen – Komonen Architects

Client/Commissioning Body
Finnish Ministry for Foreign Affairs

Total Floor Space
45,000 square feet

Number of Floors
6 (including 2 below ground)

Total Contract Cost
US $10 million

Date of Completion
1994

Simple on the outside, complex within, the Finnish Embassy in Washington, D.C., makes the most of its prestigious hillside location to create a green building with a difference.

Beneath a white canvas canopy, a wooden deck on the north-facing elevation unites the Finnish Embassy with its green surroundings by extending a staff cafeteria into the woodland.

The green glass block façade of a
simple cube represents architects
Heikkinen and Komonen's
deceptively skilful response to a site
on Massachusetts Avenue in
Washington, D. C., that features 20
different species of trees.

Set in a green plot on Massachusetts Avenue in the heart of Washington's prestigious embassy district, Heikkinen and Komonen's Finnish Embassy is a compact, jewel-like building that responds to its sloping woodland site with an unusual degree of sensitivity. More than 20 different species of trees, some more than 90 feet tall, shade the embassy, which has two partially subterranean floors on account of the slope.

Perhaps the most dramatic aspect of this tightly controlled little building is its gesture to its surroundings on the rear north-facing elevation. Here a staff cafeteria can be extended by means of a deck or landing stage protected by a white canvas canopy. This physically unites the building with the neighbouring woodland to which its solid facets already respond so well.

Externally the embassy is a simple cube but one that has been transformed into a seductive presence by careful use of materials. Gable ends are of moss green granite; external office walls are of glass tile and green-tinted glass; and all external metal surfaces, copper panels and bronze profiles have been given a green patina. As a result, all the surfaces appear to respond to the surrounding foliage. This effect combines with that of a trellis for climbing plants situated on the south-facing façade to give the embassy a very green appearance overall.

The embassy houses a staff of 50 (with parking space for all) as well as offices, conference rooms, a library and a multipurpose facility for receptions, seminars, exhibitions and concerts. Inside, the design plan is spatially quite complex, as if to compensate for the formal simplicity of the envelope. The dominant feature is a skylit central hall that traverses the building longitudinally. Copper-clad conference rooms are visually suspended from a deep blue ceiling area that houses air-conditioning equipment, while all around steel bridges, ramps and staircases form an intricate internal web.

The multipurpose facility, know as the Finland Hall, gains flexibility from a 30-metre movable partition decorated with a mural by Juhana Blomstedt. When the partition is removed, Finland Hall and the central hall combine to create a single space to accommodate larger events and receptions. The basement contains a sauna section built of jointed logs, and elsewhere this vernacular feel is extended with Finnish art and artefacts. But the truest reflection of Finnish design culture is the way the building blends into the greenery around it. ●

The exterior treatment of the building integrates with the surrounding foliage. Metal surfaces have a green patina, glass is green-tinted, and walls are of glass tile. Even the gable ends are a moss-green granite.

Section

1 Foyer/Consular Affairs
2 Grand Canyon Atrium
3 Finland Hall
4 Archives, kitchen
5 Office
6 Plant
7 Parking
8 Storage

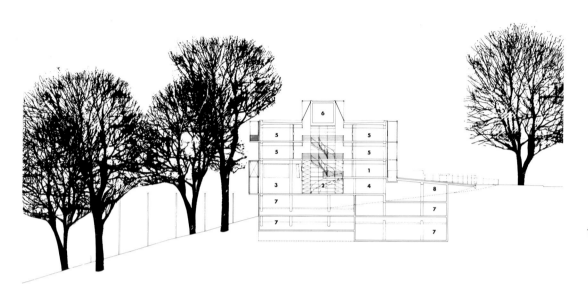

The spatial complexity of the interior plan is a counterpoint to the formal simplicity of the building envelope. Bridges, ramps and staircases form an intricate internal web.

City Library

Münster, Germany

Architect
Bolles-Wilson & Partner
Architekturbüro

Interior Designer
Bolles-Wilson & Partner
Architekturbüro

Client/Commissioning Body
City of Münster

Total Floor Space
10,000 square metres

Number of Levels
5 (including basement)

Total Contract Cost
£25.6 million

Date of Completion
November 1993

A daring piece of contextual design straddling a narrow pedestrian street on a dense historical site creates a dynamic two-part library for the capital of Westphalia.

A dense and problematic triangular site in the centre of Münster has been masterfully utilized by Julia Bolles-Wilson and Peter Wilson's design of a double-library divided into two distinct parts by a narrow pedestrian *Gasse*, or street.

Blue-tile-clad bays project from the northern wing of the library on to quiet gardens, a surprising element in a scheme full of intrigue and delight.

With so much new German public architecture subscribing to the cold high-tech logic of the construction kit, it is perhaps not surprising that the dramatic and sensual municipal library at Münster designed by architects Julia Bolles-Wilson and Peter Wilson should have attracted so much excited attention.

This is a white, shiplike building that matches form to urban context in a way that constantly intrigues and delights. The challenge of a dense triangular site in a conservative historical district of the city is turned into a glorious opportunity to intervene in the urban landscape with a slice of pure architectural invention. The library respects local landmarks, such as the Church of St Lambert, but single-mindedly goes its own way in creating its individual image.

The background to the project lies in a competition held in the mid-1980s to build a new library for the Westphalian capital. Out of more than 100 international entries, a scheme by London-based architect Julia Bolles-Wilson – ironically a native of Münster – aroused the most interest. The jury found her proposal for a double building that sits on both sides of a narrow pedestrian street, or *Gasse*, between the church and Mauritzstrasse compelling and convincing.

Bolles-Wilson and her Australian partner, Peter Wilson, both former students at the Architectural Association in London, subsequently moved to Münster and took an apartment next to the site to supervise the library's construction. The resulting five-storey building is divided in two by the specially created *Gasse*. The northern segment is given over to a large reference area and administration; the southern block to the reading areas and open book stacks of the lending library. The library's multi-level internal spaces – viewed through floors cut back progressively – are magnificent. Sloping walls held in place by giant cranked frames, white plaster surfaces

and warm birchwood acoustic panelling combine to create a rich effect.

A bridge at first-floor level links the two halves of the library and forms its entrance. North of the *Gasse*, two triangular bays rounded at their ends project on to quiet gardens. These bays create special rooms and are used most effectively in the basement children's library. But to the south, the architects have chosen a classic curved drum form, not only in practical response to the traffic flowing around the site but in recognition of the modern library tradition of Aalto and Asplund, which informs but does not impede the originality of their approach. ●

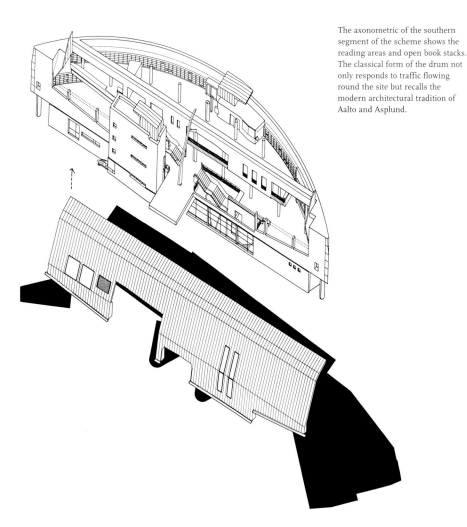

The axonometric of the southern segment of the scheme shows the reading areas and open book stacks. The classical form of the drum not only responds to traffic flowing round the site but recalls the modern architectural tradition of Aalto and Asplund.

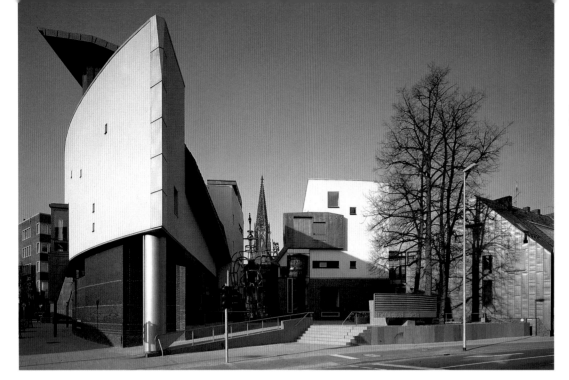

Right: The inspiring double-height reading room is suffused with natural light. The giant cranked laminated-timber portal frames, which hold up the sloping walls, stand out against a canvas of white plaster and warm birchwood acoustic panelling.

Above: View of the library through the narrow pedestrian *Gasse* which divides it in two. The building's distinct elements, connected by a bridge at first-floor level, elegantly frame the Lamberti Church in the background. The architects have responded to a rich and complex historical context with lyrical modernity.

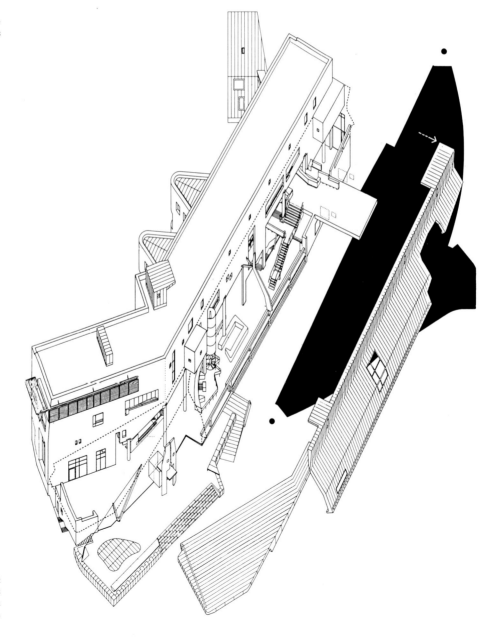

Axonometric of the northern segment of the scheme, which contains reference areas and administration facilities. Note the protruding bays.

Ehime Museum of Science

Ehime, Japan

Architect
Kisho Kurokawa

Interior Designer
Kisho Kurokawa

Client/Commissioning Body
Ehime Prefecture

Total Floor Space
24,290 square metres

Number of Levels
6 storeys plus
1 basement

Total Contract Cost
US $151.7 million

Date of Completion
September 1994

Kisho Kurokawa scatters a collection of geometric forms at the base of the mountains on Shikoku Island to create a science complex in which the sum of the parts is greater than the whole.

Main entrance to the Ehime Museum of Science as seen from the approach road. The seemingly random distribution of geometric shapes – cone, cube, crescent, sphere – conceals a scheme of precision and panache. The conical entrance hall is the first port of call for the visitor.

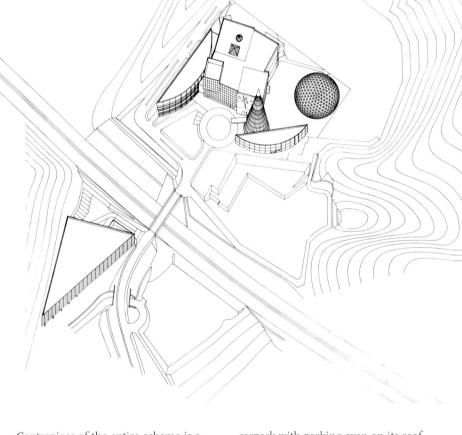

The Ehime Prefectural Museum of General Science in Japan comprises a collection of geometric forms – a cube, cone, sphere, triangle and two crescents – seemingly scattered at random at the base of the mountains on Shikoku Island by architect Kisho Kurokawa. But the unforced arrangement of elements for the new complex, which nestles in a suburb of Niihama city, is a lot more artfully contrived than initial inspection might suggest.

Kurokawa's approach has been to create a series of buildings as fragments, each individually articulated to relate to the surrounding area. To the observer, these are not deconstructed fragments or shards to express the fashionable idea of chaos, but separated components pulled apart to express the scientific concepts of assembly and inter-relationship.

Grafted on to this basic idea of geometric componentry is Kurokawa's special fascination with the Japanese tradition of asymmetry, which often recurs in his work. Thus, if you look closely, the cube-like exhibition hall is slightly tilted and shifted to emphasize the composition of four different square exterior surfaces that are finished variously in aluminium, glass and exposed concrete. According to Kurokawa, the layout of each fragment is designed to reflect the free arrangement of stepping stones in a formal Japanese garden – another expression of his country's asymmetric tradition.

Centrepiece of the entire scheme is a dramatic conical entrance hall. This has a sloping walkway tracing the spiral contours of the building. Visitors can stride down the cone, but walking up is apparently out of the question. The entrance hall is connected to the sphere – a planetarium resting on an artificial pond – by an underground passage below the pond. This is an expression of an abstract, invisible relationship between the two fragments, says Kurokawa.

The two crescent slices contain a restaurant, which relates to the entrance hall and planetarium, and an education hall, which nudges up to the exhibition hall. Across a highway that dissects the site, the triangle emerges as a multi-storey carpark with parking even on its roof. Internally, Kurokawa's rational-with-a-twist style combines hard surfaces with soft colours and unexpected angles. Overall this is a supremely confident project that is respectful of its hillside site, especially in the way the fragments break up the massing of what could have been an overwhelming complex. But it is also very determined to create a landscape on its own individual terms. ●

Above: The fourth floor of the multipurpose exhibition hall. The combination of hard surfaces and soft colours reflects a spirit of surprise and discovery.

View of the crescent-shaped exhibition centre (right) and exhibition hall cube, with outdoor exhibition space in the foreground.

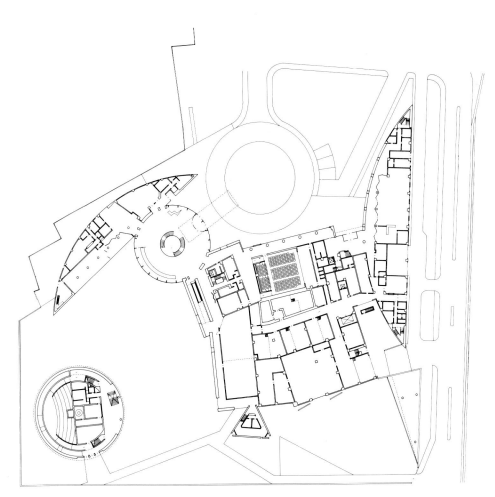

Left: First-floor plan of the complex, designed by Kisho Kurokawa with a playful sense of form. Below: Looking up inside the conical entrance hall. Visitors are permitted to descend the spiral.

Hôtel du Département de la Meuse

Bar-le-Duc, France

Architect
Dominique Perrault

Interior Designer
Dominique Perrault

Client/Commissioning Body
Conseil Général de la Meuse

Total Floor Space
14,300 square metres

Number of Floors
3 (existing building)
2 (new building)

Total Contract Cost
£10 million

Date of Completion
1994

The intervention of modern design in the classical proportions of an old mansion house creates an imaginative new council headquarters and legislative assembly in northeastern France.

Under a glass dome, the new legislative assembly at Bar-le-Duc in northern France. The illusion is of a curved structure but the dome actually consists of thousands of flat glass panels resting on an arched frame. Each panel is equipped with a thermal adjustable steel shutter, which provides shade and houses a tubular fluorescent lighting system.

By the side of the original classical building, a futuristic walkway leads to the glass dome of the legislative assembly. The glass has been designed so that elected representatives can have a view from inside but visitors on the outside cannot see in.

The regional authority headquarters at Bar-le-Duc in northeastern France have been boldly renovated and extended by architect Dominique Perrault in a scheme that powerfully inserts the spirit of modern design into the heart of a late nineteenth-century building without disturbing its classical plan and proportions. A futuristic glass-covered walkway, linking the existing building – a solid, imposing former teacher training college – with a new glass-domed structure, provides the most overt symbol of Perrault's bridge between old and new. But his intervention has actually been a lot more subtle than the sci-fi tube-like protrusions might at first suggest.

The key to the scheme lies in Perrault's decision to lower the portico to the level of the courtyard in the existing building and create a new ground floor at the level of the old basement. This required the foundations to be lowered, but it succeeded in creating an important public entry space that is light and airy and has an uninterrupted view to the rear of the building where council chambers and meeting rooms are housed in a new structure beneath a striking glass dome. The calm waters of a pond divide the two buildings which are connected by the covered walkway, and share service and maintenance functions in a common basement.

There is a symbolism in the counterpointed relationship between the original building, which houses the executive body (the entire council administration, including the chief executive's office), and the new glass dome, which houses the legislative body (elected representatives). Perrault has thus moderated the original building's impulse towards what he describes as 'the slightly aristocratic expression of the noble nature of living in large, grand mansions' with the demands of modern democracy. His scheme creates an affinity between two different French traditions in architecture, and its landscape of ponds and reflections symbolizes the importance of water in the region. ●

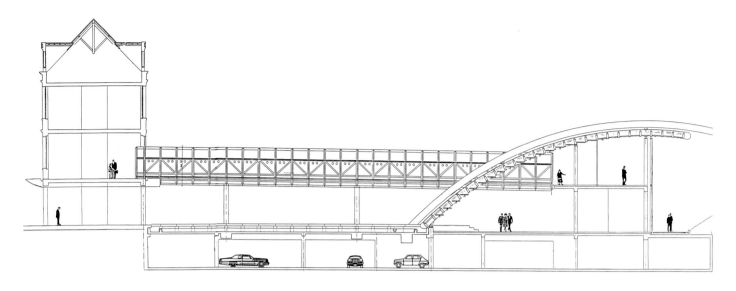

Top: The cross section shows the
different levels of the scheme, with
the executive body housed in the late-
nineteenth-century house, which is
linked to the legislative body in the
new glass dome.

The classical plan and proportions
of the original building – a former
teacher training college – are
unaffected by Dominique Perrault's
futuristic intervention of a glass-
covered walkway. Water and
reflection are key elements of
the scheme.

Above: Inside the tubular walkway a spirit of progressive modernism is your guide as you approach the seat of democracy for the region. Right: The façade of the original building shows the lowered foundations and the insertion of a new public entry foyer at the level of the old basement.

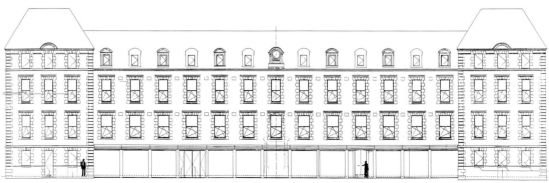

Kemper Museum of Contemporary Art and Design

Kansas City, Missouri, USA

Architect
Gunnar Birkerts and Associates

Client/Commissioning Body
Kansas City Art Institute

Total Floor Space
23,200 square feet

Number of Floors
1

Total Contract Cost
US $8.7 million (excluding landscaping and furnishing)

Date of Completion
October 1994

A dynamic new American museum responds both spatially and conceptually to the changing demands of exhibiting contemporary art with a sculptural approach that challenges convention.

The imposing entrance porch to the Kemper Museum of Contemporary Art and Design. The three columns are a contextual reference to the many other porches on Warwick Boulevard, where the building is situated.

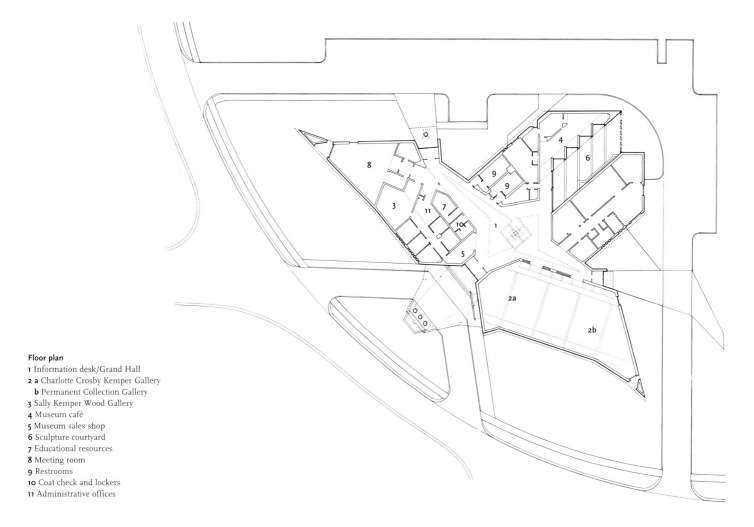

Floor plan
1 Information desk/Grand Hall
2 a Charlotte Crosby Kemper Gallery
  b Permanent Collection Gallery
3 Sally Kemper Wood Gallery
4 Museum café
5 Museum sales shop
6 Sculpture courtyard
7 Educational resources
8 Meeting room
9 Restrooms
10 Coat check and lockers
11 Administrative offices

This dynamic and adventurous museum building reflects the idea that the constant progressions of contemporary art can never be enclosed within predetermined traditional forms. Thus Gunnar Birkerts' design is a polygonal construct, apparently shaped to create a dramatic sculptural gesture, all wings, angles and points.

The lack of recognizable symmetry does indeed invite the viewer to experience the building from a number of different angles. But at the same time the roof does mark out the museum's four main exhibition spaces, and there are some references to context: the main entrance is marked with three substantial posts that allude to the many other porches on Warwick Boulevard, where the museum is situated.

Birkerts describes his unusual white concrete building as neither influenced by historical building forms nor seeking to exercise literal influence itself. Its purpose is to achieve a spatial response to allow almost limitless display and of contemporary art. Gallery spaces range in size from 250 to 4,300 square feet, and in height from 7 to 24 feet. There is also an enclosed sculpture garden with an unlimited vertical dimension.

The free-flowing interior space unfolds as the visitor progresses through it. This sense of organic development challenges expectations created by the formal compartments of more conventional museums. In addition to the main exhibition areas, the brief called for a study centre, a grand entry hall, conference centre, retail area, café, and administrative, preparation and storage spaces. A large central atrium culminates in an articulated skylight and provides an anchor to an interior space otherwise unpredictable in its effects but luxurious in its finishes.

The complex angles of the roof, with its stainless steel components; the atrium floor of quartz-flecked charcoal grey granite; a stainless steel reception desk, also designed by Birkerts; and the warm maple flooring of the main gallery – all are integrated into Birkerts' crystalline structure perfectly rationally. But at the heart of the scheme is the undefined, undefinable and ultimately restless nature of contemporary art that informs the overall spirit of a museum originally designed for the Kansas City Art Institute and now owned by the Kemper Museum Foundation. ●

The complex structural form of Gunnar Birkerts' organic museum design. This dramatic sculptural gesture, all wings, angles and points, has been designed to provide a varied spatial response to the dynamic needs of contemporary art exhibition.

The museum's enclosed sculpture garden. Birkerts observes that 'organic architecture is like listening to a piece of music. You can never take in the entire piece at once. You have to listen to it from beginning to end several times.'

SECTION 4

Opposite:
The Finnish National Opera House
in Helsinki, designed by architects
Hyvämäki-Karhunen-Parkkinen to
blend into its urban bay setting.

In a world of increasing global communications, growing
metropolitan complexity and an ever-swifter pace of life, the
cultural places we visit to expand the mind and enjoy the quiet
contemplation of art, artefacts or music away from everyday
pressures are becoming ever more scarce and precious. This
section explores the idea of the tranquil space in public buildings
and environments, a theme that has emerged in recent years as
public bodies, cultural organizations and their architects and
designers try to define a new realm in which calm appreciation
can take the place of frantic consumerism.

The majority of the projects shown here – from Art Deco
restoration to the display of Aztec sculpture – are museum
buildings or galleries; the study of often demanding subject matter
requires all the unhurried focus that intelligent interiors, lighting,
spatial and material organization can provide. But there is also a
concert hall, an opera house and a synagogue in the selection,
providing different perspectives on the creation of tranquillity
through quality design.

The new Begegnungsstätte synagogue at Wuppertal in
Germany, for example – built dramatically on the site of the
old Wuppertal synagogue destroyed by the Nazis during the
Reichkristallnacht in 1938 – achieves a state of grace as an abstract
sculptural composition in assembling a collage of different
architectural fragments to reflect the idea of tension and fracture.
Meanwhile Fumihiko Maki's Kirishima International Concert Hall,
set on a verdant sloping plain, introduces the idea of the relaxing
outdoor music village with rehearsal rooms around a courtyard.

Maki's distinctive concert hall is one of no less than four
Japanese projects shown here which are set in either a partial or
total rural landscape. These schemes may surprise given the
country's scarcity of green sites and the urban character of so

much Japanese architecture. But in Tadao Ando's stepped hillside
Chikatsu-Asuka Museum, Kisho Kurokawa's study in geometric
composition that creates two museums in the Wakayama castle
grounds, and Hiroshi Naito's vernacular Sea Folk Museum on a
wet coastal site, one can see a vigorous new modern Japanese
architecture developing that draws its inspiration from natural
surroundings and historical tradition.

Not that a city site precludes the creation of tranquil spaces.
One of the triumphs of the giant new Finnish National Opera
House is the way it blends into the Helsinki cityscape. Built over
20 years at a cost in excess of £100 million (with £5.3 million alone
spent on furniture and fittings), the opera house hides much of its
volume underground. Its public foyers, however, are models of
uncluttered clarity. And in the centre of Madrid, José Rafael
Moneo's elegant remodelling of a neoclassical palace to house the
1,600 works of the Thyssen-Bornemisza art collection achieves
interiors of genuine warmth and tranquillity.

Moneo's scheme – ideally suited to show one of the most
important private art collections in the world – cannot escape
a formal grandeur. But inspiring awe is not necessarily a
prerequisite for a tranquil setting. Ettore Sottsass adopts a very
different strategy in creating a new cloister-like gallery for a
furniture museum in Ravenna. 'We thought of using very common
materials and giving the entire building a vague, run-down feeling,'
he explains, 'so that it would not seem, in the simple countryside,
that someone had wanted to place a definitive monument. We
hope that with the passing of the years, the grass grows perfumed,
the trees in the courtyard make shade, and the walls get a bit
dirty.' Tranquillity, suggests Sottsass, is a state of mind, not a
state of perfection. ●

Thyssen-Bornemisza Collection, Villahermosa Palace

Madrid, Spain

Architect
José Rafael Moneo

Interior Designer
José Rafael Moneo

Client/Commissioning Body
Thyssen-Bornemisza Foundation

Total Floor Space
18,000 square metres

Number of Floors
7 (3 below ground)

Total Contract Cost
£21 million

Date of Completion
Autumn 1992

A former palace has been classically remodelled to display one of the world's most important art collections in a warm, inviting setting that does not resort to historical pastiche.

The upper-floor gallery of the museum is flooded with daylight from skylights. The Thyssen-Bornemisza art collection is the most important private collection in the world, with the exception of that owned by the British Royal Family. It contains around 1,600 works, from 13th-century Italian master paintings to American Pop Art.

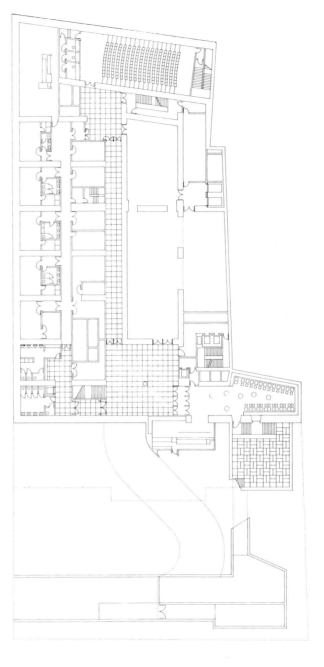

Free circulation between levels is an integral part of a scheme that corresponds to the classical proportions of the palace but has been given a complete interior remodelling by José Rafael Moneo.

First basement-floor plan, incorporating cafeteria, lecture hall, storage, temporary exhibition, office and service spaces.

Madrid's splendid Villahermosa Palace, built by Mirandola in the eighteenth century, has been a building much-buffeted by changing architectural enthusiasms. It was given its neoclassical proportions in the nineteenth century by architect Antonio Lopez Agudo, who moved the main entrance to the north façade and reorganized the floor compositions; then, a century later, in the 1970s, it was stripped internally to house a modern banking office and the entrance was shifted to the south façade.

Today, however, this fine building in the heart of the city has at last found a state of grace at the hands of architect José Rafael Moneo, whose sensitive restoration to create a home for Baron von Thyssen's art collection overcomes considerable odds with great tact and flair.

The way in which Moneo's scheme reflects Agudo's neoclassical dimensions without resorting to palatial pastiche is especially praiseworthy given what he had to work with. Although the noble, neoclassical façade of the building was in perfect condition, the offices of the former bank were utterly worthless. So Moneo was forced to reinvent the interior completely in a way that would respect the past but convincingly belong to the present.

Not surprisingly he has returned the entrance to the well-conserved northern façade, as Agudo intended, and used its symmetry as the main reference point for his interior plan. The museum is ordered around a central, glass-roofed inner courtyard that unfolds from the neoclassical dimensions of the façade, enabling Moneo to develop a uniform layout that corresponds to the old style while allowing visitors to circulate freely from the ground floor up to a third-floor terrace. The geometry of a network of internal walls repeats the rhythm of openings along the façade.

A carefully planned combination of natural and artificial light (designed by London-based Ove Arup and Partners) plays an important part in the scheme's success. On the top floor, where the museum tour begins, natural light floods through special skylights and vertical light wells. A computer-controlled system introduces fluorescent and low-voltage halogen effects, in keeping with Moneo's concern to create a warm, inviting glow. That will explain his principal use of salmon-pink stucco to decorate a sequence of rooms in a way that harmonizes with the spirit of this grand old duke's residence without displaying a trace of historicist vernacular. ●

A typical gallery in the building, one of a series grouped around a central inner courtyard. The warm stucco walls are stained with a natural pigment; the floors are marble. Low-voltage spotlights and fluorescent wallwashers provide a mix of general and decorative lighting.

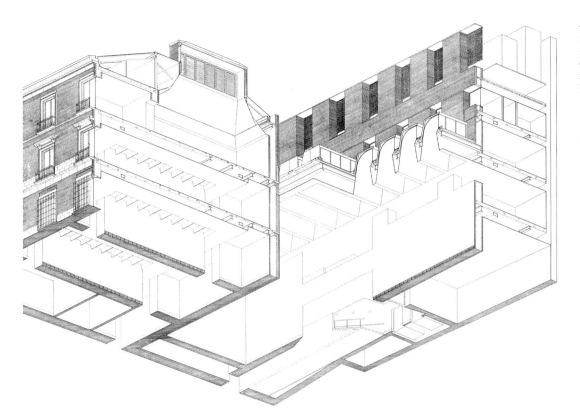

The sectioned axonometric reveals Moneo's structural reinvention. The rhythm of the nineteenth-century classical façade is extended to the geometry of the new network of interior walls and levels.

Exterior of the Villahermosa Palace, built by Mirandola on a prime Madrid site: a graceful old building has been recycled with the finesse it deserves.

Chikatsu-Asuka Historical Museum

Osaka, Japan

Architect
Tadao Ando Architect
& Associates

Client/Commissioning Body
Osaka Prefecture

Total Floor Space
5,925 square metres

Number of Floors
3

Date of Completion
March 1994

A stepped concrete plaza – the roofline of an iconoclastic new historical museum – provides the perfect vantage point to view Japan's earliest burial mounds in their natural context.

The 30-metre-high Golden Spring tower dominates Osaka architect Tadao Ando's museum dedicated to studying Japan's early burial mounds. The stepped plaza has been designed to be a regional hub of activity.

An aerial view shows the Chikatsu-Asuka Museum in its landscape: the form of the building has been lifted tectonically from its natural terrain, providing panoramic views of the surrounding countryside from its stepped roof.

The oft-repeated claim of modern architecture to open doors to a new expression while touching upon the earliest visual forms of history is given eloquent substance in this extraordinary project by Osaka architect Tadao Ando in a place called Chikatsu-Asuka in a southern part of Osaka Prefecture.

Chikatsu-Asuka was central to one of the earliest periods of Japanese history, and has one of Japan's best collections of burial mounds (kofun) dating from the sixth and seventh centuries, with more than 200 examples. The new Chikatsu-Asuka Historical Museum has been built to fulfil two purposes: to exhibit the tombs and to facilitate research into the culture of the era; and to provide a total experience as an element integral to the natural environment in which the burial mounds are found.

Tadao Ando has therefore conceived of the building in the form of a hill lifted tectonically from the natural terrain, a structure that immediately draws the eye to the surrounding vistas. The giant stepped roof of the museum provides views that set the entire group of tombs in their natural context, while also creating a dramatic outdoor plaza for plays, concerts and lectures, enabling the museum to become a hub of regional activity.

The use of exposed concrete to create a stepped landscape recalls the work of Sir Denys Lasdun at the National Theatre or University of East Anglia in the UK. But Ando's symbolism here goes beyond the idea of public spectacle or academic research to reflect the raw spiritualism of the early Japanese burial rituals in a technologically advanced late-twentieth-century monument.

Accordingly, the interiors of the museum are deliberately dark and sombre, with objects exhibited precisely as they were found in the tombs, in order to capture the sensation of being drawn into the tombs and going back – in mood at least – to ancient times. A 30-metre-high Golden Spring tower at the heart of the scheme creates black shadows that add to the sensation of discovery of early Japanese civilization. This is a project that cuts a concrete swath through a rural enclave, yet its stepped plaza shows that Tadao Ando's sometimes brutalist forms can be unusually sympathetic to humanistic reflection. ●

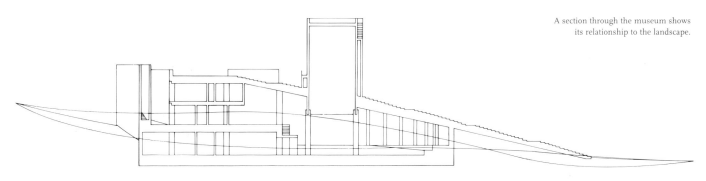

A section through the museum shows its relationship to the landscape.

The main exhibition space of the Chikatsu-Asuka Museum, with a model of a burial mound as its centrepiece. The atmosphere is deliberately rather sombre in its evocation of the raw spirituality of the past.

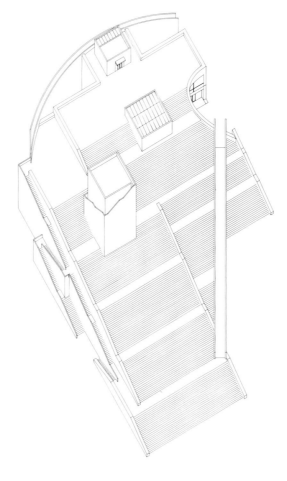

The axonometric shows the giant stepped-roof structure of the museum.

Right: Ando plays with shadow and light to capture the sensation of going back in time, and to provide quiet places for humanistic reflection.

Gallery of the Museum of Contemporary Furniture

Ravenna, Italy

Architect
Sottsass Associati

Interior Designer
Sottsass Associati

Client/Commissioning Body
Sine Loco Snc di
Raffaello Biagetti & Co

Total Floor Space
650 square metres
(Interior enclosed space:
400 square metres.
Covered portico: 250
square metres)

Number of Floors
1 (plus loft)

Date of Completion
1994

A graceful extension to a furniture museum in the Italian countryside reveals the subtle skills of the Sottsass studio in creating a cloister-style setting around a central courtyard.

A courtyard closed on three sides by blue-painted concrete portico walls separates the existing furniture museum at Ravenna from the graceful new gallery designed by Ettore Sottsass and Johanna Grawunder.

A view of the simple gallery extension shows its relationship to the existing building: a thoughtful new addition on a site of green fields and rolling vistas that is designed to grow old gracefully.

Furniture and architecture are inextricably linked in the postwar development of Italian design. Italy's most influential group of furniture and product designers – Ettore Sottsass, Mario Bellini, Gae Aulenti and Vico Magistretti among them – trained and practised first as architects. So it is fitting that the architecture of a new gallery to be attached to the existing Museum of Contemporary Furniture in the Italian countryside at Ravenna should be entrusted to the Sottsass studio, which has done so much to define the context of the Post-Modern Italian object.

Sottsass and co-designer Johanna Grawunder have met the client's requirement for extra space at the museum by sympathetically creating a new gallery extension that looks fresh but will grow old gracefully. They wanted to ensure an appropriate response to the surrounding countryside, an area of green fields and distant horizons, as well as adding experiential value to what could otherwise have been a mundane adjunct.

Working with local architects, Agora, Sottsass and Grawunder devised a way to link the new gallery – a prefabricated concrete warehouse-style structure – to the main building emotionally as well as physically. Separating the two structures is a new space of calm and reflection, a courtyard closed on three sides by concrete portico walls painted blue. In the centre of the courtyard, an olive tree sits in a raised garden area. At ground-floor level the two buildings are connected by a covered walkway. Another link – a bridge passage – is situated at the upper level.

The new building, on the fourth side of the courtyard, is a very simple structure with a continuous skylight for natural illumination. It is distinguished on the exterior wall that faces into the courtyard by a staircase – this is proposed as an independent sculpture in its own right and makes imaginative use of black terrazzo tiles and glass. Additional decorative elements include the mosaic tile finishing of another smaller courtyard, which affords access from the rear. The tiles were designed by Sottsass and made by local master-craftsmen in Ravenna.

The overall result is a new space designed not only to relate a new building to an older one in a thoughtful way but also to add a new dimension to the museum itself. The Gallery is a meeting place, an open studio for artists, and a setting of quiet contemplation. 'A kind of cloister in which to walk, rest or concentrate afresh' is how Sottsass aptly describes it. ●

The playful shapes and colours that define the new gallery and its courtyard reflect the relationship between architecture and furniture in Italian design. The new facility is envisaged as an 'open studio' for artists to gather.

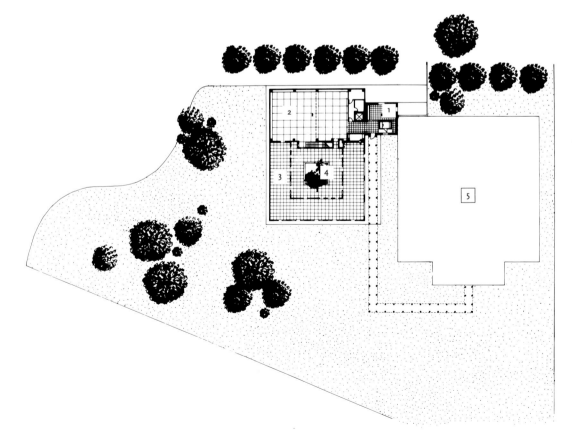

Plan of spaces:
1 Entrance courtyard
2 New gallery
3 Portico
4 Courtyard
5 Existing museum

New Wing and Restoration of the Joslyn Art Museum

Omaha, Nebraska, USA

Architect
Sir Norman Foster
and Partners

Interior Designer
Sir Norman Foster
and Partners

**Client/Commissioning
Body**
Joslyn Art Museum

Total Floor Space
58,000 square feet

Number of Floors
3

Total Contract Cost
US $15.9 million

Date of Completion
November 1994

An early 1930s Art Deco building in Nebraska, clad in pink marble, provided an unlikely but rewarding renovation challenge for one of the world's best-known modernist practices.

A view of the gallery space in the new wing of the Joslyn Art Museum, designed by Sir Norman Foster and Partners: the extension of a Nebraska Art Deco building has been achieved with a calm authority.

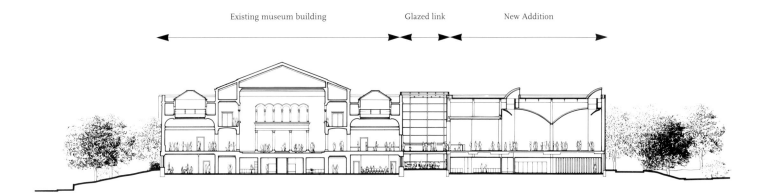

Existing museum building   Glazed link   New Addition

The Joslyn Art Museum, built in 1931 as a cultural centre for art and music, can claim to be one of the finest examples of Art Deco architecture in America. However, the passage of time had severely compromised its practicality: 60 years on, many of the facilities in this venerated pink marble building had become outdated and there was an urgent need for new space to be added.

Even so, the building's monumental effects had endured gloriously – from its introductory stone staircase leading to an imposing classical entrance, to the huge entrance lobby, top-lit fountain court and 1,200-seat concert hall.

A new building of approximately 4,600 square metres was commissioned to house new gallery spaces and management facilities for the collection. In addition, limited renovation and refurbishment work on the original building was to be undertaken. Sir Norman Foster and Partners developed a calmly authoritative master plan with characteristic rigour, based on analysis of the existing facilities and a thoughtful initial response to the site.

Over the years public use of the museum's grand east entrance had dwindled with car users tending to use a small entrance adjacent to the car park.

The original emphasis has now been restored by redirecting access roads and parking towards the main entrance. There is also a new landscaped amphitheatre for summer concerts. Interior restoration includes enhancements to the concert hall's lighting and acoustics, the updating of existing galleries, renovated restrooms and a remodelled museum shop.

Foster's new wing makes no attempt to compete or contrast with the original building. It echoes the scale of the original and duplicates its unusual pink Etowah Fleuri marble – taken from the same Georgia quarry as that used in the 1930s – in the new cladding. The two buildings are connected with a glass atrium – a recognizable product of Foster's architectural language – that provides new restaurant space, a secondary public entrance and a reception area.

Working as lead designer on the project in partnership with local architects and engineers Hennington Durham and Richardson, and main contractor Kiewit Construction Company, the Foster practice has created a thoughtful, tranquil and sympathetic complement to a building that may be defined by the manners of another architectural era but remains timeless in its essential appeal. ●

A cross-section shows how the addition of the new wing to the existing museum uses a language and a scale that neither contrasts nor competes with the original.

The glazed link between the 1931 building and its modern new addition is a transparent structure at night, providing reception and restaurant facilities.

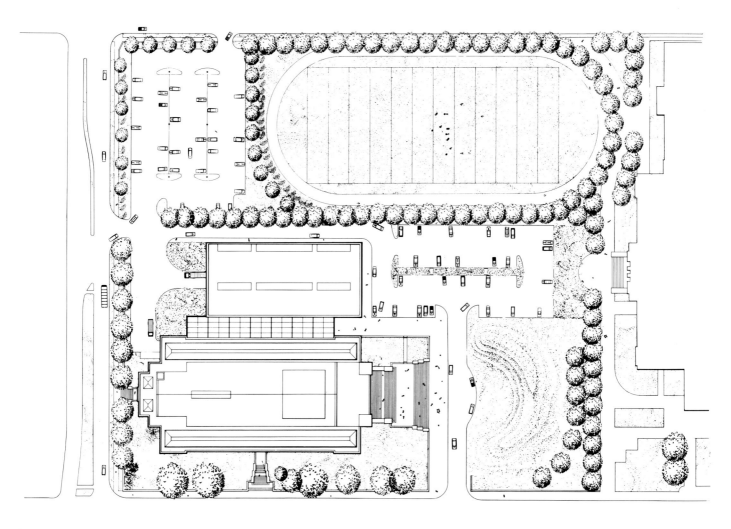

Top: The site plan shows access roads and car parking redirected to the main entrance. A landscaped amphitheatre for summertime concerts sits opposite.

Above: Foster achieved a perfect match on the façade by cladding his new wing with the same pink Etowah Fleuri marble as was used on the original museum in the early 1930s, quarried from the same Georgia site.

4.5 Sea Folk and Shima Art Museums

Tobashi, Mie Prefecture, Japan

Two museums share a site but contrast styles along a wet, windy and salty stretch of Japanese coastline, in order to reflect the art and culture of the local fishing industry.

Architect
Naito Architect
& Associates

Client/Commissioning Body
The Foundation of Tokai Suisan Kagaku Kyokai (Sea Folk Museum)
Kamegawa Construction Corporation (Shima Art Museum)

Total Floor Space
512 square metres (Shima Art Museum)
3,924 square metres (Sea Folk Museum)

Number of Levels
2 in each museum

Total Contract Cost
US $4.6 million

Date of Completion
January 1993 (Sea Folk Museum)
August 1993 (Shima Art Museum)

Boat storage facility in Hiroshi Naito's Sea Folk Museum at Tobashi: an imposing interior space reflecting the heritage of Japan's fishing industry shelters beneath a dynamic structure of precast concrete.

Nestling in hills along the Japanese coastline close to wind and water are two highly individual museums, each with their own distinct personality but linked by a common theme and architectural approach.

The Sea Folk Museum is the larger of the two, dedicated to collecting, storing and exhibiting the tools and equipment used by local fishermen in the era before rapid Japanese economic growth in the 1960s turned a thriving industry into a fact of heritage. On a hill just 100 metres away is the Shima Art Museum, designed to exhibit oil paintings by contemporary artists, with a greater emphasis on presentation than storage.

Both museums are defined by their combination of appropriately modest materials and rich spatial arrangements, and influenced by the local topography and climate, which is characterized by heavy rainfall and high humidity and salt levels. Architect Hiroshi Naito has revelled in the visual links to be made between the two, especially in the use of traditional roof tiling, but also in their contradictions.

Thus the Sea Folk Museum has an organic structural dynamism in the use of a post-tensioned precast concrete system for the main storage area and a laminated wood structure for the main exhibition space; whereas the Shima Art Museum – barely one tenth of its size – is given a much simpler, more hard-edged treatment. Its exposed concrete bearing walls are topped by laminated wooden beams and steel-tensioned steel members, and finally by a refined glass skylight – reflecting Naito's idea that 'as the building reaches its top, it increases the refinement of its details'.

The Sea Folk Museum is a sophisticated project realized with great economy and ingenuity to defy the natural elements: exterior precast concrete surfaces are sprayed with resin, while a system of Japanese cedar boards has been used in the fishing net storeroom to withstand the high humidity. The configuration of exhibition wings, research lab, repository and main entrance resembles the vernacular style of local homes in the area, which were once coated with whale oil for weatherproofing.

The Shima Art Museum, meanwhile, is organized on the ground floor with an entrance hall used to divide an exhibition zone from an atelier space. On the second level, offices and a second atelier space are linked by a steel suspension bridge. Through these two intelligent and understated museum projects, Hiroshi Naito casts a cool and tranquil light on the art and culture of the fishing villages that once dominated the region but are now fast disappearing. ●

Top: Elevation of the Sea Folk Museum, from right to left: repository, research lab, exhibition wing A, main entrance, and exhibition wing B.

The collection of pavilion buildings which together make up the Sea Folk Museum echo the local domestic vernacular. Sited in an area of high humidity and rainfall, the buildings have been sprayed with resin to withstand the harsh climate.

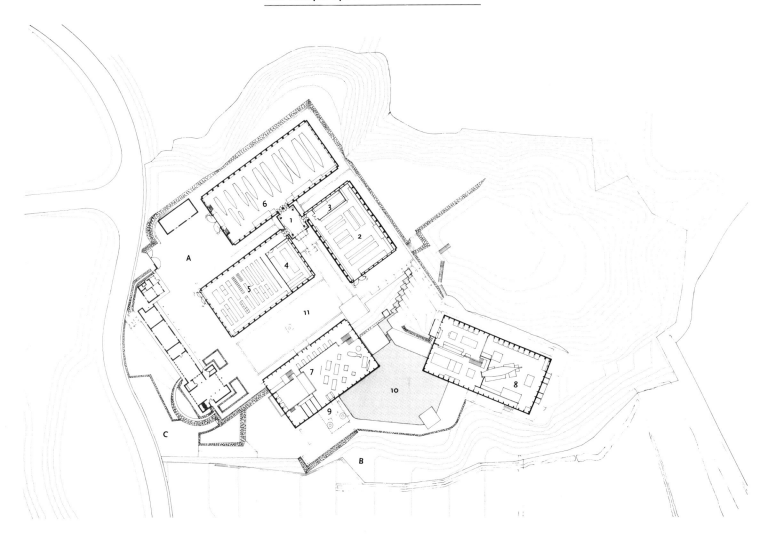

SITE PLAN
A Repository
1 Entrance room
2 Storage room – fishing nets
3 Storage room – clothes, papers
4 Storage room – tubs, casks, baskets
5 Storage room – fishing implements
6 Storage room – boats
B Exhibition hall
7 Exhibition wing A
8 Exhibition wing B
9 Main entrance
10 Water plaza
11 Courtyard
C Research lab

Japanese cedar boards line the
fishing net storage room; they help
the artefacts to withstand the
high humidity.

The plan shows how architect Hiroshi Naito developed the two contrastingly-scaled museums within a common vernacular framework: the Shima Art Museum sits 100 metres to the north of the larger Sea Folk Museum.

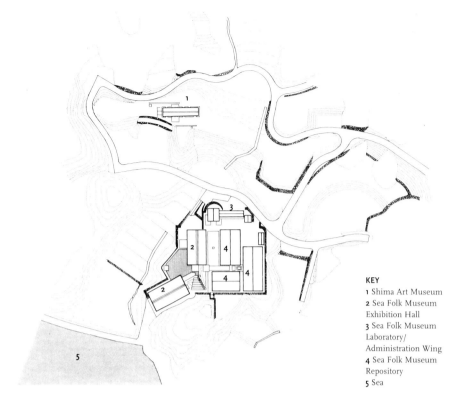

KEY
1 Shima Art Museum
2 Sea Folk Museum Exhibition Hall
3 Sea Folk Museum Laboratory/ Administration Wing
4 Sea Folk Museum Repository
5 Sea

The exterior view shows the independent wooden roof, clad with traditional Japanese tiles, which is set on cantilevered concrete walls.

The elegantly resolved Shima Art Museum interior: the accent is on display of contemporary oil paintings rather than on the storage of artefacts, as in the neighbouring Sea Folk Museum.

Right: An isometric drawing and below, exterior view of the Shima Art Museum. The structure of this simple building has been designed to increase in the refinement of its details from concrete wall up to wooden beams and glass skylight.

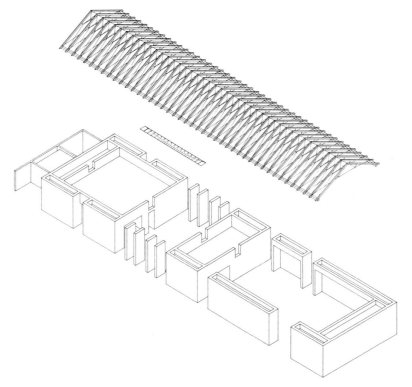

Finnish National Opera House

Helsinki, Finland

Architect
Hyvämäki-Karhunen-Parkkinen

Interior Designer
Tuula Mäkinen, Anita Karhunen, Antti Paatero

Client/Commissioning Body
The National Board of Public Building, Finland

Total Floor Space
40,450 square metres

Number of Floors
8 (6 underground)

Total Contract Cost
£101.3 million

Date of Completion
March 1993

Two decades in development, this new national opera house for Finland creates a timeless quality in the calm and considered way it responds to performers, visitors and the city itself.

Architects Hyvämäki-Karhunen-Parkkinen have created a series of tranquil, airy public foyers, flexibly designed to house smaller musical events outside main performance hours, as well as light-filled social spaces for opera audiences during intervals.

n its hundred-year history, the Finnish National Opera never had all of its facilities under a single roof until architects Hyvämäki-Karhunen-Parkkinen created this integrated opera house of international scale and prestige. Long-term efforts to find a worthy home for the opera finally crystallized in an architectural competition proposed by Helsinki's city council in the mid-1970s. More than 20 years later, the resulting Finnish National Opera House represents an exemplary exercise in public building, both externally and internally.

The new building was achieved with minimum disturbance to the existing street pattern or to the shoreline recreational areas of neighbouring Töölönlahti Bay. In order to lessen the impact on a bayside park, the bulk of the building is hidden underground. Meanwhile its visible aspects

relate well to two other urban cultural landmarks – Finlandia Hall and the Helsinki City Theatre. The overall external effect is one of sympathetic response rather than monumental intrusion. This is all the more remarkable when one considers the size and scale of the activities that are housed within.

A primary design principle was that this should be neither a theatre nor a concert hall but a dedicated opera house. The light, airy foyers, with their cool blue-grey marble floors, have been flexibly designed to house smaller public events outside main performance hours, as well as to provide generous social spaces for opera audiences during intervals.

With the exception of the seating, the auditorium uses hard wooden surfaces throughout, its walls and floor maximizing the reflection of sound. The acoustically

crucial side walls on the level of the orchestra are adjustable, as is the width of the proscenium, so making the auditorium exceptionally responsive to the needs of individual productions.

The principal stage is cruciform, with numerous technological aids, including hoists for easy transportation of equipment between basement and stage-level, lateral rolling structures for rapid scene changes, and an entire revolving stage that can itself be rolled into position when required.

Despite its long, expensive gestation period, the new Finnish National Opera House emerges as a particularly well-focused public building; it delivers state-of-the-art facilities in a calm and considered building that looks entirely at home in its urban surroundings, and provides a timeless tranquillity in the quality of its spatial and material organization. ●

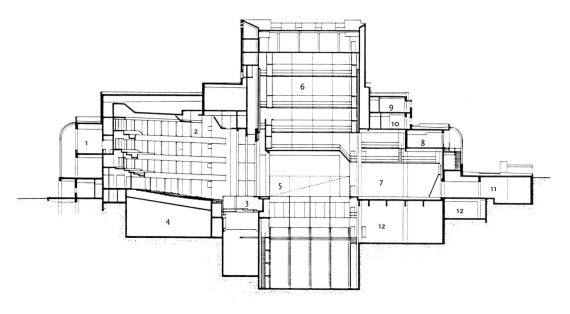

Above: A night view of the Finnish National Opera House reveals how it fits into its urban context with a minimum of disruption. Much of the building is hidden below ground.

Section through main auditorium
1 Foyer
2 Auditorium
3 Orchestra pit
4 Orchestra rehearsal room
5 Stage
6 Fly tower
7 Rear stage
8 Staff restaurant
9 Artistic direction
10 Dressing rooms
11 Loading area
12 Storage

A glass window-wall facing towards the recreational areas of Töölönlahti Bay runs along the south side of the building, and creates public foyer spaces of timeless quality. Blue-grey marble floors further enhance an ambience of calm authority.

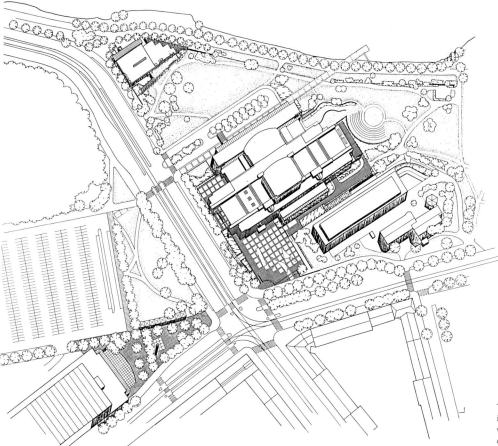

The site plan shows a sympathetic intervention in a complex urban area, with visible aspects well oriented to other urban cultural landmarks.

Ground floor plan
1 Lower entrance
2 Rehearsal hall foyer
3 Rehearsal hall
4 Loading area
5 Workshops
6 Main stage
7 Auditorium

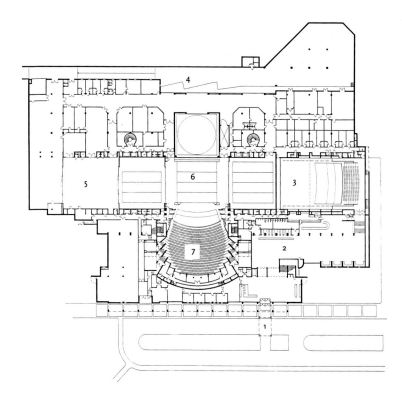

The warm tones of reddish wood in the main auditorium create an intimate, intense environment and contrast with the coolness of the public lobby areas. Hard surfaces predominate to reflect sound in a facility purpose-designed for opera.

Mexican Gallery in the British Museum

London, UK

Architect
Teodoro González
de León

Interior Designer
Miguel Cervantes

Client/Commissioning Body
Consejo Nacional
para la Cultura y las
Artes/Instituto Nacional
de Antropología e
Historia de Mexico

Total Floor Space
187 square metres

Number of Floors
1

Date of Completion
November 1994

The British Museum's extensive pre-sixteenth-century meso-American collection is given a worthy home in a richly atmospheric new gallery, which houses the artefacts of five pre-Columbian cultures.

Intensity of colour and sensuality of finish compensate for monumental scale in architect Teodoro González de León's British Museum gallery devoted to meso-American artefacts.

The gallery's rear wall is finished in blood-red stucco with dark grey English slate panels. The use of Ancaster limestone on floor plinths and as showcase background provides visual continuity. The scheme is enhanced by Fisher Marantz's sensitive lighting design.

Funded by Mexican businessmen and realized by architect Teodoro González de León, this spectacular environment has finally done justice to a collection of 180 meso-American pieces from five different cultures, maintained by the British Museum since the eighteenth century.

The overwhelming impression is one of contrasts. The gallery lies at the north end of the King's Library in what was once a cataloguing room. This utilitarian space, divided into two parts, has been transformed into an exotic spiritual place defined by rich colours, theatrical tableaux and an absence of conventional exhibition display cases.

Stone deities preside over the small entrance. A main precinct is dedicated to the display of artefacts from the Olmec, Teotihuacán, Husatec and Aztec cultures that flourished in the territory now known as Mexico between 2000 BC and the sixteenth century. A red stucco portico along the rear wall separates this from a gallery containing a sequential display of Mayan stone lintels from Yaxchilán.

Originality of display is the keynote. The main precinct houses two large plinths clad in Ancaster limestone – a pyramid and a cylinder – from which some of the larger exhibits seem to be growing. A large semi-suspended display case on one side of the main space is painted in luminous ultramarine and contains the gallery's collection of Aztec ritual masks, serpents and tiny, turquoise mosaic objects. These, placed against a dark background, are illuminated with fibre-optics that add to the dramatic, other-worldly atmosphere. Three more cases occupy the other three walls extending the full height of the gallery and cataloguing the highly distinctive regional cultures that endured in Mexico until European contact in the sixteenth century.

The gallery's small size is to some extent turned to advantage, with intensity of colour and sensuality of finish achieving what, in this case, monumentality cannot.

Practicality and effect are seamlessly blended throughout, from the blood-red stucco of the portico's wall with its splayed base to keep visitors an arm's length away from the stones, to the cool grey slate finish of the ceiling's aluminium maintenance panels. Fisher Marantz's sensitive lighting scheme enhances the whole.

Once again, a major museum collection has been revived and refocused in a new gallery that encourages quiet and intense contemplation of the artefacts, and recreates the spectacle of context lost through relocation and the passing of centuries. ●

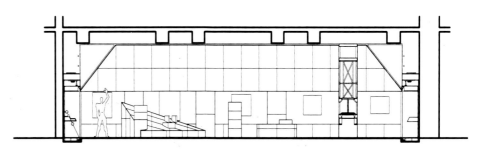

Left: An Aztec deity sculpture stands guard near the entrance. Above: Section through a cleverly planned exhibition area.

Museum of Modern Art and Prefectural Museum

Wakayama, Japan

Architect
Kisho Kurokawa
Architect & Associates

Interior Designer
Kisho Kurokawa
Architect & Associates

Client/Commissioning Body
Wakayama Prefecture

Total Floor Space
11,838 square metres
(Museum of Modern Art)
6,866 square metres
(Prefectural Museum)

Number of Levels
3 (including basement)

Total Contract Cost
£87,500

Date of Completion
1994

Kisho Kurokawa spells it out in black and white, using the abstracted style of fifteenth-century Japanese castle architecture to create two contemporary museums on an ancient castle site.

Overall view of the two museums designed by Kisho Kurokawa on the site of the ancient Wakayama Castle grounds: the abstract, monochromatic style is based on fifteenth-century Japanese castle architecture.

Entrance hall to the Museum of
Modern Art: the architect shows
sensuality and restraint in
organization, finish and detail.

Joined by the wedge of a segment-shaped entrance hall, its curved glazing defining the main point of interrelationship, these two museums on the 23,356-square-metre site of the ancient Wakayama Castle grounds provide a geometric study in contrast and asymmetry.

The larger, the Museum of Modern Art, is clad in black ceramic tiles; the Prefecture Museum in white. Designer Kisho Kurokawa's inspiration for this architectural game of chess comes from traditional black-and-white Japanese castle architecture of the fifteenth century. The source of his approach can be seen most clearly in the roofline and eaves, which quote this ancient style in an abstract way.

Both museums are two-storey buildings with a third basement level, and are set on a historic site recently vacated by the local university and still under development. Eventually a park will be opened and connected to the main museum complex by a wide pedestrian walkway that is being constructed over the road that currently runs through the site.

A stepped plaza lined by tall rectilinear light pillars takes visitors up to the main glazed entrance hall as part of an ordered external plan. But once inside the museums, a sophisticated asymmetry takes over – again a reflection of Kurokawa's concern not simply to mimic Japanese cultural tradition but to assimilate and transform it. The Museum of Modern Art has a total floor area of 11,838 square metres; the Prefecture

Museum 6,866 square metres. The asymmetry that is part of Japan's visual heritage is expressed here through the natural curved lines and unusual angles of white concrete surfaces, glass planes and furniture pieces placed with sensitivity and restraint in the carefully composed interior landscape.

But if 'the evasion of symmetry' is a Kurokawa preoccupation internally, the most overriding impression for the visitor is outside on the approach-way, where the contemporary reinterpretation of Japanese black-and-white castle architecture is reflected in those extraordinary overhanging eaves. Like Tadao Ando, Kurokawa reveals that modern Japanese architecture can have very deep roots indeed. ●

The perspective drawing sets the museum complex in its Wakayama Castle grounds setting. The new architecture relates to a much earlier building style.

The lobby of the art museum. Cool interior spaces are clearly defined.

Right: A 'fractal' handrail leads the visitor down into the Museum of Modern Art. Kurokawa's aim with the interior scheme has been 'the evasion of symmetry', in keeping with characteristics of Japan's visual heritage.

Right: An after-dark approach on the entrance plaza reveals the abstracted overhanging eaves. Note the subtle wall-top lighting to guide visitors and the 'fractal' handrail – a motif repeated inside the museums. The geometric and monochromatic quality of the scheme is both very modern and evocative of a period of Japanese architecture nearly 500 years old.

Glass-fronted entrance hall to the Prefecture Museum, part of the segment-shaped structure which defines the relationship between the small Prefecture Museum and its far larger art-museum neighbour.

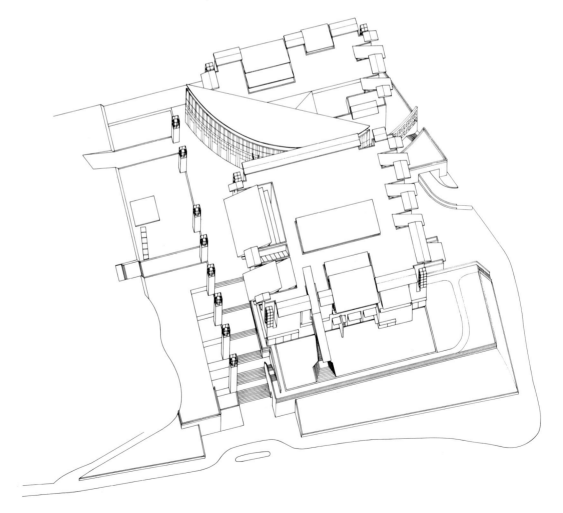

The axonometric shows how the stepped entrance plaza, lit by a row of giant light columns, borders the sequence of spaces that configure the two museums designed as a black-and-white pair.

Begegnungsstätte Alte Synagogue

Wuppertal, Germany

Architect
Busmann & Haberer

Interior Designer
Zbyszek Oksuita

Client/Commissioning Body
City Administration
of Wuppertal

Total Floor Space
381 square metres

Number of Floors
2

Total Contract Cost
£2.3 million

Date of Completion
April 1994

Wuppertal's sculptural new synagogue, built on the site of one destroyed by the Nazis in 1938, takes the form of an abstract collage symbolizing the spiritual whole amid fractures and tension.

View of the synagogue from the entrance plaza. The stone cube to the left sits directly on the site of the synagogue destroyed by the Nazis in 1938. The lead-clad rotunda in the centre is the entrance and reconciles the disparate elements of a quiet and dignified scheme intended to symbolize conflict and fracture. The rectangular building with the pitch roof is the main place of assembly.

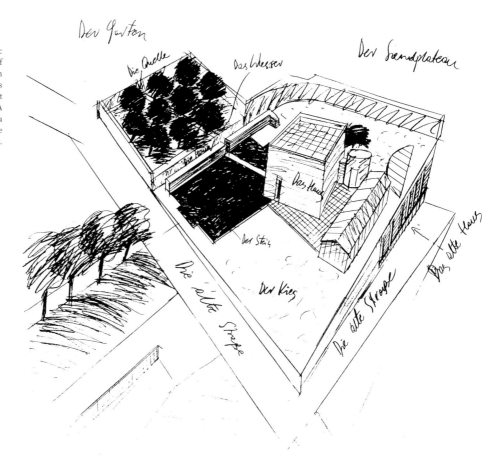

The drawing shows the dynamic relationship of the different pieces of the project, composed as part of an architectural collage and dedicated as much to painful memories of the past as it is to present possibilities. A walled orchard, an entrance plateau and a lower street level form the three levels of the scheme.

Every new synagogue built in postwar Germany must enter delicate cultural negotiations with the past as well as the present. Such is the weight of Nazi tyranny on Jewish history that these projects must inevitably become a place of remembrance as well as a contemporary house of worship. Wuppertal's new synagogue, built on the site of one destroyed in 1938, confronts its painful symbolism head-on through a formal artistic conception developed in collaboration with a sculptor.

The scheme has been conceived by architects Busmann & Haberer and architect-artist Zbyszek Oksuita as a collage of different elements from different times that eloquently represents the idea of fractures and conflicts rather than a formal sacred whole. *Begegnungsstätte* means 'meeting place', and a primary aim of the building is to discuss and advance an understanding of the Jewish fate in Germany within an environment that shows clearly the tensions that exist between different elements.

It is a measure of the project's success that, given this philosophical dynamic, a tranquil totality is achieved in which worshippers and visitors can meditate on past and future destinies. The geometry of the synagogue is divided into three levels: entrance plateau, orchard and lower street level. The entrance plateau is covered in grey gravel and provides the base for an ensemble of different architectonic shapes: a lead-clad rotunda, which is the main entrance and connects the disparate parts; a long rectangular concrete building, which houses a place of assembly and other facilities; and a stone, cube-like house, which sits on the site of the destroyed synagogue and symbolizes its original floor plan by means of black granite plates placed in front of the ruins of the old foundation walls.

The walled orchard, meanwhile, has apple trees and a canal to represent different aspects of Jewish mythology. The lower street level rebuilds a piece of the urban jigsaw that surrounded the original historical synagogue and disappeared when the street was widened in the 1950s. This level has a façade reminiscent of a turn-of-the-century Wuppertal apartment house and holds seminar rooms, a foyer, a small office and kitchen. In counterpointing such an array of formal elements, the entire scheme takes on the abstract quality of a modern sculpture. But, as people move through wide and narrow spaces, it becomes clear that this is not a static memorial – it is about the living as well as the dead. ●

View of the lower street level which represents the fusion of different eras in the history of the Jews in Wuppertal. Behind a façade that recreates a turn-of-the-century Wuppertal apartment house are the synagogue's seminar rooms, a foyer, a small office and a kitchen.

Left: On a sombre grey-gravel plateau, the ensemble of different architectonic shapes has the deliberate tranquillity of a memorial. Architects Busmann & Haberer collaborated with artist Zbyszek Oksuita in the conception of the scheme. Below: Poignant, mute interior space on the site of the destroyed original synagogue. *Begegnungsstätte* means 'meeting place' and a key aim of the architects has been to 'rebuild a living place of remembrance'.

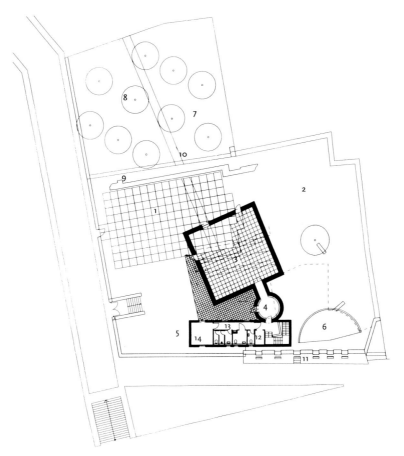

Site plan
1 Black-granite terrace
2 Gravel terrace
3 Meeting room
4 Rotunda entrance
5 Long house
6 Round plateau over seminar room
7 Orchard
8 Apple orchard
9 Remains of old synagogue
10 Canal
11 Lower street façade
12 Cloak room
13 Toilets
14 Chair storage

Kirishima International Concert Hall

Aira, Kagoshima Prefecture, Japan

Architect
Fumihiko Maki
Maki and Associates

Client/Commissioning Body
Kagoshima Prefectural Government

Total Floor Space
4,904 square metres

Number of Levels
3 (including basement)

Date of Completion
June 1994

With its distinctive profile, leaf-shaped plan and spatial integration of audience and performers, this plateau-sited building presents an imaginative reworking of the modern concert hall.

Night view of the Concert hall from the southeast: the faceted panels of Fumihiko Maki's polygonal stainless-steel roof create an intriguing image in the landscape without being a monumental imposition.

Fumihiko Maki's Kirishima International Concert Hall sits on a gentle north-easterly slope of the Kirishima Plateau in Southern Kyushu, Japan, its site of nearly 5,000 square metres affording superb panoramic views of the verdant terrain. Seen in its entirety, the concert hall avoids the imposing monumentality of many such buildings. It relies instead upon a distinctive profile, incorporating a polygonal stainless-steel roof that blends effortlessly into the natural surroundings and recalls the combination of craft tradition and high technology evident in other Maki buildings, notably the Fujisawa Metropolitan Gymnasium and Nippon Convention Centre in Tokyo.

But while the building's form may reflect the architect's interest in reinventing old tea kettles and other tactile artefacts of Japanese culture as the raw material for modern rooflines, its primary purpose is as a venue for chamber ensembles and small orchestras, with a section also dedicated to musical education and rehearsal.

The audience approaches from a foyer and entry hall that provides views of the Kirishima mountains directly ahead, heightening the sense of place and occasion. Rehearsal rooms are positioned around a courtyard, creating the tranquil atmosphere of an outdoor music village. Through the courtyard the approach to the amphitheatre is clearly visible, giving a feeling of continuity and progression to the process of arrival.

Inside the auditorium the benefits of the building's unusual shape start to become apparent. The leaf-shaped plan allows for segmentation of the balcony seating whose right and left profiles step down towards the stage, emphasizing the focal point. The familiar 'shoebox' shaped auditorium is here deformed, so standard acoustic calculations on reverberation time have had to be adapted. However, the leaf shape lends itself to a superior acoustic effect in which sound reaching the left and right ears of the audience has a similar quality. The result is greater acoustic expansiveness. Acoustics are further enhanced through the use of triangulated ceiling panels; they are an important design motif, but also impart a smoothness to the sound quality.

Texture, light, volume and muted colour are superbly managed in a scheme whose ambiguous spatial definitions – a Maki trademark – take on a different character by day and night. The Kirishima International Concert Hall not only confirms Fumihiko Maki as the most accomplished and influential modern Japanese architect since Kenzo Tange, but, more generally, reaffirms the idea of architecture as frozen music. ●

Gently ascending two-storey foyer area, with curtain wall panels providing fragmented views of the rural surroundings.

Right: Entrance plaza with small hall in the foreground. Directly ahead, the view of the Kirishima mountains heightens the sense of occasion.
Below: South elevation.

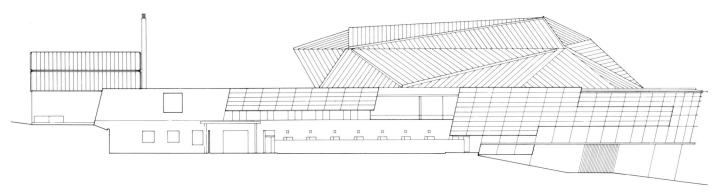

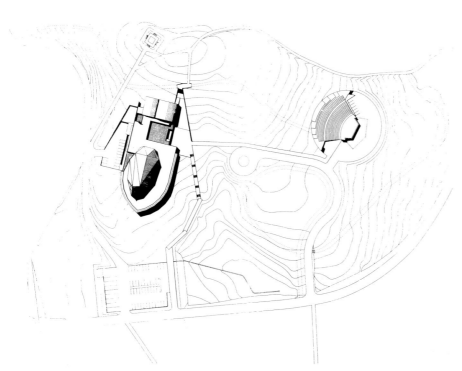

The site plan shows the relationship of the Kirishima International Concert Hall with the verdant terrain of Kirishima Plateau. The shape, from the air, seems like that of a traditional Japanese artefact.

Interior view of the main concert hall. The leaf-shaped plan lends itself to superior acoustics and unifies the balcony seating with the stage, enhancing the sense of focus and creating a bond between audience and performers.

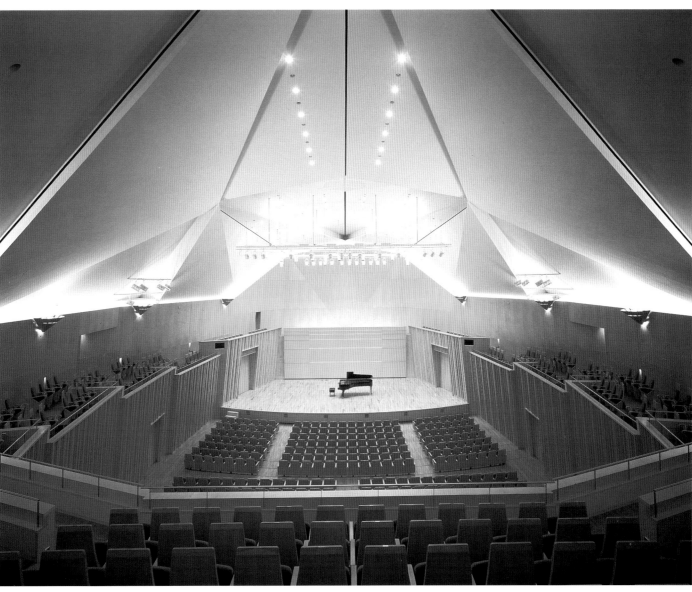

The Art of Interaction

The Imax Theatre of Port Vell, designed by Jordi Garcés and Enric Sòria: a setting for social interaction and a focal point in the commercial regeneration of the Barcelona waterfront.

This final section looks more closely at one of the most significant aspects of the new generation of public buildings and interiors: the concern to interact with people, and not simply impose civic values and symbols on them. This art of interaction, as it is termed here, manifests itself in many ways – from hands-on exhibits in museums to architectural schemes for cinemas and libraries that dissolve the boundaries between the building and the street, or define circulation routes as a kind of narrative journey.

Whatever form it takes, this interactive art of the architect is rewriting the rules of engagement with the public. In the old days, such was the power of authority vested in brick and stone, grand arch and stern façade, that people visited public buildings with a sense of awe, even trepidation. Today the boot is on the other foot: the public building visits the people. The ingenious foldaway pavilion for the Hong Kong Tourist Authority, designed by Apicella Associates to tour 50 European cities a year, is transported by road on two trailers. Climate-controlled mobile structures of this kind literally deconstruct the monumental idea of the civic building, replacing it with a more fluid, lightweight architectural alternative.

Even where new public buildings remain rooted to the spot, there is a concern to constantly reinvent the public spaces in and around the envelope of the building, making way for plazas and parks, nooks and crannies for public performance and interaction. Both Moshe Safdie's Vancouver library complex and Garcés and Sòria's Imax Theatre at Port Vell, Barcelona, are imposing, grand-scale edifices in their own right. But each creates an entire human world eddying around its base. The classical elliptical wall wrapping around the Vancouver library forms a mall-like public sanctum, while wooden walkways around the Imax Theatre draw visitors to the newly developed waterfront.

A key part of the process of achieving a more interactive public architecture is in arousing individual curiosity in a building, most notably through contrasts – of light and shade, hard and soft, new and old, transparent and opaque. Behnisch & Partner's informal building for the Charitable Service of the Lutheran Church in Stuttgart adopts that strategy, as does O'Donnell and Tuomey's Irish Film Centre in the heart of Dublin, which blends a modern cinema complex into a historic Quaker meeting house. In designing the Orléans Mediathèque in France, the architects, du Besset and Lyon, say they placed their faith in human curiosity: this special and spectacular building has been conceived as an intellectual journey through a series of unusual spaces that contrast in form, colour and texture.

Total immersion in an experience, a 'saturation of the senses', is another keynote of the art of interaction in public building or exhibition design. This can either be entirely simulated – as in MET Studio's high-tech Environment Theatre for Taiwan's National Museum of Natural Science – or it can be entirely natural; the Ibaraki Nature Museum in Japan exploits a marshland site to create viewing platforms beside flocks of birds and hilltop discovery areas where children can witness first-hand the excavation of fossils.

The Ibaraki scheme, shaped like a prehistoric beast in the woods, also demonstrates how buildings with a readily communicable image can create an immediate dialogue with people. The Florida Aquarium's elegant shell-shaped glass dome and Toyo Ito's curved aluminium tube-like museum on the shores of Lake Suwa make a similarly direct impression. The two highly sculptural street projects – a futuristic police booth near Tokyo and a boat-like bus stop in Hanover – show a creative approach to interaction succeeding on the smallest scale. ●

Vancouver Library Square

Vancouver, British Columbia, Canada

Architect
Moshe Safdie and
Associates;
Downs/Archambault and
Partners Associated
Architects

Client/Commissioning Body
City of Vancouver

Total Floor Space
650,000 square feet

Number of Levels
7

Total Contract Cost
Cdn $100 million

Date of Completion
May 1995

Moshe Safdie's coliseum-style library for Vancouver creates user-friendly architecture by wrapping a classically-detailed elliptical wall around a central rectangular block.

Night view of Vancouver Library
Square: Moshe Safdie's monumental
design, modelled as a contemporary
reading of the coliseum in Rome, is
people-friendly in the way it draws
the visitor from a public piazza into
the enclosed spaces of the building.

An aerial view of the scheme reveals the way a four-tiered, colonnaded, elliptical wall wraps around a central rectangular library block. A federal government-leased tower is also part of the development, and is clad in the same sandstone-coloured precast concrete. The design, which won a major vote of confidence in a public referendum, is intended to anchor a downtown expansion of the city.

A seven-storey swirl of glass and granite shaped like a latter-day coliseum, Moshe Safdie's controversial new library complex brings a distinct touch of ancient Rome to the centre of Vancouver. This is an audacious project in every sense, wrapping a free-standing, elliptical, four-tiered, colonnaded wall around a rectangular library block at the heart of the scheme. The library's roof serves as a large public garden.

It is a building that arouses strong emotions. Protesting architecture students turned up to its opening satirically dressed in togas. Standing on a site earmarked to anchor an eastward expansion of the downtown area of the city, it is a landmark design that you may love or hate but cannot ignore. This is important. According to its chief librarian, the new building is the result of a 'community-interactive' approach in which people were balloted on its design. And in its built form, the library centre is undeniably community-interactive in the way users are drawn from an inviting external piazza into a cavernous mall-like arcade which curves beneath a glass roof.

Bridges spanning skylit light-wells connect study areas in the 12-feet-wide elliptical wall to the rather minimalist central library block, which contains stacks and services and is simply finished. The roof-level public garden is supplemented by a staff cafeteria and lounges that open on to their own private gardens. A second elliptical wall defines the east side of the site, enclosing the arcade. As well as the 350,000-square foot public library, Safdie's new complex contains a 300,000-square foot federal government tower (clad in the same sandstone-coloured precast concrete and using the same abstracted classical detail as the elliptical walls); retail and service facilities; and underground parking for 700 cars.

Critics have questioned whether Safdie has gone over the top and created a Caesar's Palace that is too florid and too foreign for its local environment. But the new library was given a giant vote of confidence in a public referendum and has been exceptionally popular since its opening, drawing large crowds to facilities inside the building and to events staged in its public spaces. As the local Vancouver newspaper put it: 'The exterior's nod to antiquity is soothing in this CD-Rom world.' The library has an unsubtle monumentalism, but it stops short of kitsch. There is even something serene in its user-friendly reddish-brown envelope, reflecting Safdie's commitment to people in architecture, not just political correctness. ●

Site plan. The outer wall follows the elliptical shape of the development on its rectangular block, and literally embraces the central library building.

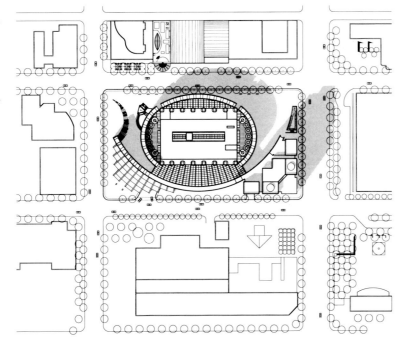

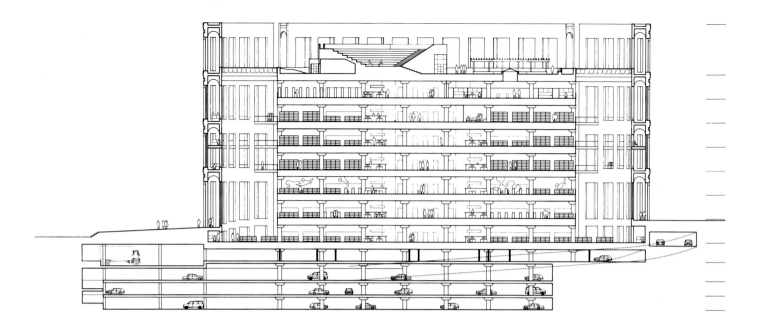

A longitudinal section reveals the scale of the scheme.

Left: A reading room in the library's outer wall reveals a simplicity in interior finish and furnishings, in contrast to the rich, ornate quality of the building's envelope.
Right: Inside the glass-covered mall-like arcade that curves around the library block. This cavernous light-filled space is overlooked by reading rooms and has been the scene of many public events.

The Environment Theatre

Taichung, Taiwan

Interior designer
MET Studio

Client/Commissioning Body
The National Museum of Natural Science, Taiwan, Republic of China

Total Floor Space
500 square metres

Number of Floors
1

Total Contract Cost
US $2.5 million

Date of Completion
August 1993

State-of-the-art display technology creates a total interaction with the natural world in the revolving Environment Theatre, a key attraction at Taiwan's National Museum of Natural Science.

The interdependence between human beings and nature is vividly expressed in this flexible multimedia theatre made of steel and ply, which is part of the new National Museum of Natural Science in Taiwan.

The Environment Theatre, which seats 150 people on a revolving platform, is approached across a bridge of backlit sandblasted glass panels. Its essential form is of a circle inside a square room, leaving space in the four corners, one of which is used as an entrance lobby.

Taiwan's museum-building programme is a fast-track late-twentieth-century version of the kind of approach that built the South Kensington museum campus in London more than 100 years ago. In a Pacific Rim country where economic advances have long run ahead of cultural progress, major new museums are now being built at a rate of knots to redress the balance; there have been no less than two in the coastal city of Taichung alone.

These are the Museum of Fine Art, which is an improvement on its rather grim counterpart in Taipei, and the National Museum of Natural Science, which uses state-of-the-art display technology to study and interpret what its director calls 'the interdependence between nature and human beings'.

The Environment Theatre, created by London-based exhibition designers MET Studio, is one of the National Museum of Natural Science's principal attractions. This is a flexible multimedia gallery that seats 150 people on a revolving platform 15 metres in diameter and two metres above floor level, surrounded by a 360-degree cyclorama screen of 21 metres in diameter. As the stage revolves, the Environment Theatre constantly mutates into different configurations of moving screens and gauze panels as dramatic visual images are computer-choreographed using a battery of slide and video projectors, laser graphics and lighting effects.

The windowless theatre, with virtually all surfaces painted black, features three different 12-minute shows, each designed to totally engross visitors in understanding the rhythms of the natural world. The installation was built entirely of steel and ply, with a bridge between the entrance lobby and revolving platform decked in sandblasted glass panels back-lit in blue light.

This multi-disciplinary project, for which MET Studio coordinated a large specialist team of sound, audiovisual, video, laser and lighting consultants, has played a key role in raising exhibition standards in Taiwan, and in helping to raise public awareness of conservation issues – a national objective. But its lasting impression is of achieving total interaction with the audience through new technology by completely immersing them in such experiences as walking through a rainforest. ●

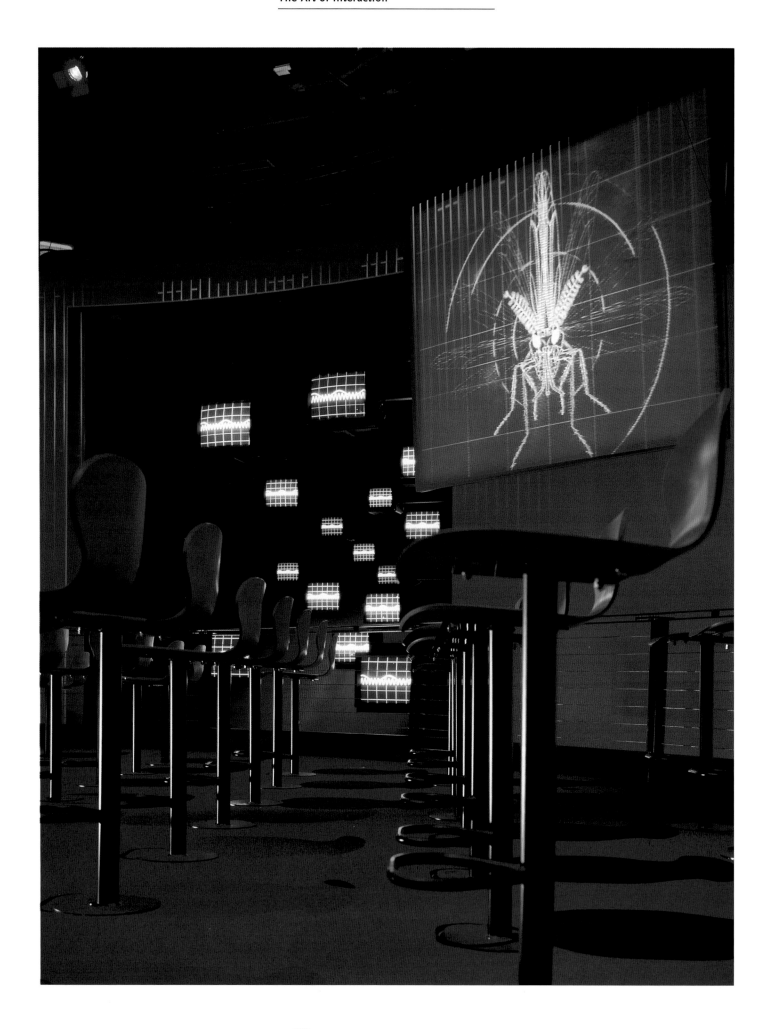

The plan shows the circular multimedia theatre's span through 360 degrees inside a windowless black box.

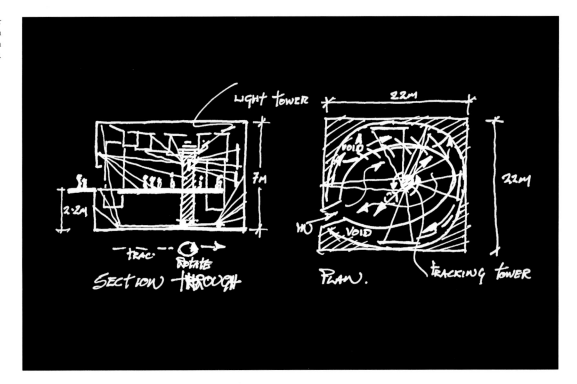

Left and below: MET Studio's design of the Environment Theatre utilizes state-of-the-art display technology to create a seamless, wrap-around 'experience'. Laser and light effects, moving screens and gauzes, and audio and video techniques are computer-choreographed for maximum impact.

The Imax Theatre of Port Vell

Barcelona, Spain

Architect
Jordi Garcés – Enric
Sòria Arquitectes

Interior Designer
Jordi Garcés – Enric
Sòria Arquitectes

Client/Commissioning Body
Teatro Imax
Barcelona SA

Total Floor Space
2,500 square metres

Number of Floors
2

Total Contract Cost
US $4.5 million

Date of Completion
February 1995

The blank white façades and wooden decks of the Imax Theatre evoke a plush ocean cruiser newly moored at Port Vell, part of the commercial development of Barcelona's seafront.

Visitors enjoy the sunshine and sea views on the wooden promenade in front of the Imax Theatre at Port Vell. Clad in white aluminium panels, the stark geometric massing of Garcés and Sòria's building is a soaring, self-absorbed landmark on the regenerated Barcelona waterfront.

On deck at the Imax Theatre: the architects wanted their design to evoke a boat moored in the harbour. The canvas umbrellas and wicker furniture soften the impact of a building whose blank façades suggest traditional Spanish warehousing, when viewed from a distance.

The commercial development of Port Vell marks the latest stage in reclaiming Barcelona's coastline from the industrial wastelands. Within a master plan jointly drawn up by the port authority and city hall, a number of new developments are now redefining the waterfront, among them the Maremagnum commercial centre, an aquarium and a wavy, timber-decked link. Amid this new collection of buildings, one stark white structure stands out: the Imax Theatre designed by Jordi Garcés and Enric Sòria.

In contrast to the sea-lapped glass and granite all around it, the Imax Theatre is clad in modular white aluminium panels. It emerges in the centre of Port Vell, surrounded by water, an object substantially taller than neighbouring buildings and oddly indifferent to its context, like a giant plush cruiser newly moored at port and somewhat scornful of other craft. What makes it work with its surroundings is the way its decks – the wooden public walkways and thoroughfares – draw people into and through to its leisure facilities, while providing panoramic views of the sea.

Its form has been based, say the architects, on strict functionalist criteria. The characteristics of Imax film technology dictated the layout, plan and spatial volumes. The Imax Theatre is actually four buildings in one. Three are moderately proportioned (11 metres high) and are grouped around an entry foyer, an open patio with extensive skylight above. One is an administrative block with ground-floor entrance booth and first-floor offices; a second is a commercial block, with ground-floor bar and shop, restaurant and restrooms on the first floor, and terrace and balcony overlooking the marina; the third is a service block.

Out of this three-way composition juts the tallest and most visible element of the project. This is the hexagonal prism of the grand projection room, 26 metres high, with precisely sloped seats and large screens, and space and equipment for production and projection.

Fit for its purpose the scheme may be, but the blank façades and stark geometric forms of traditional Spanish warehouse architecture have also influenced the white-box style of design. Garcés and Sòria have taken a serious and clinical approach for a building type that often inspires more outlandish imagery. But then the architects were keen to float their own ideas: 'We wanted the vision of Imax to evoke more a boat than a conventional building.' ●

Entry-level floor plan.

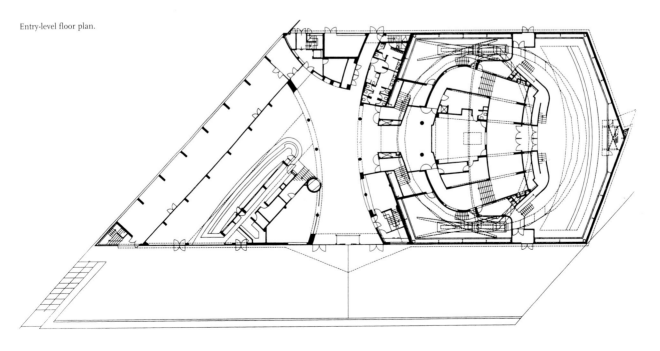

Perspective through the Imax Theatre at Port Vell. Three elements – the administration, commercial and service blocks – form a low-level structure. The fourth, the hexagonal grand projection room, is the tallest and most visible aspect of the project, 26 metres in height.

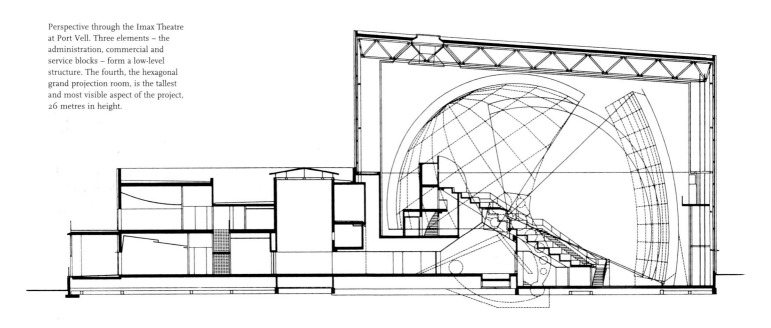

Wooden floors and furniture, raw and stained concrete lend an informal air to the sheltered decks that give the white hulk of the Imax Theatre its human aspect and provide views of craft in the harbour.

Inside the precision-raked main
projection auditorium. The needs of
cinema technology dictated the slope
of the walls and screens, and the
configuration of the seating.

Extension of the Charitable Service of the Lutheran Church

Stuttgart, Germany

Architect
Behnisch & Partner

Interior Designer
Behnisch & Partner

Client/Commissioning Body
Charitable Service of the Lutheran Church in Württemberg

Total Floor Space
6,500 square metres

Number of Floors
5

Total Contract Cost
£7 million

Date of Completion
1994

Relaxed and informal, this stand-alone Stuttgart extension to a charity's headquarters contrasts hard and soft, light and shade, in order to create a suitably humane environment.

An interior gallery for social gatherings is placed at a point where the building's three 'work wings' converge. An informal, humane spirit pervades an environment designed with subtle variations in light, colour and material.

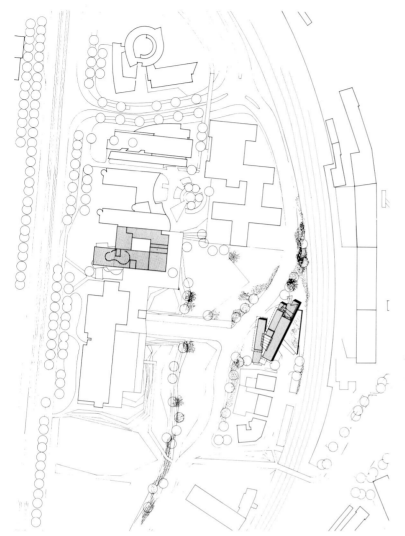

A decade after architects Behnisch & Partner designed the main administrative building of the Württemberg Charitable Service of the Lutheran Church, the Stuttgart practice has completed an extension in much the same informal, humane spirit. The organization is a charity that helps the elderly, sick and handicapped, and the building's architecture and interiors seek to create a casual, intimate environment with subtle variations in light, colour and material.

The site of the new stand-alone extension is awkwardly shaped and adjacent to railway lines, but it is opposite the original building and shares with it a fine view of Stuttgart down through a valley basin. In form, it comprises three staggered east-west oriented 'work wings' that unite in the southeast section of the plan. At their point of contact, a sloping glazed structure creates a series of small galleries for social gatherings and a large indoor foyer space under a glass roof from which a staircase connects to all floors.

The ground floor incorporates a foyer, coffee bar and conference room for meetings and training courses; upper floors are dedicated to office space, although here the aim has been to avoid the repetitive tendencies of most workspaces and create more unusual, pleasant, open-plan areas with opportunities for staff to congregate. A cafeteria, dining hall and kitchen are located at roof level.

In keeping with the aim to create a low-key environment that is not precious or intimidating, the architects avoided using precious materials. The concrete-and-glass building is clad in aluminium-sheet panels. A cantilevered north façade shelters the main entrance. Internally, there is a play on hard and soft, light and dark, using expanses of concrete, sheet-metal and glass partitions interspersed with the warmer, softer tones of wood – birch for furnishings and boards, maple for parquet floors, and beech for staircases. This is a scheme that relaxes, even transcends, the functionalist German aesthetic with a little caring and daring. Yet it remains undeniably true to the utilitarian Lutheran spirit. ●

Shimosuwa Municipal Museum

Shimosuwa, Japan

Architect
Toyo Ito, Toyo Ito &
Associates, Architects

Interior and Exhibition Designer
Toyo Ito, Toyo Ito &
Associates, Architects

Client/Commissioning Body
Shimosuwa-cho

Total Floor Space
1,983 square metres

Number of Floors
2

Total Contract Cost
US $12.5 million

Date of Completion
June 1993

Toyo Ito's aluminium-clad lakeside museum nestles beneath the mountains on a narrow shorefront strip of reclaimed land. Its purpose: to commemorate a town's centenary.

Built to commemorate the centenary of the town of Shimosuwa on a very narrow strip of reclaimed land 200 metres in length, Toyo Ito's municipal museum has the look of an elongated sea creature caught between mountain and lake.

Entrance to the museum, which sits by a prefectural highway that runs along the shoreline. This view accentuates the image of the upturned hull, one of a number of water-borne visual metaphors in the scheme. The beguiling structure is clad in aluminium panels on a skeleton of steel.

Toyo Ito's waterside Shimosuwa Municipal Museum has a living, ethereal quality as though it has just emerged from the water on to the banks of Lake Suwa. It has the look of an elongated sea creature clad in aluminium scales, or an upturned ship's hull, left high and dry by a receding tide. The form, however, is not arbitrary. Ito has designed the building on a narrow strip of reclaimed land 200 metres in length but with very little depth. The museum, built to commemorate the centenary of Shimosuwa, a town in Nagano prefecture, is separated from the lake by a prefectural highway that runs right along its shore.

The museum has been designed to accommodate two permanent collections. One consists of artefacts and materials on the history of Lake Suwa. The other is a collection of exhibits chronicling the life of a local Japanese poet, Akahiko Shimaki (1876 – 1926). The building consists of two distinct elements. Behind the gently curving, elongated structure that faces the lake to the south and contains a linear series of exhibition spaces, there is a cube-like storage facility on the mountain-facing side.

Ito's exhibition interiors subtly reflect the content of the two permanent exhibits. Fishing implements and skates used on Lake Suwa, for instance, are displayed on bases of frosted glass, evoking the lake's frozen winter surface. An ocean of blue carpeting surrounding the showcases of manuscripts and photographs of the poet suggests the lake's summer appearance. In this way, Ito seamlessly combines interior and exterior concerns.

But the lasting impression of this project is the external form of Ito's extraordinary building, its boat-shaped volume curved towards the water. A computer-aided design system was used to calculate the cutting of aluminium panels which clad a steel skeleton of arcs, joints and radial lines and are set at intervals of three metres along its length, wrapping the whole surface. At times Ito's museum looks exactly like a computer wire-frame model. But then the setting sun catches the structure, and you know it is something that could only have been created by the human imagination. ●

Left: Main entrance lobby area of the Shimosuwa Municipal Museum. Hard, cool, shiny surfaces suggest glassy frozen water on a lake. Below: The façade viewed from the water, suggests the influence of computer-aided design in the development of the wire frame.

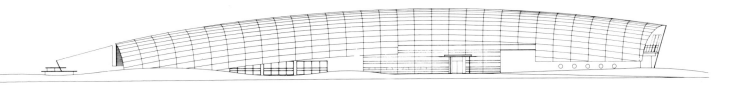

Right: The ground floor plan reveals the two distinct elements of the building. The gently curving structure, which faces the lake to the south, contains a linear series of exhibition spaces. Behind it on the mountain side, a cube-like block provides storage facilities.
Below: A view into the main entrance lobby area is enhanced by subtle lighting.

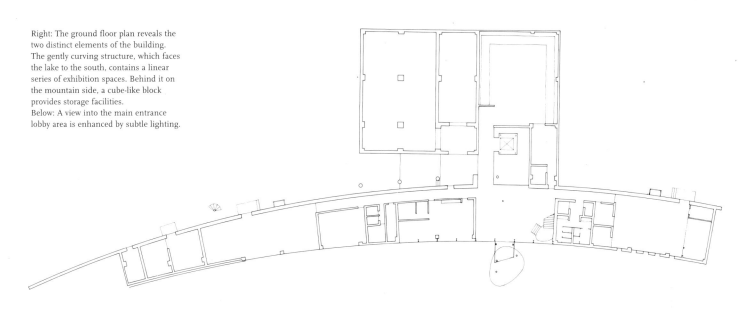

5.6 Pavilion Hong Kong, Mobile Touring Structure

Hong Kong

Architect
Apicella Associates

Interior and Exhibition Designer
Apicella Associates

Client/Commissioning Bodies
Hong Kong Tourist Authority
The CP Group
(production company)

Total Floor Space
220 square metres

Number of Floors
2

Date of Completion
June 1995

Lorenzo Apicella's foldaway public pavilion for the Hong Kong Tourist Authority is designed to tour Europe and takes the idea of lightweight public architecture to a mobile and memorable conclusion.

The ultimate in lightweight, flexible public architecture: the Pavilion Hong Kong, designed by architect Lorenzo Apicella to tour European cities. The building folds out from two standard 40-foot lorry trailers. The travelling aluminium structure reflects both the traditional and modern character of Hong Kong.

View of the main ground-floor exhibition area, with meeting areas at balcony level. The colourful and inviting pavilion has been designed to withstand extremes of temperature.

The five-stage construction sequence demonstrates how the building 'grows' out of the trailers. Hydraulics are used to raise the first-floor frame of the two-storey pavilion and to open out floor panels for an atrium space. Aluminium bridges brace the two structural frames. A double-skin inflatable membrane forms the roof and sides of the atrium.

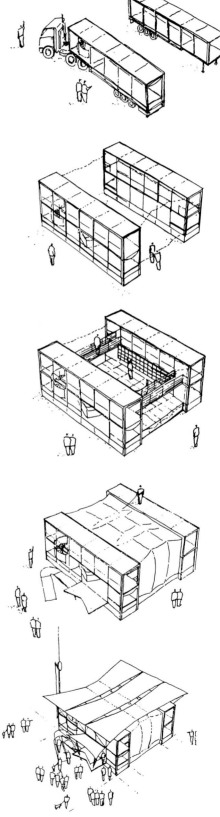

Lightness, fluidity and accountability have been growing themes in public architecture in recent years, but this building for the Hong Kong Tourist Authority takes the reversal of the monolithic presence to its logical conclusion. It is completely portable – a friendly, colourful mobile pavilion trailer designed to travel around promoting the city of Hong Kong to holiday-makers and conference organizers in 50 European cities a year.

Architect Lorenzo Apicella has designed the ultimate statement of taking public architecture to the people. The modern steel-and-glass pavilion 'grows' from two standard 40-foot lorry trailers, which only minutes before were speeding down the autobahn, into a structure three times their original volume. The construction sequence, in which hydraulics are used to raise the first-floor frame of the two-storey pavilion and open out floor panels for an atrium space, requires only a small crew to perform. Aluminium bridges brace the two structural frames, while a double-skin inflatable membrane forms the roof and sides of the atrium.

According to Apicella, the use of a fabric membrane with a lightweight aluminium structure reflects both the traditional and modern character of Hong Kong. The pavilion has also been designed to withstand reasonable extremes of summer and winter climates across Europe; it is in operation 320 days a year. The membrane skin enables warm air to be pumped in without heat loss in winter through air-conditioning units powered by an acoustically insulated main generator. 'Fly' canopies on the roof pull up the inflatable membrane at three points where there are circular polycarbonate rooflights that allow natural ventilation in summer.

The main exhibition level is on the ground floor, with meeting areas on an upper balcony level. At first glance the overall visual effect, says Apicella, is of 'an extraordinarily modern Oriental city'. This is not the first time this innovative London architectural practice has tackled such a project – previous foldaway buildings have included a mobile bank and a travelling auditorium. ●

Mediathèque d'Orléans

Orléans, France

Architect
Pierre du Besset and
Dominique Lyon

Interior Designer
Pierre du Besset and
Dominique Lyon

Client/Commissioning Body
City of Orléans

Total Floor Space
7,800 square metres

Number of Levels
4 floors
2 mezzanines
2 levels of basement

Total Contract Cost
£7.8 million

Date of Completion
May 1994

The programme to build a new generation of media libraries across France has an imaginative new addition in the heart of Orléans, complete with enormous horizontal latticed bow window.

Decorated with aluminium sunscreens, du Besset and Lyon's new multimedia library makes its presence felt in the centre of Orléans. A giant latticed bolster of a bow window runs horizontally across its façade at first-floor level, symbolizing the highly stylized creative intent of the scheme.

Before winning a French Ministry of Culture competition to design a new multimedia library for Orléans, the architectural partnership of Pierre du Besset and Dominique Lyon could claim only one major built project – the editorial offices of *Le Monde* newspaper. But the imaginative quality of this scheme, with its amazing horizontal latticed bow window protruding from the building, has catapulted the pair into a new league. The Mediathèque d'Orléans is an exceptional development in a number of ways. The variety and unpredictability of its forms, spaces, colours and finishes reflects Dominique Lyon's comment that 'we placed our faith in human curiosity'.

The first thing that strikes you is its unusual response to a tricky site. It faces on to the city's Place Gambetta and incessant ring-road traffic, and is surrounded by a tower, church, shopping centre and housing denoting a jumble of different periods. But the media centre does not retreat and close itself off from the ring road; instead it opens the road up. There is no main façade or hierarchy to the concrete-and-iron structure delicately adorned with undulating aluminium sunscreens. As one critic observed, 'From whichever angle you view it, the Orléans media library always appears to be facing you.'

The façade actually has three feature protrusions. Above the horizontal latticed bolster that so catches the eye, there is a panoramic picture window; below it, a square glass keep. The interior of the media centre, flooded with soft indirect light, is laid out as the architectural equivalent of an intellectual journey. As the architects explain, 'A mediathèque is a place where each individual must search out the means of expanding his

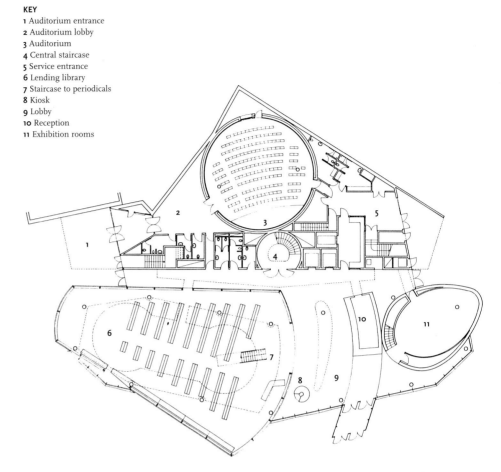

knowledge. Our building attempts to express this process.'

Thus a light-filled reception lobby opens into a space from which visitors can ascend a staircase into a bright yellow turret at mezzanine level to read periodicals. The ground floor includes a 200-seat auditorium and exhibition room, and a bright orange stair tower leads to an unfolding sequence of rooms at the upper levels composed to play tricks with texture, colour and organization. Facilities here include a green main reading room, and a children's library and music/video lending library, both covered in silver vinyl fabric. There is a sense of enclosure but the enormous feature windows mean that the city is never far away.

As if the architects' approach were not creative enough, there is also a collaboration with an artist, Victor Birgin, whose video installation sits close to the entrance to the main reading room. Du Besset and Lyon have created an object-building of desire in the heart of Orléans, which engages people in a narrative architecture designed to reward the spirit of intellectual curiosity. ●

Inside the latticed bow window
at first-floor level. A circular
information desk sits among the
furniture in the bright main reading
room of the Mediathèque d'Orléans.

The new library is set in a tricky urban context at Place Gambetta in Orléans. The jumble of ring-road traffic, a rather nondescript church and anonymous shopping developments encouraged the architects to break free of subtle contextual solutions to create their own individual and challenging form.

Below: The children's library on the second floor. The scheme delights in its contrasts of colour, shape and material.

View from the entrance lobby up a staircase into the bright yellow drum of the periodicals reading area at mezzanine level. The architects have designed the building in the form of a narrative journey, arguing that they have placed their faith in the drive of human curiosity to negotiate the building.

Right: Bright colours and robust finishes add lustre to a functional stairwell in the Mediathèque d'Orléans. Stairways are a key element in the unfolding narrative of the building.

5.8 Irish Film Centre

Dublin, Ireland

Architect
O'Donnell and Tuomey

Interior Designer
O'Donnell and Tuomey

Client/Commissioning Body
Irish Film Centre

Total Floor Space
2,000 square metres

Number of Floors
3 over basement

Total Contract Cost
£1.6 million

Date of Completion
January 1993

The twentieth-century spirit of cinema is blended into an eighteenth-century Quaker meeting house in O'Donnell and Tuomey's subtle scheme in the historic heart of Dublin.

Restaurant in the Irish Film Centre. Architects O'Donnell and Tuomey have created a metropolitan centre of cinematic culture within the walls of an old Quaker meeting house in the historic heart of Dublin.

In a clever piece of urban editing, a former Quaker meeting house in Dublin city centre dating back to the eighteenth century has been expertly renovated to create the Irish Film Centre. Architects O'Donnell and Tuomey have designed new elements but seamlessly integrated them into what already existed. The result is a deftly considered scheme in the heritage-rich Temple Bar area of Dublin which pays homage to the modern cinema tradition of the 1920s and 30s with its neon-lit features, but remains essentially a historic house. It is also a project that reflects the aim of its designers in continuing the public realm of the city into and through the building. 'We are interested', they explain, 'in the way architectural form operates as a backdrop for life and movement.'

At ground-floor level, the Centre's facilities are organized around a pivotal circular foyer that leads into an enlarged glass-roofed urban courtyard, its strong day-lit ambience a deliberate contrast to the flickering darkness of the Centre's two cinemas. Indeed the play on natural and artificial light is one of the project's key themes, as is the relationship between solidity and lightness. The use of brick, limestone, naturally pigmented plaster and waxed steel represents an essentially robust architecture, which is offset by lighter elements. As well as two cinemas, the Centre contains archive film storage, a bar, bookshop and an upper-floor restaurant, plus offices and ancillary administration areas tightly squeezed into the plan.

The red brick façade on the west of the block, designed to echo surrounding warehouses, represents the strongest external manifestation of the scheme. But this is not a project intended to be a monolithic civic statement; the Irish Film Centre is primarily a skilful series of interior interventions and connections, a secret passageway of culture through which the denizens of Dublin's vibrant art scene can be drawn.

The exploded axonometric shows the new elements introduced to a scheme which is primarily about a skilful series of interior interventions and connections.

Since completing the project, the architects O'Donnell and Tuomey have returned to Temple Bar to design a sister facility, the £3-million new-build National Photography Gallery, which contains an archive, college and gallery in 2,500 square metres of space. This second, complementary complex opened in October 1995. ●

Left: Inside the glass-roofed urban courtyard, a foyer setting for social interaction. A key feature of the design is the counterpoint between solidity and lightness in materials. The use of neon refers to the golden age of 1930s cinema.
Below: Axonometric of the scheme.
Right: Informal bar area, with view through to the foyer beyond.

Ibaraki Nature Museum

Iwai-city, Ibaraki Prefecture, Japan

Birds flying across the surrounding marshlands become the principal exhibit in this interactive museum of nature, shaped like a prehistoric beast lying low in the trees.

Architect
Mitsuru Man Senda & Environment Design Institute

Interior Designer
Mitsuru Man Senda & Environment Design Institute

Client/Commissioning Body
Ibaraki Prefectural Museum

Total Floor Space
12,771 square metres

Number of Floors
3

Total Contract Cost
US $194 million

Date of Completion
November 1994

Closest to the lake is the 'head' of the Ibaraki Nature Museum, containing a restaurant which opens out on to a formal garden. The building achieves a genuine integration with its natural surroundings despite its large scale.

An aerial view of the museum, which was designed with five pods attached to a central spine, an abstract suggestion of a prehistoric beast lying low in the marshlands of Sugao. Its position at a point where a series of swamps and lakes drain into the vast Tonegawa River creates the perfect platform for the observation of nature. Below: Perspective through the museum.

An hour's drive from Tokyo, the Ibaraki Nature Museum has been built beside the marshlands of Sugao, a series of swamps and lakes draining into the Tonegawa River, as a very deliberate and successful exercise in harmonizing architecture with nature. The site of the building, just 16.4 hectares, is dwarfed by the vast 230-hectare lake beside it and there are stunning views across the Kanto plain. In this museum the main exhibit is, indeed, the marsh outside with its flocks of migrant birds skimming the water.

The purpose of this well-composed, user-friendly complex is environmental and ecological education. It has been designed to stand no higher than the surrounding woodlands, its surfaces are clad with dark earth-coloured tiles, and its bulk has been broken down into five separate sections, or pods, that run off a central spine. Sitting in its green context, these vertebrae help to give the building the abstracted look of a prehistoric creature; the head, closest to the lake, contains the entrance, a restaurant and an audio-visual 'reflection' hall. The main body of the building is shrouded by trees.

The brief specified two demands: first, a 'joyful' nature museum; and second, 'a facility for families to cultivate environmental literacy'. So this is very much a hands-on, interactive museum, with play equipment, a fresh-water aquarium and an external Discovery Plaza on a hill, where children can experience the excavation of fossils, all contributing to the sense of engagement. Six different exhibition themes are accessed from a central spine in such a way that the architect likens the plan to reading the chapters of a book.

The largest exhibition hall sits next to the lake, providing fine natural views from several levels, including a 'birdwatch cage' on the first floor. Discovery and enjoyment are the keynotes of the entire Ibaraki Museum experience. But in the quest to entertain and amuse, this is a facility that never trivializes its subject matter. Indeed, its clever appropriation of the surrounding marshland for exhibition purposes is achieved with simplicity and restraint. ●

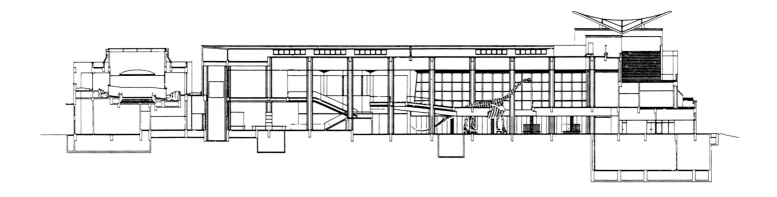

Travelling along an exhibition walkway. The serious aim of environmental education is approached in a highly imaginative and entertaining way. Six different exhibition themes are accessed from a central spine.

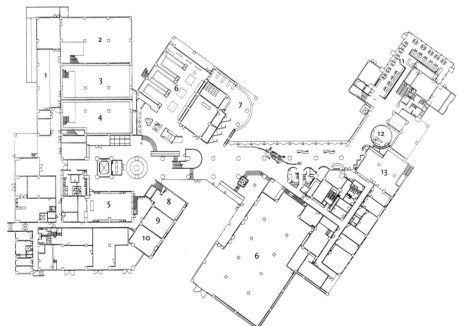

Ground floor plan
1 Specimen store
2 Geological specimen store
3 Stuffed animal store
4 Plant specimen store
5 Study room
6 Exhibition room
7 Library
8 Plant research laboratory
9 Animal research laboratory
10 Earth science research laboratory
11 Restaurant
12 Museum shop
13 Office

Vista through the main public area of the museum. The accent is on encouraging each visitor to discover more. Different levels and walkways connect to the various exhibits.

The Florida Aquarium

Tampa, Florida, USA

Architects
Hellmuth Obata &
Kassabaum (HOK)
Esherick Homsey Dodge
and Davis (EHDD)

Client/Commissioning Body
The Florida Aquarium
Inc.

Total Floor Space
152,000 square feet

Number of Levels
3

Total Contract Cost
US $39.3 million

Date of Completion
March 1995

An elegant shell-shaped glass dome provides a fitting symbol for a new waterfront aquarium designed to take the visitor on a winding journey up and through a range of aquatic habitats.

Main waterfront entrance plaza to the Florida Aquarium. Its shell-shaped glass dome and exotic exterior colours, chosen to evoke the architecture of Mexico and Central America, project a sense of adventure to the visitor.

With its glass dome shaped like an exotic shell, exterior canopies in the form of sails, and windows designed as large portholes, the new Florida Aquarium takes its mission to tell the story of the sunshine state's diverse water habitats quite literally. The maritime metaphors, however, are not laboured. The elegance of the distinctive dome is the architectural keynote of a scheme located on a waterfront and designed very much with people in mind.

The project is the joint work of two American architectural practices – HOK and EHDD – who designed the reinforced concrete structure as an envelope for the aquarium's exhibition progamme, devised by Joseph A. Wetzel & Associates. Two major enclosed habitat exhibitions are organized around a large, spacious public lobby that serves as a reception and orientation area as well as a break-out space for visitors before and after experiencing the main exhibits.

One, the Florida Wetlands exhibit, sits beneath the faceted glass dome to ensure the maximum daylight necessary to sustain native habitats for hundreds of species of sea and plant life under near-to-natural conditions in a controlled environment. The other is the spectacular Coral Kingdom – a 500,000 gallon tank in a two-storey 'black box' area – which enables visitors to pass through the simulated depths of a coral reef via graduated ramps. Even the exterior of the aquarium has a sense of adventure, its tropical hues based on colours more often seen in Mexico and Central America.

The architects arranged for the visitor flow from the entrance area to give a dramatic sense of rising up and winding through exhibit layers of marine life, plants and free-flying birds at the second level. A book store, cafeteria, live performance areas and outdoor terraces complete the facilities in a building that has been designed with conviction to educate and entertain in equal measure about the Florida habitats of stream and swamp, coast and open sea. ●

The spacious, sweeping public lobby area around which the Florida Aquarium's two main exhibitions are organized.

Axonometric of the scheme reveals how the two covered exhibits are connected by the central entrance lobby area. The exotic shell roof sits above the Florida Wetlands exhibit, providing the natural light needed to maintain the many species of sea- and plant-life in near-to-natural conditions. Below: A dark and inspiring journey through the Coral Kingdom, the other main exhibit.

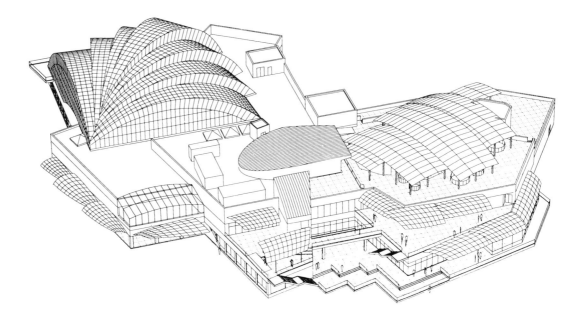

Above: A view of a side elevation of the Florida Aquarium from the opposite river bank reveals the faceted contours of the shell-like glass-and-steel roof.
Right: Upper-level plan of the main exhibition routes.

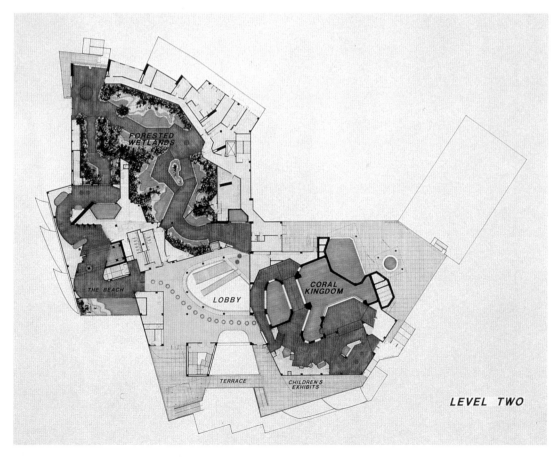

Police Booth/ Bus Stop

Tokyo, Japan/Hanover, Germany

Architect
Police Booth:
Norihiko Dan
Bus Stop:
Massimo Iosa Ghini

Client/Commissioning Body
Police Booth: Tokyo
Metropolitan Police
Department
Bus Stop: Foundation of
Lower Saxony

Date of Completion
Police Booth:
December 1993
Bus Stop: April 1994

And finally: a futuristic police booth in a Tokyo dormitory town and a sculptural bus stop across the road from Hanover palace share a symbolic concern to interact with the public.

Massimo Iosa Ghini's sculptural Hanover bus stop: this boat-like structure on a concrete base will one day be covered in ivy.

Norihiko Dan's police booth stands guard on a public plaza next to the railway station of a Tokyo commuter town. Its bold sci-fi appearance suggests an alien object, but the machine-like solution is very well-crafted.

Below: Police booth elevation, showing the suspended triangular roof. Bottom: The plan cleverly encloses bedroom, bathroom, office and reception in a confined space.

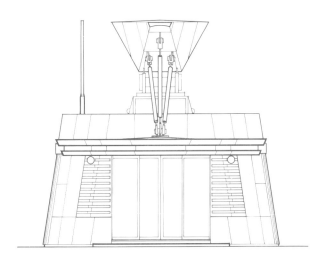

As a coda to this book, these two small-scale projects show that the new interactive spirit in public architecture extends to the street and is embodied in such schemes as police booths, bus stops and street furniture.

Norihiko Dan's bizarre space-age police box has landed in the dormitory town of Minami Osawa, and occupies a position on a plaza next to the train station from which thousands of commuters travel daily into the centre of Tokyo. In its symbolic presence it shares many characteristics with Italian designer Massimo Iosa Ghini's eco-futuristic bus stop in Hanover, Germany – one of nine diverse, eye-catching, individualistic new bus stops commissioned for the city at a total cost in excess of £1 million.

Norihiko Dan's well-crafted mini-police station houses office, reception room, bathroom and bedroom in a single-storey structure topped with an exaggerated triangular roof. Its purpose is to reassure and interact with the local community. The architect says he chose the stand-alone, streamlined form because he saw little point in trying to blend into such an expressionless and anonymous urban context – Minami Osawa was built in less than five years. The steel-panelled exterior was specified for ease of maintenance; police officers simply hose it down.

Iosa Ghini's bus stop, meanwhile, stands opposite one of Hanover's few remaining classic buildings, Wangenheim's city palace, built in 1833. Its sculptural form draws the old palace into a new discourse on the disappearing boundaries between art, architecture and design in the public domain. The bus stop has a green boat-like top asymmetrically hollowed out of synthetic material; this fills with water which drains through a pipe down the concrete structure to a bed of ivy on the brick base. It is the architect's intention that the ivy will completely cover his design, which has a little wooden birdhouse at its point. So far the ivy's progress is very slow. But given Iosa Ghini's novel artistic approach to a piece of street architecture normally so nondescript that it disappears into the landscape, nobody is complaining. ●

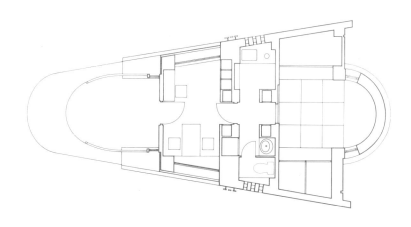

Biographies

Alsop & Störmer Architects

Albert Bridge House, 127 Albert Bridge Road,
London SW11 4PL, UK
William Alsop founded his own architectural
practice in 1980. He was born in 1947 in
Northampton, studied at the Architectural
Association in London (1968–73) and subsequently
spent periods in the studios of Maxwell Fry, Cedric
Price and Roderick Ham. He is currently Professor
of Architecture at the University of Vienna and has
been associated, in various teaching capacities, with
the Royal Melbourne Institute of Technology, the
San Francisco Institute of Art, the St Martin's
School of Art, London, the Bremen Academy of Art
and Music, and Hanover University. His major
projects vary in scale from museum and urban
planning designs in Hamburg to the Real World
Leisure Park in Sydney and a retail and housing
development in Normandy. Recent selected projects
include the CrossRail platform for Paddington
Station, London; the Regional Headquarters and
Metro Station in Marseilles, as well as studies for
the Blackfriars Railway Bridge and the Hungerford
Pedestrian Bridge. William Alsop is a member of
the Royal Institute of British Architects, Fellow of
the Royal Society of Arts, a Bernard Webb Scholar
(Rome) and has been awarded the William van
Allen Medal for architecture.

Tadao Ando Architect and Associates

5-23 Toyosaki 2-chome, Kita-ku, Osaka, Japan
The self-taught Japanese architect and interior
designer Tadao Ando (b. 1941) founded his own
architectural practice in 1969 after extensive travel
in the USA, Europe and Africa. He worked on small
housing schemes throughout the 1970s and early
80s, and received the annual prize from the
Architectural Institute of Japan in 1979 for his Row
House, Sumiyoshi, and the Japanese Cultural
Design Prize (1983) for the Rokko Housing scheme.
Today he is internationally known for his large-
scale, poetic and homogenous cultural and public
buildings such as the Church on the Water,
Hokkaido (1988); the Church of the Light, Osaka
(1989); the Naoshima Contemporary Art Museum,
Okayama (1992), and the Chikatsu-Asuka Historical
Museum, Osaka, for which he received the Japan
Art Grand Prix in 1994. He is currently working
on the FABRICA (Benetton Research Centre),
Treviso, Italy. His designs have been in exhibitions
worldwide, most notably 'Intercepting Light and
Nature', New York, 1985, and 'Breathing Geometry',
London, 1986. He was visiting professor at the
universities of Yale (1987), Columbia (1988) and
Harvard (1990) and is an Honorary Fellow of the
American Institute of Architects and the Royal
Institute of British Architects.

Apicella Associates

9 Ivebury Court, 325 Latimer Road, London
W10 6RA, UK
Apicella Associates Ltd, formerly Apicella Associates
Architecture and Design, London, was founded
by Lorenzo Apicella in 1989. Apicella studied
architecture at Nottingham University, Canterbury
College of Art and The Royal College of Art in
London before moving to the United States to
work for Skidmore, Owings and Merrill. From
1986 to 1989 he was head of the architecture and
interior design group Imagination Design &
Communications, collaborating with such clients
as Harrods, British Telecom, Forte plc, Ford and
British Steel. Lorenzo Apicella currently serves on
the RIBA Awards Panel, has been chairman of the
National Awards jury on four occasions and most
recently served as an international juror for the
American Institute of Architects' Awards in San
Diego. He has taught widely within the UK and
has been visiting critic at Canterbury, London
and Oxford. Apicella Associates' current projects
range across the full spectrum of design from
furniture to urban planning.

Ron Arad Associates

62 Chalk Farm Road, London NW1 8AN, UK
Ron Arad was born in Tel Aviv in 1951, and
studied at the Jerusalem Academy of Art and the
Architectural Association, London, from 1974 to
1979. In 1981 he founded One Off Ltd, with
Dennis Groves and Caroline Thorman, and in 1983
designed One Off's first showroom in Neal Street,
Covent Garden. In 1988 he won the Tel Aviv Opera
Foyer Interior Competition with C. Norton and
S. McAdam, and the next year formed Ron Arad
Associates in order to realize the project, moving
premises to Chalk Farm, London. As well as the
design and construction of the new One Off Design
Studio, furniture gallery and workshop in 1990,
recent projects have included furniture designs –
for Poltronova, Vitra, Moroso and Driade – such as
the Big Easy range and Los Muebles Amorosos de
Moroso as well as the design of various interior
installations and domestic architectural projects,
including a house in Schopfheim for a German
publisher. Ron Arad was the editor of the 1994
International Design Yearbook and is a guest
professor at the H.S.F.A.K in Vienna. His work
has been shown in major design shows throughout
the world.

Austin-Smith:Lord

5-6 Bowood Court, Calver Road, Warrington,
Cheshire WA2 8QZ, UK
The architect, interior and landscape designers,
planners and planning supervisors Austin-
Smith:Lord work from offices in Warrington, Mold,
Cardiff and London. The practice was established in
1949 by Mike and Inette Austin-Smith; Peter Lord
joined four years later. In 1989 the practice of
Chamberlin Powell Bon and Woods, noted for their
work at the Barbican Arts Centre, London, moved
into partnership with Austin-Smith:Lord and today
they work together on projects that include public
and government buildings, offices, warehousing
and transport areas, hotels, leisure and recreation
facilities, banks, restaurants and cafeterias.

Behnisch & Partner

Büro Sillenbuch, Gorch-Fock-Strasse 30, 70619
Stuttgart, Germany
Günter Behnisch was born in Dresden in 1922. He
studied at the Technical University of Stuttgart and
set up his own office in 1952. In 1979 he founded
Behnisch & Partner along with Winfried Büxel,
Manfred Sabatke and Erhard Tränkner. Today
the practice concentrates on large-scale public
commissions. Recent projects include banks in
Frankfurt, Munich and Stuttgart; schools; sports
facilities, and the German Flight Safety Bureau.
Behnisch is a member of the Akademie der Künste,
an Honorary Doctor at the University of Stuttgart,
a member of the International Academy of
Architecture in Sofia and an honorary member of
the Royal Incorporation of Architects in Scotland.
In 1992 he was awarded the Gold Medal by the
Architectural Academy in Paris.

Benthem Crouwel Architekten BV

Weerdestein 20, 1083 GA Amsterdam,
The Netherlands
Benthem Crouwel Architekten was founded in 1979
by Jan Benthem (b. 1952) and Mels Crouwel (b.
1953) who both studied at the Technical University
of Delft. Their practice is involved mainly with
public works in the fields of urban design, utility
buildings, offices and museums. Recent projects
include the AHOY Exhibition Centre (1993); the
West Terminal at Schiphol Airport (1993); and the
Museum Nieuw Land at Lelysted (1994). They are
currently working at Schiphol Airport on a railway
station and World Trade Centre.

Gunnar Birkerts and Associates Inc. Architects

292 Harmon Street, Birmingham, Michigan
48009–3800, USA

Gunnar Birkerts was born in Riga, Latvia, in 1925
but moved to Germany to study at the Technische
Hochschule in Stuttgart where he received a
Diplomingenieur Architekt degree in 1949. In the
same year he moved to the United States, where he
worked for various architectural practices until 1959
when he opened his own office, Birkerts & Straub,
which became Gunnar Birkerts and Associates in
1962. He received early acclaim in the 1950s –
being given the Young Designer of the Year
Award by the Akron Institute of Art in 1954 and
winning first prize at the International Furniture
Competition in Cantù, Italy – and in 1961 he was
made Assistant Professor of Architecture at the
University of Michigan. To date Birkerts has
received numerous honorary fellowships from such
organizations as the Latvian Architects Association,
and has held teaching posts throughout the USA,
including Distinguished Professorships at the
University of Illinois and at the Association of

Collegiate Schools of Architecture. He was the first recipient of the Bruce Alonzo Goff Professorship of Creative Architecture at the University of Oklahoma. In 1991 Birkerts was selected as architect for the Kemper Museum of Contemporary Art and Design for the Kansas City Art Institute and was elected Member of the Latvian Academy of Sciences. His projects – which include the Law School, Ohio State University; the US Embassy, Caracas, Venezuela, and the Thompson Library at the University of Michigan-Flint – have won 57 major awards and have been the subject of international reviews. Birkerts is currently working on projects in Italy, America and on the National Library, Riga, and a Central Market master plan, also in Riga.

Architekturbüro Bolles-Wilson & Partner

Alter Steinweg 17, 48143 Münster, Germany
Architekturbüro Bolles-Wilson was founded in 1987 by Julia B. Bolles-Wilson and Peter Wilson, architects who had previously worked together in their own London-based practice, Wilson Partnership. Peter Wilson was born and studied in Melbourne, Australia. Before working with Julia Bolles he had further training at the Architectural Association where he was Unit Master from 1978 to 1988. Julia Bolles was born in Münster and studied at the University of Karlsruhe. Postgraduate studies were followed by a teaching position at the Chelsea School of Art, which ended when she started working with Peter Wilson in 1980. Projects include a government office in Münster (1991–95); an exhibition stand at the Osaka Expo' 1990, and a waterfront design and restaurant in Rotterdam which was completed in 1995.

Busmann & Haberer

Aachener Strasse 24, 50674 Cologne, Germany
Peter Busmann was born in Hanover in 1933. He studied architecture in Braunschweig and Karlsruhe, and founded his own practice in Cologne in 1962. Since 1972 he has been in partnership with Godfrid Haberer. Haberer was born and studied in Stuttgart. He was project leader for Behnisch & Partner from 1968 before joining Busmann. The practice has received many national awards, including a distinction in the German Prize for Architecture (1991) and the architecture prize of the BDA Nordrhein-Westfalen (1992).

Coop Himmelblau

Seilerstatte 16/11a, Vienna A-1010, Austria
Coop Himmelblau was founded in 1968 by Wolf D. Prix (b. 1942, Vienna) and Helmut Swiczinsky (b. 1944, Poznan, Poland). The firm has worked on a series of study and building projects in the fields of architecture, design and the arts. It has become well known for its open, avant-garde architecture and has participated in many international exhibitions, including the 1988 Museum of Modern Art 'Deconstructivist' architecture show and the 1993 solo exhibition at the Georges Pompidou Centre, Paris. During the last five years it has become increasingly involved in large-scale projects, such as the Paris Melun–Senart City Planning Scheme; the Ronacher Theatre Renovation Project in Vienna; the Hygene Museum in Dresden, and the Art Academy, Munich. In 1988 Prix and Swiczinsky opened an American office in Los Angeles working on West Coast/Pacific Rim projects which include a five-storey restaurant/bar in Japan. The office is currently working on several design proposals and has recently completed a 6,000-square foot hilltop residence in Malibu, California.

Norihiko Dan and Associates

Jyowa Takanawa Bldg, 6F, 1-5-4 Takanawa, Minato-ku, Tokyo 108, Japan
Norihiko Dan was born in Kanagawa Prefecture in 1956 and graduated from Tokyo University where he later received a Master of Architecture from the Maki Laboratory. He undertook further studies at Yale University before setting up his own practice in 1986. He has been visiting critic at many Japanese universities, including the Waseda as well as at Kanazawa College of Art, and today is a lecturer at the Tokyo Institute of Technology. Although work to date is mostly small scale he is beginning to receive international recognition and has taken part in the exhibition 'Emerging Japanese Architects of the 1990s' which toured the USA, Canada and Spain. He has also held a one-man show at the Gallery MA, Tokyo, entitled 'Archipelago – The Work of Norihiko Dan'.

de Architekten Cie

Keizersgracht 126, 1015 CW Amsterdam, The Netherlands
de Architekten Cie is a Dutch architectural firm headed by Pi de Bruijn, Frits van Dongen, Jan Dirk Peereboom Voller (formerly Netherlands Deputy State Architect) and Carel Weeber, all of whom studied construction engineering at the Technical University of Delft. Their designs have won significant acclaim nationally and include housing and mixed-use projects in Amsterdam, the House of Representatives in The Hague, the Faculties of Economy and Planning for the University of Amsterdam, railway stations, interior design schemes and urban planning.

Studio de Lucchi

Via Pallavicino 31, 20145 Milan, Italy
Michele de Lucchi was born in Ferrara, Italy in 1951 and graduated from Florence University in 1975. During his student years he founded the 'Gruppo Cavat', a group concerned with avant-garde and conceptual architecture. He worked and designed for Alchimia until the establishment of Memphis in 1981. Today he produces exclusive handmade, art-oriented products, industrial consumer items for Olivetti and furniture in wood, metal, stone and other materials for companies serving specialized markets. His architectural activities range from shop design to large-scale office buildings and private apartment blocks. De Lucchi's work has received many awards and he has published and exhibited widely and internationally. Due to his activities and vast experience in the most important period of Italian design, de Lucchi has been invited to lecture at such design schools and universities as the Domus Academy, Milan, and the University of Detroit.

Atelier Christian de Portzamparc

1 rue de l'Aude, 75014 Paris, France
Christian de Portzamparc was born in 1944 and studied architecture at the Ecole Nationale Supérieure des Beaux-Arts in Paris. His early research into the 'theory of the city' has influenced the work of his practice to date. Some of his first designs include the water tower at Marne la Vallée; the rue des Hautes Formes (1969) and the urban plan for the residential block 'La Petite Roquette' in Paris. The design of the latter formed part of de Portzamparc's Programme for New Architecture (PAN VII), 1974. The Conservatoire Erik Satie (1983) was the first in a series of designs devoted to music and dance and was followed by the Ecole de Danse de l'Opéra de Paris (1983), the Opéra Bastille and the Cité de la Musique which, standing at the entrance to the Parc de la Villette, is one of Mitterrand's Grands Travaux. During the 1980s de Portzamparc also worked on interiors – such as the Café Beaubourg and a boutique for Emmanuel Ungaro in Paris – but in recent years has returned to urban development. In 1991 an exhibition was held in Tokyo dedicated to his urban projects. Recent schemes include a cultural centre in Rennes, the headquarters of DDB Needham Worldwide and law courts in Grasse. Christian de Portzamparc has held various teaching posts, including a professorship at the Ecole Spéciale d'Architecture in Paris, and has received the Commandeur de l'Ordre des Arts et des Lettres, the Grands Prix National d'Architecture, the Pritzker Prize and the Grand Prix d'Architecture de la Ville de Paris in recognition of his achievements.

Pierre du Besset–Dominique Lyon Architectes

77 rue de Charonne, 75011 Paris, France
Pierre du Besset (b. 1949, Paris) and Dominique Lyon (b. 1952, Paris) both graduated from the Ecole des Beaux-Arts, and worked for Jean Nouvel before founding du Besset–Lyon Architectes in 1986. Dominique Lyon also worked for Frank Gehry. Du Besset and Lyon's work has become well known throughout France for its individuality and variety and the practice has been invited to take part in some of the most prestigious design competitions in France, from the French Pavilion in Seville to the Jussieu University Library in Paris. Major completed projects include the Médiathèque d'Orléans (1994); Le Monde newspaper headquarters (1990), and 'La Maison de la Villette' in the Parc de la Villette (1987). The studio is currently working on two social housing projects – 55 units in the Parisian suburb of Gagny and 101 units in Euralille – both due to start construction in 1996.

J. Dubus et J.P. Lott S.A.R.L.

2 rue Custine, 75018 Paris, France
The Parisian architects Jean Dubus (b. 1949) and Jean-Pierre Lott (b. 1962) founded their partnership in 1986. Since then they have worked extensively throughout France, Spain, Algeria and Nairobi, and they are currently completing the French Embassy in Phnom Penh, Cambodia. Their practice deals mainly with large-scale public and educational facilities, and recent schemes include the Lycée Polyvalent d'Osney; the Palais de Justice at Fort de France, and a university restaurant in Evreux. They are currently working extensively in Evreux, adding to their list of schemes a further extension of the university faculty as well as city law courts.

Ecart

111 rue Saint-Antoine, 75004 Paris, France
The Ecart Group was founded in 1978 by Andrée Putman who was born in Paris. Putman studied music under Poulenc before becoming first a journalist and later a design consultant for the mass-market chain Prisunic and co-founder of Créateurs et Industriels, which introduced the work of Issey Miyake and Jean Muir, among others, to France. The Ecart practice is divided into three specific disciplines. Ecart SA is the design office, specializing in interior and product design varying from hotels to boutiques, corporate offices to private houses, and museums to governmental offices. Notable designs include the Office of the Minister of Culture (1984); Ebel Headquarters (1985); Morgans Hotel (1985) and the Im Wasserturm Hotel (1990). Ecart International re-edits furniture and objects by such designers as Eileen Gray and Mariano Fortuny and edits designs by Ecart SA (designers regularly used include Patrick Naggar, Paul Mathieu and Michael Ray). Andrée Putman licensing division designs objects distributed throughout the world, including rugs, upholstery

fabrics, tableware and bathroom accessories. Recent projects by Ecart SA include the Cartier Foundation exhibition areas (1993); the Centre d'Art Plastiques Contemporaines in Bordeaux; the Sheraton Hotel, Paris-Roissy (1994); the Bally Boutiques concept (1993–94) and the brand images of Baccarat and Swarovski.

Environment Design Institute
Mita Sonnette Bldg 3F, 1-1-15 Mita, Minato-ku, Tokyo 108, Japan
Mitsuru Man Senda (b. 1941, Yokohama) was head of the Environment Design Institute from 1968 to 1984, during which time he gained a doctorate in engineering. He graduated from the Architectural Department of the Tokyo Institute of Technology in 1964, after which he spent four years in the practice of Kiyonori Kikutake Architects and Associates. He has held various teaching positions in Japan and today is Professor of Architecture in the Engineering Department of the Tokyo Institute. He has been given various prizes within Japan and in 1993 was awarded the Architectural Institute of Japan Kazumigaseki Memorial Prize and Grand Expo Prize, Supreme Order of Merit, for his Shinshu Expo Alpiko Plaza.

Esherick Homsey Dodge and Davis Architecture and Planning
2789 25th Street, San Francisco, California 94110, USA
Joseph Esherick founded his own practice in 1946 and expanded to include associates George Homsey, Peter Dodge and Charles Davis in 1963; they became partners in 1972. Charles Davis FAIA is the current Senior Design Principal of EHDD. He studied Architecture and Design Administration at the University of California, Berkeley, is the director of the San Francisco chapter of the American Institute of Architects and has taught at the University of Hawaii and UC Berkeley. Today the company has grown substantially in size and scope and has added four principals: Joram Altman, Jim Hastings, Ed Rubin and Blair Spangler. Early work was mainly residential projects in the San Francisco Bay Area but by the late 1960s more complex schemes were being undertaken, including one of the earliest urban shopping complexes, The Cannery, San Francisco. During the 1970s EHDD's work included Bay Area Rapid Transit stations and the award-winning Garfield School, San Francisco. Their present involvement in aquarium design evolved from the Monterey Bay Aquarium, one of the most widely acclaimed and visited facilities of its kind in the USA. Another area of expertise is the design of university libraries, including the University of California, Santa Cruz Science Library for which they were awarded the Library Building Award in 1993. Current work includes the new Museum of Marine Biology/Aquarium in Taiwan, and the Wuksachi Village at Sequoia/Kings Canyon National Park, California.

Sir Norman Foster and Partners
Riverside Three, 22 Hester Road, London
SW11 4AN, UK
Sir Norman Foster was born in Manchester, England in 1935 and studied architecture and city planning at the University of Manchester and at Yale University. He established Team 4 in 1963 – with his late wife, Wendy, and Su and Richard Rogers – and founded Foster Associates in 1967. Today he is internationally famous for his high-tech designs, many of which, such as the Hong Kong and Shanghai Bank (1979–86), and Stansted Airport (1981–89) have resulted directly from competitions. Projects include the Sackler Galleries at the Royal Academy of Arts, London, which was

named the RIBA building of the year in 1993; the Centre d'Art/Cultural Centre, Nîmes; the Reichstag remodelling, Berlin; ITN Headquarters, London; Cranfield University Library; the new wing to the Joslyn Art Museum in Omaha, Nebraska, and the Cambridge University Law Faculty. Master plans include the King's Cross development, London. Current projects include the new headquarters for Commerzbank in Frankfurt and an airport at Chek Lap Kok for Hong Kong – covering an area of 1,248 hectares, it is the largest project in the world. Norman Foster received a knighthood in the Queen's Birthday Honours in 1991, and his work has won over 60 awards and citations. He is a well-known figure on the international lecturing circuit. Although primarily concerned with large-scale architectural projects, Sir Norman Foster is also involved in furniture design.

Massimiliano Fuksas Architecte
76 Bis, rue Vielle du Temple, 75003 Paris, France
Massimiliano Fuksas was born in 1944 in Rome, where he also studied for and received an architecture diploma in 1969 from the University La Sapienza. He opened his own studio two years before leaving university and today has offices in both Paris and Rome. His work strongly reflects his interest in the problems associated with successful town planning in the outskirts of large cities and he is currently continuing his series of city regeneration projects with schemes for the Neusser Strasse in Munich and for the neighbourhood around the train station in Padua, Italy. Earlier works include cultural and sporting centres, factories, museums and university facilities.

Jordi Garcés–Enric Sòria Arquitectes
c/Boqueria, 1-ler Piso, 08002 Barcelona, Spain
Jordi Garcés was born in Barcelona in 1945, studied at the Escuela Técnica Superior de Arquitectura in Barcelona, and graduated in 1970. In the course of his studies he worked in the offices of Martorell-Bohigas-Mackay and with Ricardo Bofill and since 1970 has worked in collaboration with Enric Sòria. Garcés was Professor of Projects in the Escuela Eina from 1971 to 1973; at the Escuela Técnica de Arquitectura, Barcelona, until 1975; and until 1987, was Doctor of Architecture at the Universitat Politécnica of Catalonia where today he holds the Chair. Enric Sòria was born in Barcelona in 1937 and, like Garcés, graduated from the Escuela Técnica Superior de Arquitectura and worked for Martorell-Bohigas-Mackay. He is the author of *Conversation with José Antonio Coderch de Sentmenat* and editor of the catalogue of drawings of the Escuela Técnica, where he was also Professor of Projects and Drawings from 1976. Notable projects from the Garcés–Sòria partnership include the Museum of Science, Barcelona; Museum Picasso, Barcelona; a hotel on the Plaza de España, Barcelona; Museum of Science in Santa Cruz de Tenerife, and the Cinema Imax, Port Vell de Barcelona. Jordi Garcés and Enric Sòria's joint work has been published in the principal architectural periodicals and has been the subject of many conferences and exhibitions.

Prof. Gerber & Partner
Harenberghaus, Königswall 21, 44137 Dortmund, Germany
The German architect and designer Eckhard Gerber was born in Oberhain, Thüringen in 1938. He studied at the Braunschweig Technical University and later held a scholarship with the design company Reemtsma in Hamburg. He opened his first studio, Werkgemeinschaft 66 in 1966, which was followed by Prof. Gerber & Partner at Dortmund-Kley in 1979. Today the firm also has

offices in Berlin, Leipzig, Braunschweig and Stuttgart. Gerber's early interest was in urban development and architecture, and he was awarded a special prize for young artists of Nordrhein-Westfalen in 1975. He has held two professorships to date – first at the University of Essen, where he taught a basic course of designing for architecture and landscape architecture, and later at the Bergische University, where he concentrated on architecture alone. He is a member of the BDA and DWB and a frequent adjudicator at design competitions throughout Germany. He has received much acclaim for his work, including most recently the BDA-Prize Niedersachsen (1994) for his state and university library in Göttingen as well as the IAKS-Auszeichnung (silver) for sport and leisure facilities for his Neckartal Sports Hall in Wernau. Built projects include numerous large-scale public, educational and state facilities. He is currently working on two church designs in Germany as well as landscape schemes and a college in Lüneburg.

Teodoro González de León
Amsterdam No. 63, Colonia Hipódromo Condesa, Mexico D. F., 06100, Mexico
Teodoro González de León was born in Mexico City in 1926. He studied at the School of Architecture of the National University of Mexico from 1942 to 1947 during which time he carried out his practical training in the offices of Carlos Obregón Santacilia, Carlos Lazo and, later, Mario Pani. In 1948 he was awarded a scholarship from the French government and worked in Le Corbusier's Atelier in Paris, where he participated in the construction of the Unité d'Habitation Marseille and was in charge of the building of the Manufactures St Die, France. He returned to Mexico in the 1970s, and since then his architectural practice has received much national acclaim. González de León is an Honorary Fellow of the American Institute of Architects and of the National College of Mexico and is the recipient of numerous major awards. In 1989 he was given the First Prize at the International Academy of Architecture and the Gold Medal and Diploma from the Centre for Human Settlement (United Nations); and in 1994 the Grand Prix of the International Academy of Architecture 'for all entries submitted'. He has shown his work both nationally and internationally. Recent projects include the National Court and Tribunal of Justice, Mexico City (1992); a building for Hewlett-Packard, Mexico City, in collaboration with J. F. Serrano (1993, second stage under construction); the Site Museum of the archaeological zone of Tajín, Veracruz, Mexico (1992); the Mexican Embassy in Guatemala, also with Serrano (1993); the Mexican Gallery, British Museum, London (1994); the renovation of the exhibition halls of the Palacio de Bellas Artes, Mexico City, in collaboration with Serrano (1994), and a villa in Moscow for the International Dwelling Complex 'INTERBAU-Moscow' (1994).

Michael Graves
341 Nassau Street, Princeton, New Jersey 08540, USA
Michael Graves was born in Indianapolis, Indiana, and received his architectural training at the University of Cincinnati and Harvard University. Since the formation of his practice in 1964 he has become an influential figure, in part responsible for moving urban architecture away from abstract modernism towards more contextual and traditional themes. He has produced designs for over 200 projects, including office buildings, hotels and convention centres, private residences, sports facilities, institutional buildings, retail spaces, theatres, libraries, museums and other cultural

facilities. Through his affiliated company, Graves Design, he has produced an extensive collection of furniture and consumer products, collaborating with such manufacturers as Alessi, Arkitektura, Swid Powell, Baldinger and Atelier International. Major projects include the Walt Disney World Swan and Dolphin Hotels, Orlando, Florida; the Disney Company Corporate Headquarters, Burbank, California; the Crown American Offices, Johnstown, Pennsylvania; the Whitney Museum of American Art, New York; a master plan for the Detroit Institute of Arts; the Denver Public Library; and the Clark County Library in Las Vegas. Forthcoming schemes will include work in Japan and Taiwan, as well as the corporate headquarters for Thomson Consumer Electronics in Indianapolis. Graves is the Schirmer Professor of Architecture at Princeton University and a Fellow of the American Institute of Architects. He has received many awards, including fifteen Progressive Architecture awards and nine American Institute of Architects National Honor awards.

Gwathmey Siegel & Associates Architects
475 Tenth Ave., New York, NY 10018, USA
Gwathmey Siegel & Associates was founded in 1967 by Charles Gwathmey and Robert Siegel, who are both Fellows of the American Institute of Architects and recipients of the Medal of Honor from its New York chapter. Charles Gwathmey studied at the University of Pennsylvania and Yale University and has held numerous teaching posts including positions at Princeton and Columbia universities as well as visiting professorships at Yale and Harvard. Robert Siegel trained at the Pratt Institute and Harvard University. Their designs range in scale from arts and educational facilities and major corporate buildings to furniture systems and decorative art objects. In 1982 the firm became the youngest architectural practice to be given the Firm Award, the highest accolade of the American Institute of Architects, for innovative detailed design showing appreciation of environmental and economic concerns. Recent projects include the Contemporary Resort Convention Center at Walt Disney World; additions to the faculties of Cornell University; the Busch Reisinger Museum and Fine Arts Library addition to the Fogg Museum at Harvard University, and the restoration of and addition to Frank Lloyd Wright's Guggenheim Museum in New York. Works in progress include the Henry Art Museum at the University of Washington, Seattle; the Social Sciences Building at the University of California at San Diego, and the Science, Industry and Business Library at the New York Public Library.

Heikkinen–Komonen Architects
Kristianinkatu 11-13, 00170 Helsinki, Finland
Heikkinen–Komonen Architects was founded in 1974 by Mikko Heikkinen (b. 1949) and Markku Komonen (b. 1945) who both received Master's degrees from the Helsinki University of Technology in 1974 and worked for various architectural practices within Finland before forming their partnership. Heikkinen has held teaching posts at Helsinki University and in 1992 was given a New York residence scholarship by the Finnish Foundation of Visual Arts. He is a visiting critic at the Philadelphia College of Textiles and Science, University College, Dublin, the University of Virginia and the Städelschule, Frankfurt. Komonen has been the Professor of Architecture at Helsinki University of Technology since 1992 as well as visiting teacher at the University of Houston (1983–93). He was also the Editor-in-Chief of *Arkkitehti* magazine (1977–80) and Director of the Exhibition Department of the Museum of Finnish

Architecture (1978–86). Early projects include renovations and retail and exhibition designs in Finland, but in the 1990s the pratice has undertaken increasingly larger commissions, such as a Health Unit in Guinea, Africa; fair pavilions for Marimekko in Düsseldorf, Frankfurt, Copenhagen and Paris, and the Finnish embassies in Washington and Berlin.

Hellmuth, Obata & Kassabaum (HOK) Inc.
One Metropolitan Square, 211 North Broadway, St Louis, Missouri 63102-2231, USA
Hellmuth, Obata & Kassabaum was founded in 1955 and today employs over 1,300 people. Their area of expertise covers work for major corporations, developers, state and local agencies, sports facilities, hospitals, colleges and universities, the US government and governments in Canada, the Caribbean, Central and South America, the Middle East and Asia. The firm offers services in architecture, engineering, interior design, graphic design, planning, landscape architecture, facility programming/management and consulting. Gyo Obata FAIA, is co-chairman of the firm. He received a Bachelor's degree in architecture in 1945 from Washington University and a Master's in architecture and urban design from the Cranbrook Academy of Art. He has Honorary PhDs from Washington and the University of Missouri. George Hellmuth (now retired) received a Bachelor's and Master's degree from Washington University and also studied at the Ecole des Beaux Arts at Fountainebleau, France. He was given the Gold Medal Award by the St Louis chapter of the AIA. George Kassabaum FAIA (died 1982) also studied at Washington University. He served as a national president of the AIA (1968–69) and as chancellor of the College of Fellows of the AIA (1977–78). HOK's major recent projects include the Federal Reserve Bank in Minneapolis; the Los Angeles County Replacement Hospital; the Department of State US Embassy in Moscow, and a high-rise for the Principal Life Insurance Company in Des Moines, Iowa.

Hyvämäki-Karhunen-Parkkinen Architects
Lönnrotinkatu 35D, 00180 Helsinki, Finland
Eero Hyvämäki was born in 1938, Jukka Karhunen in 1945 and Risto Parkkinen in 1938, and all studied architecture at the Technical University in Helsinki. They founded their partnership in 1968 after having jointly entered various architectural competitions. Today their offices deal mainly with large-scale public buildings – town halls, libraries, meeting facilities, universities and transport systems ranging from urban planning to design, and including detailed plans, furniture and light fittings. Most recently completed works include Itäkeskus (1992); the eastern commercial subcentre of Helsinki and the adjacent swimming baths in an excavated underground dome (1993); the Helsinki Opera House (1993), and the Central Bureau of Investigation (1994). The practice has recently won the competition for the Technical University of Hamburg, Germany, and was awarded first prize in a competition for a new head office building for LM Ericsson in Finland.

Iosa Ghini Srl
via Caprarie No. 7, 40124 Bologna, Italy
Massimo Iosa Ghini was born in Borgo Tossignano, Italy, in 1959 and graduated with a degree in architecture from Milan Polytechnic. Before working with Ettore Sottsass and Memphis in 1986, he was involved in drawing cartoons for international magazines, such as *Heavy Metal* (New York), *Alter Linus* (Milan) and *Ryuko Tsushin* (Tokyo), and creating set designs for cultural

television programmes in Italy. In 1987 he launched his first furniture collection, Dinamic, for Moroso, which received awards worldwide. Since then he has been a leading figure in the design world, holding one-man shows internationally and judging design awards. In 1991 he presented a collection of furniture that represented his research on the moulding of wood. Important interior design projects include the planning of the fashion-store chain Fiorucci and the planning and design of the Renault Italy showrooms. Since 1992 he has held various major retrospectives, including one at the Steininger Gallery, Munich, on the occasion of the presentation of the comic book *Captain Sillavengo*, and a second on drawings, canvases and design objects at the Axis Building, Japan. Also in 1992 he was invited to take part in the 'Busstop' exhibition along with other leading design figures. In 1994 Ghini began his collaboration with Ferrari designing exhibition show-rooms and factory interiors and the following year was selected to design the corporate visual identity of Omnital, part of the Olivetti Group responsible for the GSM cellular phone network in Italy. As well as being active in interior design, Iosa Ghini has worked for most of the leading furniture and product manufacturers including Moroso, Fiam, Poltronova, Swatch and Silhouette.

Toyo Ito & Associates, Architects
1-19-4, Shibuya, Shibuya-ku, Tokyo 150, Japan
Toyo Ito was born in Nagano, Japan in 1941 and graduated with a degree in architecture from Tokyo University in 1965. After working for Kiyonori Kikutake (1965–9), he established Urban Robot in Tokyo which became Toyo Ito & Associates in 1979, the year he won a Japan Airlines design commission. Ito has designed numerous residences in Japan and, since the mid-1980s, larger scale architectural projects, receiving awards for his house in Kasama (1981); the Silver Hut, Tokyo (1984); the Nomad restaurant, Tokyo (1985/6); the guest house for the Sapporo brewery, Hokkaido (1989), and the Yatsushiro Municipal Museum (1991). Other major projects include the Tower of Winds, Yokohama (1986); the I and T Buildings, Asakusabashi and Nakameguro (1989–90); the Opera House, Frankfurt (lighting 1991); the U-Gallery, Yugawara (1991); the F-Building, Tokyo (1991); JAL office interiors, New York (1992); Hotel P. Hokkaido (1992); an amusement complex in Nagayama (1992); Shimosuwa Municipal Museum, Nagano (1993); Tsukuba South Parking Building, Ibaragi (1994), and the Fire Station in Yatsushiro, Kumanoto. Schemes currently under construction are the Nagaoka Municipal Culture and Art Hall, Niigata and the O-Dome Akita. Ito is a visiting lecturer at the University of Tokyo and at Japan Women's University. Exhibitions include the Pao dwelling project, Tokyo, and 'Transfiguration' Europalia '89, Belgium. A monograph on Ito was published by Editions du Moniteur in 1991 and his work featured in 'Architecture in a Simulated City' (1992) INAX. Ito is a visiting lecturer at leading universities throughout the world, including the University of Tokyo, Japan Women's University and Columbia University, USA.

Kiyonori Kikutake, Kikutake Architect and Associates
PO Box 1128, 19F, Sunshine-60 bldg, 3-1-1 Higashi-Ikebukuro, Toshma-ku, Tokyo
Kiyonori Kikutake was born in 1928 in Japan. He is currently Professor of Architecture at the Waseda University in Tokyo and has spent periods lecturing abroad in Hawaii and Austria. Well-known for his concept of the 'Marine City' and 'Floating Systems' projects as well as his work on metabolic architecture and the idea of the 'Sky House', he has

been made Honorary Fellow of the American Institute of Architecture and is President of the Japan Institute for Macro-Engineering. Recent architectural projects include the Hotel Cosima and the Kurume City Hall and he is currently working on the Shimane Museum and the Kitakyusyu Media Dome.

Kisho Kurokawa Architect & Associates
Aoyama Bldg 11F, 1-2-3 Kita-Aoyama, Minato-ku, Tokyo, Japan
Kisho Kurokawa was born in Nagoya in 1934 and studied architecture at Kyoto University. In 1960, while studying for a doctorate at Tokyo University, he formed the Metabolist Group, whose philosophy, closely linked with Buddhism, viewed urban architectural forms as organisms capable of growth and change, a belief that is echoed in his designs to date. Major projects include the National Bunraku Theatre, Osaka; the Roppongi Prince Hotel, Tokyo; the Japanese–German Culture Centre in Berlin, and the national museums of modern art in Nagoya, Hiroshima and Wakayama. As well as his architectural works, he has designed distinctive furniture for Tendo and Kosuga and has exhibited in New York, Paris, London, Dublin, Moscow, Milan, Florence, Rome, Budapest and Sofia.

Maki and Associates
3-6-2 Nihonbashi, Chuoh-ku, Tokyo, Japan
Maki and Associates was founded in 1965 by Fumihiko Maki. Maki was born in 1928 in Tokyo where he was educated and received a Bachelor of Architecture from the University. He continued his education in the USA where he gained a Master of Architecture from both the Cranbrook Academy of Art in 1953 and from the Harvard University Graduate School of Design in 1954. Before returning to Japan, Maki worked for Skidmore, Owings and Merrill in New York and for Josep Lluis Sert, and in 1958 began teaching at Washington University in St. Louis at which time he received the Graham Foundation Travelling Fellowship. From 1962 to 1965 Maki served as an Associate Professor at Harvard University. In conjunction with his practice in Tokyo, Maki has served as professor at the University of Tokyo and has taught and lectured extensively outside Japan at Columbia University, the University of California at Berkeley and the Technical University of Vienna, amongst others. He is a member of the Japan Institute of Architects and an Honorary Fellow of both the American Institute of Architects and the Royal Institute of British Architects. Major completed projects to date number the National Museum of Modern Art, Kyoto (1986); the Tokyo Metropolitan Gymnasium (1990); YKK Research Center, Tokyo (1993); the Centre for the Arts, Yerba Buena Gardens, San Francisco, and the Isar Büropark, Munich (1994).

Rick Mather Architects
123 Camden High Street, London NW1 7JR, UK
The London-based architect, Rick Mather (b. 1937), studied architecture in the USA and urban design at the Architectural Association in London before opening his own office. He maintains a varied architectural and planning practice, working mainly on residential and commercial schemes including both new-build and renovations, with a special interest in urban design and an expertise in low-energy, 'green' buildings and advanced techniques in the use of glass. Notable award-winning projects include an all-glass structure in Hampstead; student residences, the Schools of Education and Information Studies and the Climatic Research Unit at the University of East Anglia; the Zen restaurants in London, Hong Kong and Montreal;

the office development 'La Lumière' in London, and the renovation of the Architectural Association. He is currently working on numerous projects, such as the new business school of ISMA at Reading and a new academic building for the French Lycée in Kensington. He has held teaching posts at leading design colleges in the UK and is currently Royal Institute of British Architects external examiner for Cambridge and other universities in England. He has been the recipient of many prizes, most recently the Civic Trust Award (in 1995) and a third Royal Institute of British Architects Award (in 1994). His designs have been exhibited worldwide.

Mecanoo Architekten
Oude Delft 203-2611 HD, Delft, The Netherlands
Mecanoo architekten was founded in 1982 by a group of young architects who won an architectural competition for the Kruisplein in Rotterdam. The housing and commercial spaces schemes were completed in 1985. Today the practice is involved in a wide range of urban design, including social and commercial housing projects, public utilities, residential schemes, interior design, restoration and landscape design. Their work includes the Restaurant/Grand-Café Boompjes, Rotterdam (1990); a Public Library, Almelo (1994); Isala College, Silvolde (1995), and the Faculty of Economics and Management, Utrecht University (1995).

Richard Meier & Partners
475 Tenth Avenue, New York, NY 10018, USA
Richard Meier was born in Newark, New Jersey, in 1934. He studied architecture at Cornell University after which he worked for architects Davis, Brody and Wisniewski in New York, and later Skidmore, Owings and Merrill and Marcel Breuer. In the late 1950s and early 60s he worked as an artist with Michael Graves but set up his own architectural practice in New York in 1963. He has been professor of architecture at Harvard and Yale universities as well as at the Cooper Union, and in the 1970s was a member of the New York Five – with Peter Eisenman, Michael Graves, Charles Gwathmey and John Hejduk – who advocated a modernist ideal strongly reminiscent of Le Corbusier's Cubist designs of the 1920s. Much of Meier's work at this time, such as a tea set for Alessi in the style of Malevich and Hoffmannesque metalwork and ceramics for Swid Powell, was derivative of previous twentieth-century designs. Architectural work includes the Museum for Kunsthandwerk, Frankfurt (1984); the High Museum, Atlanta (1984); the Getty Center in Los Angeles (1985), and the City Hall in The Hague (1985). Richard Meier's work has been the subject of many solo exhibitions worldwide and he has been the recipient of such accolades as the Arnold W. Brunner Memorial Prize, the Reynolds Memorial Award and the Pritzker Architecture Prize. His life story has been the subject of a monograph and television film.

Atelier Mendini Srl
via Sannio 24, 20137 Milan, Italy
Alessandro Mendini was born in 1931 in Milan where he later studied architecture at the Polytechnic. He was the publisher of the design magazines Casabella, Modo and Domus as well as directing the journal Ollo. For many years he has been the theorist of avant-garde design, co-founding the Global Tools Group in 1973 as a counter-movement to established Italian design. In 1978 he started his collaboration with Studio Alchimia in Milan and developed the so-called 'banal design' which sought to change items in daily use into new and ironical objects – a notable example is the early

version of the Proust Chair painted in a divisionist technique for the Bauhaus Collection in 1980. In 1983 he became Professor of Design at the University of Applied Art in Vienna and was also made a member of the scientific committee of the Domus Academy. In the late 1980s he established the Genetic Laboratory for Visual Surprises in order to research and question established ideas of taste and form. His own work covers architecture, furniture, product, tableware and interior design and he is currently design advisor for Swatch and Alessi, amongst others. Additional clients include Zanotta, Fiat, Zabro, Driade, Poltronova, Elam and Abet Laminati. In 1990 he set up Atelier Mendini with his brother Francesco Mendini designing projects such as the Groninger Museum and, with Yumiko Kobayashi, the Paradise Tower, Hiroshima. Alessandro Mendini's work has been the subject of countless exhibitions and one-man shows worldwide.

MET Studio
6-8 Standard Place, Rivington Street, London EC2A 3BE, UK
MET Studio is an award-winning design consultancy, specializing in exhibition and interior design for museum, corporate, government and leisure clients worldwide. The company was formed in 1982 and is led by Managing Director Alex McCuaig, who, together with Museums Director Deirdre Janson-Smith and Leisure Director Vic Kass, supervises a team of concept planners, researchers, architects, interior, exhibit and graphic designers. MET Studio also work with modern artists and sculptors and artists whose specially commissioned work is often integrated into projects. The Studio has recently been awarded the 1995 Minerva Award for the Best Environment for its work on the Environment Theatre at the National Museum of Natural Science, Taiwan. In 1994 it won the Best Exhibition Award at the Design Week awards for its work on the Life Sciences Exhibition for the Wellcome Trust in London. The Life Sciences gallery also won the Best Education Initiative prize at the 1994 IBM Museum of the Year awards as well as a Special Award for Lighting Design. Recent projects include an exhibition for Hong Kong Telecom; a travelling exhibition for the Wellcome Trust; the National Museum of Prehistory, Taiwan; the refurbishment of the QE2; the 'Evolution of Plants' exhibit at Kew Gardens; the Electronic Theatre at the Science Museum, London, and the D&AD Festival Exhibition 1995 at the Saatchi Gallery, London.

José Rafael Moneo
Calle Cinca 5, Madrid 28002, Spain
José Rafael Moneo was born in Tudela, Navarre, Spain, in 1937. He obtained his architectural degree in 1961 from the Madrid University School of Architecture. As a student he worked with architect Francisco Javier Sáenz de Oiza in Madrid and Jørn Utzon (architect of the Sydney Opera House) in Hellebæk, Denmark. In 1963 Moneo was awarded a two-year fellowship at the Spanish Academy in Rome and upon his return took up the first in a long line of teaching appointments that has included chairs in Madrid, Princeton and Lausanne. In 1985 he was named Chairman of the Architecture Department of the Harvard University Graduate School of Design where he remains active as Professor and in 1991 was granted the honorary Sert Professorship. Rafael Moneo's best-known works number the Diestre Factory in Zaragoza (1967); the Previsión Española Insurance Co. Building in Seville (1987); the central offices of the Bank of Spain in Jaén (1988); the San Pablo Airport in Seville (1992); the Atocha Railway

Station (1992); the Davis Art Museum of Wellesley College in Massachusetts (1993), and the refectory of the Monastery of Santa Maria de Guadalupe (1994). Currently under construction are the Barcelona Concert Hall; the Museum of Modern Art and Architecture in Stockholm, and the 'Kursaal' Concert Hall and Cultural Centre in San Sebastian (1990). Moneo has received many accolades, most recently the 'Laurea ad Honorem' from the School of Architecture in Venice. He is a member of the American Academy of Arts and Sciences and of the Accademia di San Luca di Roma as well as an Honorary Fellow of the American Institute of Architects and of the Royal Institute of British Architects. Moneo's works have been published widely and a collection of his essays, which originally appeared in the magazines *Oppositions* and *Lotus* and in his own periodical *Arquitectura Bis*, is due to be brought out by CLUVA Press in Milan and MIT Press, Cambridge, Massachusetts.

Naito Architect & Associates
No. 301 Matsuoka Kudan Bldg 2-2-8 Kudan-Minami, Chiyoda-ku, Tokyo 102, Japan
Naito Architect & Associates was founded in 1981 by Hiroshi Naito who was born in 1950 in Yokohama. He graduated from the Waseda University and in the same year was the recipient of the Murano Award. He later studied under Professor Takamasa Yoshizaka at the Graduate School of Waseda University. Before opening his own office he worked in the architectural studio of Fernand Higueras in Madrid as Chief Architect and for Kiyonori Kikutake in Tokyo. Today he lectures at Waseda University. Major works include the Gallery TOM (1984); domestic housing projects (1984, 1990); Autopolis Art Museum (1991); the Sea-Folk Museum (1992), and the Shima Art Museum (1993). He has been awarded the design prize of the Architectural Institute of Japan (1993) and the Education Minister's Art Encouragement Prize for Freshman of Art (1993).

O'Donnell and Tuomey
20A Camden Row, Dublin 8, Ireland
The Dublin-based architectural practice O'Donnell and Tuomey specializes in cultural and educational schemes and the re-use of existing buildings. Sheila O'Donnell was born in 1953 and obtained a Bachelor of Architecture from University College Dublin, and a Master's degree from the Royal College of Art, London. She worked for Spence and Webster and Stirling Wilford and Associates before forming her current partnership. O'Donnell was visiting critic at Princeton University (1987) and currently lectures at University College Dublin. John Tuomey was born in Tralee in 1954 and also received a Bachelor of Architecture from University College Dublin, where he lectures today. Like O'Donnell, he worked for Stirling Wilford and Associates and was visiting critic at Princeton University (1987 and 1993). He also spent a period at the Office of Public Works, Dublin, and was visiting design critic at Harvard University from 1988 to 1989. Tuomey has been external examiner for the Architectural Association, Cambridge and Oxford, and was President of the Architectural Association of Ireland from 1992 to 1993. Both O'Donnell and Tuomey are Fellows of the Royal Institute of Architects, Ireland. They have received numerous awards and commendations including the RIAI Gold Medal commendation for the Laboratory at Abbotstown (1991); the RIAI Irish Architecture Award; the Andrea Palladio International Award-Finalist, and the *Sunday Times* Building of the Year Award – all for the Irish Film Centre (1993); and the RIAI Award for the

Blackwood Golf Centre in County Down (1995). The practice is currently working for University College Cork, developing an existing convent building and associated lands.

Pei Cobb Freed & Partners
600 Madison Avenue, New York, NY 10022, USA
Ieoh Ming Pei was born in China in 1917. He moved to the USA to study architecture at the Massachusetts Institute of Technology and received a Bachelor of Architecture degree in 1940. He then studied at the Harvard Graduate School of Design under Walter Gropius – at the same time teaching in the faculty as assistant professor – and gained a Master's degree in 1946. In 1955 Pei formed I. M. Pei & Associates, which became I. M. Pei and Partners in 1989. The practice has designed over 150 projects in the USA and abroad, more than half of which have won awards and citations. As well as working for corporate and private investment clients, the practice has executed numerous commissions for public authorities and religious, educational and cultural institutions. Its most important buildings include the Bank of China, Hong Kong; the East West Wing of the National Gallery of Washington, D.C.; the Grand Louvre in Paris, and the United States Holocaust Memorial Museum, Washington, D.C. Works recently completed are the Federal Triangle, Washington, and the San Francisco Main Public Library. Pei is a Fellow of the American Institute of Architects, a Corporate Member of the Royal Institute of Architects, and in 1975 he was made a member of the American Academy. He has honorary degrees from leading universities in the USA, Hong Kong and France.

Dominique Perrault
26-34 rue Bruneseau, 75013 Paris, France
Dominique Perrault was born in Clermont-Ferrand in 1953 and studied architecture at the Ecole des Beaux-Arts, Paris. He also gained a certificate of advanced studies in town planning from the National School of Bridges and Roadways, Paris, as well as a Master's degree in history from the School of Advanced Studies in Social Sciences. Before opening his own studio in 1981 he worked for Martin van Treck, René Dottelonde and Antoine Grumbach, the consulting architects for the CAUE de la Mayenne. In 1983 Perrault was the winner of the 'Programme for New Architecture' (Pan XII), France, and the 'Album of Young Architecture', sponsored by the Ministry of Housing, France. In 1986 he was made consultant architect for the Loiret District Council. Today he is also the consultant architect for the city of Nantes and is on the Council for Urban Planning in the city of Salzburg. Perrault has been a member of the board of the French Institute of Architecture and of the Scientific and Technical Committee, ESA, in Paris since 1988. He has been the recipient of numerous awards in honour of his achievements, including second prize from the Foundation of the Academy of Architecture for his project for the Bibliothèque de France. In 1993 he was awarded the Grand Prix National d'Architecture.

Antoine Predock Architect
300 Twelfth Street, NW, Albuquerque, New Mexico 87102, USA
Antoine Predock studied at the University of New Mexico, Albuquerque, and at Columbia University, New York, and founded his own practice in 1967. He is a Fellow of the American Institute of Architects and his work has received numerous awards and citations. Recent projects include the Institute of American Indian Arts, Santa Fe; the Student Affairs and Administrative Service Building

at the University of California, Santa Barbara, and the New Mexico Hispanic Cultural Center, Albuquerque. He has held educational positions at various universities in the United States, including Harvard (1987); and UCLA (1989–90 and 1990–91) and is a well-known figure on the lecturing circuit. Predock's work has been published widely and he has exhibited nationally and internationally.

Richard Rogers Partnership
Thames Wharf, Rainville Road, London W6 9HA, UK.
Richard Rogers founded his own practice with John Young, Marco Goldschmied and Mike Davies in 1977. Since then they have built a wide range of projects ranging from low-cost industrial units to prestigious headquarters buildings; from highly technical laboratories to landscape proposals; from cultural centres to office developments, and from airport planning to the restoration of historic monuments. Their most notable and ground-breaking schemes include the Pompidou Centre (1977), which has attracted more visitors than the Louvre and Eiffel Tower combined, and the Lloyds building, London. Recent public commissions have included the European Court of Human Rights, Strasbourg, and the Law Courts in Bordeaux, and their work with historic buildings can be seen in the award-winning conversion and restoration of Billingsgate Fish Market in the City of London into a bankers' dealing room (1988). Other schemes in London number the Headquarters Building for Channel 4 Television and offices for Daiwa and Lloyds Register of Shipping, and they are currently working on designs for Heathrow Airport's Fifth Terminal and modifications for Terminal 1. The Partnership's interest in urban planning has recently won them the South Bank Centre Competition, a scheme that drew on experience gained in master-planning such projects as the Potsdamer Platz, Berlin, and the Lu Jia Zui business district in China. Richard Rogers received the Royal Gold Medal for Architecture from the Royal Institute of British Architects and was made Chevalier, l'Ordre National de la Legion d'Honneur in 1986. He was Chairman of the Tate Gallery (1986–89) and of the Building Experiences Trust (1989–94), and became vice-chair of the Arts Council in 1994. He received a knighthood for services to architecture in the 1991 Birthday Honours List and was awarded the Ordre des Arts et des Lettres (1995).

Hartmut & Ingeborg Rüdiger
Zeppelinstrasse 5, 38106 Braunschweig, Germany
The architectural partnership Hartmut & Ingeborg Rüdiger was founded by Hartmut Rüdiger (b. 1949) and Ingeborg Rüdiger (b. 1950) in 1980. Both studied at the Technical University in Braunschweig where Hartmut held the post of assistant professor from 1976 to 1980. The practice has taken part in 80 architectural competitions and has been awarded more than 30 prizes. They are also involved in urban landscaping (work includes a new design for the Königstrasse in Duisburg) and town planning (in Berlin-Adlershof). Principal projects include the Gothaer Lebensversicherung, Braunschweig (1985); Haus der Geschichte (1992); Centre for Art, Media and Design, Braunschweig (1993), and a series of residential schemes in Wolfenbüttel (1995).

Moshe Safdie and Partners, Inc., Architect and Planners
100 Properzi Way, Somerville, Massachusetts 02143, USA
Moshe Safdie was born in Haifa, Israel in 1938 and graduated from McGill University in Montreal, Canada. He worked his apprenticeship with Louis Kahn in Philadelphia but returned to Montreal in 1967 to design the master plan for the World Exposition. Moshe Safdie and Associates was founded in 1964 and early work concentrated on

issues of housing and the planning of new towns, including the pioneering residential complex Habitat '67 and the Coldspring area of Baltimore, Maryland. He established an office in Jerusalem in 1970, and since then he has undertaken various schemes in Israel. Recent work includes such major cultural and civic projects as the Ben Gurion Airport, Tel Aviv; the Vancouver Library Square, British Columbia; the Skirball Cultural Center, Los Angeles; the Musée des Beaux Arts, Montreal; the National Gallery of Canada and the Ottawa City Hall, Ottawa; the Ballet Opera House, Toronto, and the New City of Modi'in, Israel. Moshe Safdie's work has received acclaim internationally and he is the author of several books on architecture. In 1978, having taught at McGill, Yale and the Ben Gurion universities, Safdie became director of the Urban Design Program at the Graduate School of Design, Harvard University, and from 1984 to 1989 he was Ian Woodner Professor of Architecture and Urban Design.

Architekten Schweger & Partner
Postrasse 12, 20354 Hamburg, Germany

The architectural firm of Schweger & Partners was founded in 1964 (becoming Architekten Schweger and Partner in 1987) when Peter Schweger formed a project team for the purpose of designing the technical college in Hamburg-Bergedorf. Born in 1935 in Mediasch, Rumania, Schweger attended the Technical University in Budapest and later the University of Zürich. He founded his own practice in Zurich in 1959 and was also involved in research for A. Körber-Stiftung in Hamburg. Today he is Professor at the Technical University of Hanover's Institute for Design and Architecture and his firm offers services that include urban planning, building design and project management. Recent prize winning schemes include the Reichstag and the Headquarters of the Deutsche Bauindustrie in Berlin, the Promotion Park in Bremen and the Centre for Arts, Alte Kraftpost, Pirmasens.

Short Ford & Associates
Prescott Studios, 15 Prescott Place, London SW4 6BS
Short Ford & Associates was founded in 1992 by Brian Ford and Charles Short. Charles Short was born in 1955 and educated at Cambridge University and had a year-long fellowship at the Harvard University Graduate School of Design. He returned to Cambridge to take a Diploma in Architecture, which he received with first class honours. Before founding his own practice Charles Short worked for Basil Spence and Colin St John Wilson & Partners, was a partner at Edward Cullinan Architects and was a founding partner of Peake Short & Partners. He has held various teaching posts and is at present visiting professor at De Montfort University and external examiner at Manchester University School of Architecture. Brian Ford (b. 1949) trained at Canterbury College of Art School of Architecture and the Royal College of Art, Department of Design Research from which he received an MA for his work in passive solar heating. He was employed by Robert Mathew Johnson Marshall; Ian Hogan and Partners, Max Fordham & Partners and was an associate in Peake Short & Partners with Charles Short. He, too, is well known on the lecturing circuit and is currently visiting professor at De Montfort and tutor and lecturer at the Architectural Association Graduate School Environment and Energy Studies Programme. Short Ford & Associates' recent projects number various faculties for De Montfort University, including the Queens

Building which received the Green Building of the Year Award in 1995; an advanced housing study, Beaumont Leys for Leicester City Council; Simonds Farsons Cisk Ltd Brewery Process Building, Malta; the Winery Building, Malta; Palazzo Parisio, Malta, and the Torrent Pharmaceutical Research and Development Centre, Ahmedabad, India. Currently the practice is undertaking work for Manchester University that includes an analysis for the redevelopment of the campus.

Sottsass Associati
via Melone no. 2, 20121 Milan, Italy
Sottsass Associati was founded in 1980 by Ettore Sottsass, together with Aldo Cibic, Marco Marabelli, Matteo Thun and Marco Zanini. Mike Ryan and Johanna Grawunder have been junior partners since 1989 and James Irvine and Mario Milizia since 1992 and 1993, respectively. Sottsass Associati initially concentrated on furniture and industrial and interior design, but it has since expanded and is now active in the fields of graphic design, corporate identity and architecture. Ettore Sottsass was born in Innsbruck in 1917 and graduated from the University of Turin in 1939. Well known for the 'radical architecture' of the Memphis Group, his concern with experimentation and research has also distinguished Sottsass Associati's work over the years. Marco Zanini was born in Trento in 1954 and graduated in architecture from Florence University. After a period of travel and work experience in the United States he started work in Milan, first as assistant to Ettore Sottsass and then as one of the founders of Sottsass Associati. Since this time he has designed products for Knoll and Esprit and has worked on various domestic and industrial interior design projects. In 1988 he held a one-man show of drawings and watercolours at the Galleria Antonia Jannone in Milan. Sottsass Associati's clients include Knoll, Cassina, Zanotta, Philips, Olivetti, Apple Computers, Zumtobel and NTT. Several architectural projects have also been completed including the Wolf House in Colorado; the Oshima Residence in Tokyo; Cei House in Empoli, and renovations of buildings in Milan, Austria, Germany and France. The practice has been successful in numerous architectural competitions such as 'The Peak' in Hong Kong; the Accademia Bridge in Venice; the MK3 building in Düsseldorf; Twin Dome City in Fukuoka, and the interior design of the Flower Dome Stadium in Osaka.

Philippe Starck
27 rue Pierre Poli, 92130 Issy-les-Moulineaux, France
Philippe Starck was born in Paris in 1949. He attended the Ecole Camondo to train as an interior designer but did not complete the course. He went on to work as a fashion designer for the Pierre Cardin furniture collection. In the early 1970s he formed his own company which made inflatable objects. In the 1980s he was designing avant-garde nightclub interiors and won recognition for his work on Les Bains and La Main Jaune which was inspired by the science fiction of Philip K. Dick. After a period of activity in New York, he returned to France where he has since built up an international reputation and today he runs his own intentionally small design company, Starck Ubik. He has been responsible for major interior design schemes, including François Mitterrand's apartment at the Elysée Palace, the Café Costes, and the acclaimed Royalton and Paramount hotels in New York. He has also created domestic and public multipurpose buildings such as the headquarters

of Asahi Beer in Tokyo. As a product designer he works for companies throughout the world, collaborating with Alessi, Baleri, Baum, Disform, Driade, Flos, Kartell, Rapsel, Up & Up, Vitra and Vuitton. His many awards include the Grand Prix National de la Création Industrielle. His work can be seen in the collections of major design museums worldwide. Recent projects include the Delano Hotel in Miami and a new flat-pack, build-it-yourself wooden house, available through the Trois Suisses mail-order catalogue. Starck has recently become artistic director of Thomson Consumer Electronics.

TAK Associated Architects Inc.
3F Nishiki-cho, 1 Chome Bldg, 1-7 Kanda, Nishiki-cho, Chiyoda-ku, Tokyo 101, Japan
Takahiko Yanagisawa was born in 1935 in Nagano Prefecture, Japan, and graduated from Tokyo University of Fine Arts, Department of Architecture in 1958, joining in the same year Takenaka Corporation Design Department. He moved to the Takenaka USA offices in San Francisco in 1968 and later worked for Conklin and Rosant in New York. On his return to Japan he was made Head of the Design Department at Takenaka Corporation and by 1985 he was Principal Architect. Completed projects at this time include the MOA Museum at Atsumi, the Ote Center Building and the Minobusan Kuonji Temple, all of which received BCS awards. In 1986 he founded TAK Associated Architects which specializes in the design of cultural facilities. Currently under construction are the New National Theatre, New Tokyo Metropolitan Museum of Art, the Tokyo Opera City and Utsubo Kubota Memorial Museum. The Mitaka Center for the Arts, Tomioka City Museum-Ichiro Fukuzawa Memorial Museum and other projects are at the design stage. Yanagisawa is the President of the Kanto-Koshinetsu chapter of the Japan Institute of Architects and belongs to the Architectural Institute of Japan. He is a frequent ajudicator of design competitions and lectures at the Ministry of Construction, Construction College in the Architectural Design Department.

Zimmer Gunsul Frasca Partnership
1191 Second Avenue, Suite 800, Seattle, Washington 98101, USA
Zimmer Gunsul Frasca Partnership is a Portland, Oregon-based architecture, planning and interior design firm with additional offices in Seattle, Washington and Los Angeles. Since its foundation almost 30 years ago, the practice has worked on nationally recognized projects representing a broad range of planning efforts and building types for clients in industry, business, research, health care, recreation and the public sector. Major schemes include the Vollum Institute for Advanced Biomedical Research, the Justice Center, the California Museum of Science and Industry, the Fred Hutchinson Cancer Research Center, the Portland International Airport Expansion, and the Banfield Light Rail Transitway. Current projects include large-scale public buildings, such as the Oregon Convention Center and Museum of Science & Industry, as well as the Washington County Criminal Justice Complex and the Doernbecher Children's Hospital. Zimmer Gunsul Frasca has received over 150 national, regional and local design awards and was the recipient of the American Institute of Architects' highest accolade, the Firm Award, in 1991.

Credits

Denver Central Public Library, Denver, Colorado, USA
Design architect: Michael Graves Architect. Project
team: Karen Nichols (senior associate); Tom Rowe
(senior associate/project architect); John Diebbol
(senior associate); Mary Yun, Meryl Blinder,
Keoni Fleming, Andy McNabb, Saverio Manago,
Stephanie Magdziak, Jane Maybank, Carole
Nicholson, Brian Pinkett, Karin Rhae, Pamela
Carter Rowe, Kirsten Thoft, Andrea Wang. Architect
of record: Klipp Colussy Jenks DuBois Architects
P.C. Project team: Brian Klipp (directing principal);
Cornelius (Kin) DuBois (principal in charge/project
architect); Otis Odell (associate project architect);
Peter Incitti, Garey Dickenson (project manager);
Laureen Ferris, Juana Gomez, Brett Linscott, Wayne
Pierce, Tom Siebert, Diane Travis. Interior design:
Engel/Kieding Design Associates, Inc. Client: City
and County of Denver Department of Public Works.
Construction manager: Hyman/Etkin Construction.
Structural and civil engineer: S. A. Miro, Inc.
Mechanical engineer: The Ballard Group.
Associate mechanical engineer: John L. Altieri.
Electrical engineer: Gambrell Engineering.
Lighting consultant: Clanton Engineering, Inc.
Graphic Design: Weber Design Partners.
Kitchen design: Thomas Ricca Associates.
Soils engineering: Aguirre Engineering.
Surveyors: Kelly Surveying Associates, Inc.
Lighting: NeoSource (custom); Columbia,
Edison-Price, Kurt Versen, LiteControl, GE Lamps
(standard). Custom furniture: Blanton & Moore,
Craftwood, Transline. Landscape design: Badgett
and Coover-Clark Architects. Acoustics: David L.
Adams and Associates. Elevator consultant:
Lerch, Bates & Associates.

**Hôtel du Département, Bouches-du-Rhône,
Marseilles, France**
Architect: Alsop & Störmer. Project team: William
Alsop, Francis Graves and Stephen Pimbley
(directors), Jonathan Adams, James Allen, Sonia
Andrade, Peter Angrave, Hilary Bagley, Russell
Bagley, Stephan Biller, Florence Bobin, Pierre-
André Bonnet, James Brearley, Joanne Burnham,
Xavier d'Alençon, Jason Dickinson, Sybil Diot-
Lamige, Robert Evans, Roger Farrow, Colin Foster,
Cristina García Borja Goyarrola, Ivan Green, Astrid
Huwald, Stephen James, John Kember, David Knill-
Samuel, Nigel Lusty, Harvey Male, Paul Mathews,
Roger Minost, Philippe Moinard, Suzy Murdock,
Simon North, Sophie Palmer, Victoria Perry,
Emmanuelle Poggi, Sanya Polescuk, Geoffrey
Powis, John Prevc, Matthew Priestman, Stuart
Rand-Bell, Christian Richard, Anne Schmilinsky,
Diana Stiles, Peter Strudwick, Gary Taylor, George
Tsoutsos, Nicki Van Oosten, Laurence York Moore,
Petra Wesseler. Interior design: Alsop & Störmer,
Ecart. Project team: Andrée Putman, Gérard
Borgniet, Gilles Leborgne, Elliot Barnes, Marion
Guidoni, Roure Bové, Charles Bové, Thierry
Ciccione, Martin Roure. Client: Conseil Général

des Bouches-du-Rhône. Consulting engineers:
Ove Arup & Partners International. Engineering
sub-consultant: O.T.H. Méditerranée. Quantity
surveyor: Hanscomb Ltd. Concrete structure:
CBC/MCB. Cladding: Cabrol. Mechanical
contractor: Albouy/AIC/TNEE. Electrical contractor:
Cegelec. Lifts: Otis Elevator Co. Woodwork: Delta
Menuiseries. Decoration: Bareau. Flooring and
walls: Gambini. Paintwork and mirrors: Cantareil.
Signage: Lettre & Lumière. False ceiling: Wanner
Isofi. Lighting: Concord.

Suntory Museum, Osaka, Japan
Architecture and interior design: Tadao Ando.
Client: Suntory Co. Ltd. Subcontractors: Takenaka
Corporation; Obayashi Corporation. Consultants:
Makoto Karasawa Acoustic Design Associates
(acoustic engineers).

Kunstmuseum, Wolfsburg, Germany
Architecture and interior design: Architekten
Schweger & Partner. Project team: Prof. Peter P.
Schweger, Franz Wöhler, Hartmut Reifenstein,
Bernhard Kohl, Wolfgang Schneider, Philipp Kahl
(project director); Alexander Mayr, Prof. Wilhelm
Meyer, Rolf Achilles, Ulrike Andreas, Ingeborg
Biedermann, Michael Giebeler, Christine Hansen,
Hannelore Hedde, Dieter Heinrichs, Erika
Kamprad, Dr Rudolf Krebs, Frank Morgenstern,
Peter Oschkinat, Bettina Peschka, Matthias
Schmitz, Thomas Ventker, Arne Wellmann. Client:
Volkswagen Art Foundation. Advisor: Architektur-
Kunst-Museum, Dr Carl Haenlein. Project
management: VW Wohnungs GmbH. Project
control and building supervision: Ing. Gesellschaft
für Projektmanagement. Structural design: Bendorf
& partner Ing.-Gesell m.b.H. Landscape design:
Prof. Gustav Lange. Lighting design: Christian
Bartenbach GmbH; Adrans. Colour consultant: H &
H Janiesch. Advisor on the façade: Michael Lange
Beratender Ingenieur VBI. Heating, ventilation and
sanitation: Passau Ingenieure GmbH. Electrical
planning: Ing.-Büro Paulus GmbH. Specialist
advisors: Brandschutz (fire prevention); Dipl.-Ing
Klaus Kempe.

Bibliothèque Nationale de France, Paris, France
Architect: Perrault Architecte. Project team:
Dominique Perrault, Daniel Allaire, Gabriel
Choukroun, Guy Morisseau, Yves Conan,
Constantin Coursaris, Maxime Gasperini,
Pablo Gil, Luciano d'Alesio, Claude Alovisetti,
Emmanuelle Andréani, Judith Barber, Philippe
Berbett, Jérôme Besse, Jean-Luc Bichet, Charles
Caglini, Jean-François Candeille, Hristo Chinkov,
Alexander Dierendonck, Céline Dos Santos, Marie-
France Dussaussois, Laura Ferreira-Sheehan,
Corrina Fuhrer, Catriona Gatheral, Dominique
Guibert, Serge Guyon, Dominique Jauvin, Anne
Kaplan, Christian Laborde, Maryvonne Lanco,
Corinne Lafon, Olivier Lidon, Zhi-Jian Lin, Pierre

Loritte, Patrice Marchand, Thierry Meunier, Brigitte
Michaud, Franck Michigan, Rosa Precigout, René
Puybonnieux, Martine Rigaud, Hildegard Ruske,
Jérôme Thibault, Catherine Todaro, Louis van Ost,
Inge Waes. Client: Bibliothèque Nationale de
France. Project management: Socotec. Project
control: ODM. Lighting and acoustics: Jean-Paul
Lamoureux. Tropical forest technical centre: CTFT.
Structural engineer: Sechaud & Bossuyt. Electrical
engineer: GTME. Climatic engineering: Danto
Rogeat. Lifts: Otis. Woodwork and metalwork:
Construction bois Baumert; Jacqmin. Landscape
design: Sauveterre-Horizon. Tree planting: SNMV.
Scenography: Didier Onde/Sophie Thomas.
Interiors: Dennery (350-seat conference area,
North/South reading rooms); Bel SA (lecture,
research and public East/West reading rooms);
Ateliers Normand (200-seat conference room); SPR
Entreprise (reception and personnel restaurant);
Bredy SA (public reading rooms). Suppliers: Sibt
(wood); Mazda (external lighting); Sammode
(internal lighting).

**City Theatre De Harmonie, Leeuwarden,
The Netherlands**
Architect and interior design: de Architekten Cie.
Project team: F. J. van Dongen with R. Dijkstra,
R. Hilz, E. Winkler (design); F. Segaar (project
manager). Client: The Leeuwarden City Council.
Contractors: GTI (electricity); Wolter & Dros
(heating); Lödige Holland BV (lifts); Flashlight
(lighting); Piëe Muziek (music); Interstage Henk
Wiegers BV (upholstery and curtains). Consultants:
Technical Management (electrical and heating);
Adviesbureau Peutz (acoustics), Hans Wolff &
Partners (lighting and theatre technology).
Construction: D3BN.

**Los Angeles Convention Center Expansion,
Los Angeles, California, USA**
Design architect: Pei Cobb Freed & Partners.
Project team: James Ingo Freed (partner-in-charge,
design); Werner Wandelmaier (partner-in-charge,
management); Michael D. Flynn (partner-in-charge,
technology); Thomas Baker (associate partner,
design); Robert Milburn (senior associate,
management); Philip Toussaint, Roy Barris, Richard
Dunham, Reginald Hough, Nancy Sun, Gianni
Neri, Abby Suckle, Mark Diefenbacher, T. Fang,
Christa Giesecke, Robert Hartwig, Jennifer Nadler,
Taka Okuda, Christopher Olsen, Michael Rose,
Charles Roser, Jeffrey Rosenberg, Randy Seitsinger,
Debra Taylor. Associate architects: Edward C.
Barker & Associates. Executive architect: Gruen
Associates. Client: Los Angeles Convention &
Exhibition Center Authority. Project management:
Leo A. Daly/Robert E. McKee, Inc. General
contractors: Hyman/Mortenson Co.; George
Hyman Construction Co.; M.A. Mortenson Co.
Subcontractors: Harmon Contract; Bruce Wall
Systems Corporation (curtain wall). Metal wall

panels: H. H. Robertson, Inc. Structural steelwork: American Bridge. Ornamental metals: Columbia Fabricating. Mechanical contractor: JWP Mechanical Services. Electrical contractor: Kirkwood Dynalectric. Roofing: Letner Roofing. Skylight: O'Keeffe's Inc. Acoustical ceilings: Performance Contracting. Terrazzo: Roman Mosaic. Consultants: John A. Martin & Associates; Martin & Huang Intl. (structural); Syska & Hennessy, William J. Yang & Associates, Carlos Rodriguez & Associates, (M/E/P/ fire protection); Fisher Marantz Renfro & Stone (architectural lighting); David E. Gaines (roofing); Sasaki Inc. (landscape design:); Follis Design, C. J. Beck Marketing & Communications (graphics). Artists: Alexis Smith (terrazzo pavement in South and West lobby); Matt Mullican (6 granite panels in Meeting Room bridge); Pat Ward Williams (sculpture in Gilbert Lindsay Plaza).

European Court of Human Rights, Strasbourg, France.

Architects: Richard Rogers Partnership. Project team: Richard Rogers, Laurie Abbott, Peter Angrave, Eike Becker, Mike Davies, Elliot Boyd, Karin Egge, Marco Goldschmied, Pascale Gibon, Lennart Grut, Ivan Harbour, Amarjit Kalsi, Sze-King Kan, Carmel Lewin, Avtar Lotay, John Lowe, Louise Palomba, Kim Quazi, Pascale Rousseau, Yuli Toh, Sarah Tweedie, Andrew Tyley, Yoshiyuki Uchiyama, John Young. Client: Court of Human Rights Strasbourg, Conseil de l'Europe, Ville de Strasbourg. Site architects: Atelier d'Architecture Claude Bucher. Structural and services engineers: Ove Arup and Partners; Ominium Technique Europeén. Quantity surveyors: Thorne Wheatley Associates. Landscape consultants: David Jarvis Associates; Dan Kiley. Lighting consultants: Lighting Design Partnership. Lighting: Zumtobel Staff. Acoustic consultants: Sound Research Laboratories; Commins Ingemansson.

Tokyo Edo Museum, Tokyo, Japan

Architecture and interior design: Kiyonori Kikutake. Advisors: Seiichi Hoshino, Takeshi Ito, Motoko Ishii, Kei Tenporin, Syuhei Aida, Ichiro Kato, Yukio Hasegawa, Takemochi Ishii, Akira Ishihuku, Takashi Tamura, Tomio Kimura, Minami Tada, Ikko Tanaka, Kiyoshi Awazu, Makoto Suzuki, Shigeo Fukuda. Client: Tokyo Metropolitan Government. Main Contractor: JV Construction for the Tokyo Edo Museum. Contractors: Kajima, Tekken, Zenidaka, Muramoto, Matsumura, Toha, Skata, Inoue, Okamoto. Structural design: Gengo Matsui; O. R. S. Mechanical design: P. T. Morimura and Associates' Pte. Ltd. Exhibition plan: Total Media Development Institute Co. Ltd.

Museum of the History of the Federal Republic of Germany, Bonn, Germany

Architect and interior design: Architekten BDA, Hartmut & Ingeborg Rüdiger. Project team: Claus Bartholomäus, Kerstin Sölter, Barbara Heckel (interior design); Jan Christoph Friedrich, Nina Stullich. Client: Bundesrepublik Deutschland. Contractors: Walter Bau, Bereichsbüro (construction); DIG Deutsche Innenbau (interior construction/plastering); Rausch & Schild (façade); Eberspächer (steel construction and roof glazing); Sassenscheidt (model and glass façade); Trimborn & Söhne (metal construction and lobby roof); Bliersbach (heating); Lodewick (sanitation); Krantz (air-conditioning); Thiele (insulation); Rheinelektra (electrical construction); Kerel Keramik und Elementbau (tiling); Hapke-Parkett (wooden flooring); Grenzhäuser (flooring); Marmor Kiefer (stone flooring); Arge Toffolo-Ranft (terrazzo flooring); BT Jäger & Schorp (paintwork); Idea, Lüchtefeld, Wiener (interior decoration); META-bau

(doors). Collaborating engineers: Ing. Büro Harms & Partner (building control); Ing. Büro Dr. Hage (structural engineer); Ing. Büro HTW (mechanical engineer); Ing. Büro Alhäuser & König (electrical engineer); Ing. Büro Bartenbach (lighting); Büro Wehberg-Eppinger-Schmidtke (landscape architect).

East Wing of the Cité de la Musique, Parc de la Villette, Paris, France

Architect and interior design: Atelier Christian de Portzamparc. Project team: Christian de Portzamparc, François Barberot, Bertrand Beau, Olivier Blaise, Benoit Juret, Florent Leonhardt, Etienne Pierres. Client: Etablissement Public du Parc de la Villette. Structural and mechanical engineer: SODETEG. Scenographer: Dubreuil and Le Comte. Lighting engineer: Gerald Karlikoff. Lighting: Zumtobel Staff. Concrete structure: Bateg Delta. Metallic structure: Baudin Chateauneuf. Roofing and wall covering: Cegelec. Waterproofing: Etandex. Concrete finish: Robert. Acoustic corrections: Millet et Cie. Paintwork: S.P.R. CVCD: T.N.E.E. Tunzini. Plumbing and sanitation: Dolbeau. Electricity: Enterprise Industrielle (high voltage); G.T.M.E. (low voltage). Stage lighting: Scénilux. Lifts: Otis. Fixed seating: E.I.S. False ceilings: Steel. Ceilings: Compagnie Générale du Staff. Stone cladding: Pradeau Morin. Metal fittings/glass casing/façades: Sotrame. Lock fittings: Alufer. Carpentry: Giffard. Wooden floors: Europarquet. Plastic flooring, carpets: France Sols. Wall and floor tiling: SN S2R. Plasterwork: Stabli. Armchairs: Christian de Portzamparc, manufactured by E.I.S.

Tokyo Tatsumi International Swimming Centre, Tokyo, Japan

Architect and interior design: Mitsuru Man Senda & Environment Design Institute. Client: Tokyo Metropolitan Government. Structure: Kozo Keikaku Engineering Inc. Facility design: Morimura Sekkei Inc. Contractors: Shimizu, Dainihon, Katsumura, Maruishi (architecture); Taiseioncyo, Nakasetsu, Nanayo, Nakano, Shinrei (ventilation); Kawakita, Misawa, Sato, Masuda (electrical); Arihara Jitugyo (water treatment). Large-screen picture system: Panasonic Inc. Electric indicator system: Hattori Seiko. Roofing/stainless-steel/welding process: Shinwa Industry. Tiles: INAX Co., (water-permeable ceramic); Karumu Inc. (Aluminium-Sinter Acoustic). Truss: Tomoe Co. Landscape design: Atelier Soichiro Nakatani. Furniture design: SIP. Lighting design: Kaoru Mende of Lighting Planning Associates Inc. Sculpture: Aijiro Wakita from Studio A.
Signage: Shin Matsunaga of Shin Matsunaga Design Office.

Aldham Robarts Learning Resource Centre, Liverpool, UK

Architect, interior and landscape design: Austin-Smith:Lord. Project team: Glenn Ombler, Ernie Dickinson, Alec Colbeck. Client: Liverpool John Moores University. Main contractor: Norwest Holst Construction, Ltd. Quantity surveyor: Walfords, Liverpool. M & E: Ove Arup and Partners. Subcontractors: CWS Engineering (M & E installation); Arcon Aluminium (windows/planar glazing); Luxcrete Limited (glass blocks); MPC International Ltd (aluminium seam roofing); Perkins Plasterers (plasterwork); MG Ceilings Ltd (suspended ceiling); B & J Painters Ltd (paintwork); JAD Flooring Ltd (soft flooring); Brenden Myles (glazing); Teide (AG) Ltd (metal fabrications); Balustrading Ltd (balustrades); T. D. Johnson (landscaping); Royden Engineering Ltd (structural steelwork); Thorsman Ltd (raised flooring); Nord-Plan Ltd (mobile shelving).

Musée des Graffiti – Entrée de la Grotte de Niaux, Ariège, France

Architect: Massimiliano Fuksas. Assistant architects: J. L. Fulcrand, G. Jourdan, J. Capia, Architectes. Client: Conseil Général de l'Ariège. Main contractor/metal structure: Saint Eloi. Structural engineers: Ove Arup and Partners. Landscape Design: F. Zagari; A. Marquerit. Stonework, reinforced conrete, plumbing, electricity and foundations: Pereira; Tensolesco.

Bellevue Regional Library, Bellevue, Washington, USA

Architect and interior design: Zimmer Gunsul Frasca Partnership. Project team: Dan Huberty, Robert Frasca, Eve Ruffcorn, Brooks Gunsul, Stan Zintel, William LaPatra, Dale Alberda, Chris Chin, Sharron Duggan, Kevin Gernhart, Kim Jennings, Terri Johnson, Bertha Martinez, Robert Zimmerman, Carl Freeze. Client: King County Library System. Main contractor: Gail Landau Young. Structural/civil engineers: KPFF Consultant Engineers. Mechanical engineers: Notkin engineers. Electrical engineers: Sparling & Associates. Landscape architects: Jones & Jones. Stainless steel roof: Follansbee Steel. Wood-slat ceilings: Howard Manufacturing. Sandstone: Southland Stone USA. Granite: Cold Spring Granite Co. Brick veneer: Mutual materials. Continuous clerestory glass: Herzog Aluminium. Architectural casework: O. B. Williams. Carpet: Collins & Aikman; Tiffany Carpet Tiles. Wood decking: Potlach. Furniture: Fixtures Furniture (staff lounge); Gunlocke (lounge seating and conference chairs); Kinetics (coffee and end tables); Krueger (stacking chairs); Neo Bau (reading tables); Nevers (lectern); Smith & Hawkins (vestibule benches); Thonet (reading chairs and benches) Herman Miller (systems furniture); MJ Industries (shelving).

ESIEE Engineering College, Amiens, France

Architect: J. Dubus et J-P. Lott S. A. R. L. Project architect: Michel Rémon. Client: City of Amiens. Main contractor: Quille (Bouygues). Engineer: Sechaud & Bossuyt. BET: Cordier. Acoustics: Yaying Xu. Furniture: Kristian Gavoille. Lighting: Zumtobel Staff.

Nieuw Land Poldermuseum, Lelystad, The Netherlands

Architect: Benthem Crouwel Architekten BV bna. Project team: Jan Benthem, Mels Crouwel, Cees van Giessen, Ton Liemburg. Client: Stichting Initiatiefgroep Nieuw Land. Exhibition design: Donald Janssen Ontwerpers BV. Structural Engineer: Ingenieursgroep Van Rossum. Electrical services: Koldijk. Mechanical services: Technisch Installatiebureau Verkaart. Main contractors: Bouwcombinatie Nieuw Land v.o.f.; Heijmans Bouw B.V; Cooperatief Bouwbedrijf. Lighting: Philips Nederland BV. Window walls: Timmer-fabriek Houkesloot. Interior carpentry: Bruns BV. Steel construction/stairs: Metaalbedrijf Pompstra.

Constable Terrace, Low Energy Student Residences, University of East Anglia, Norwich, UK

Architect: Rick Mather Architects. Project team: Rick Mather, Douglas McIntosh (project architects); Glyn Emrys, Roberto Pascual Spada, Mark Annen, Chris Bagot, Charles Barclay, John Cockings, Susan Ducermic, Michael Delaney, James Slade, Thomas Verebes, Voon Wong. Client: University of East Anglia. Main contractor: R. G. Carter. Quantity surveyor: Stockings & Clarke. Structural engineer: Dewhurst MacFarlane Partnership. Services consultant: Fulcram Engineering. Electrical subcontractor: Drake & Scull. Mechanical subcontractor: Haden Young. Roof: High Profile Systems. Ironmongery: Elementer Industrial Design Ltd. Lift: Kone Lift Ltd. Metal windows and doors: Velfac UK Ltd; Vista Brunswick; Aluminart Ltd. Door and carpentry: Drayton Joinery. Steelwork: St Cowells; May Gurney & Co. Ltd. Insulation: Rockwool. Flooring subcontractor: Lees Flooring. Signage: Lundsigns. Furniture: Charter Furniture; Marland Contract Furniture.

Isala College, Silvolde, The Netherlands
Architect: Mecanoo Architekten b.v. Project team: Francine Houben, Chris de Weijer, Erick van Egeraat (project architects); Sjaak Janssen (project manager); Maartje Lammers, Gert Wiebing, Birgit de Bruin, Enrico Cerasi, Annemiek Diekman, Paddy Tomesen, William Richards, Bernard Venster, Toon de Wilde. Client: Katholieke Stichting Voor Voortgezet Onderwijs, Regio Oude Ijssel. Main contractor: Klaassen Bouwmaatschappij in Dinxperlo. Construction: ABT adviesbureau voor bouwtechniek. Consultant for installations: Ketel Raadgevend Ingenieurs.

State and University Library, Göttingen, Germany
Architect: Prof. Gerber & Partner. Project team: Eckhard Gerber, Jürgen Friedemann, Gerhard Tjarks (partners); Volker Hachenberger (project management); Jörg Angst, Inke Borgwardt, Volker Brockmeier, Karin Bröer, Georg Brücher, Klaus Brückerhoff, Egbert Driessen, Remus Grolle-Hüging, Gregor Hickmann, Siegbert Hennecke, Klaus Hesemann, Andreas Kuhn, Marita Langen, Achim Linden, Thomas Riffelmann, Franz Schlüter, Martin Schmirander, Udo Sundermann, Magdalena Ströbel, Carolin Tiedtke, Sylvia Werner. Client: Land Niedersachsen. Project supervision: Harms & Partner. Wing-unit planning: Neuhaus-Schwermann. Structural engineer: Ing.-Ges Neuhaus-Schwermann, Ing.-Büro Duwe. Structural survey: Ing.-Büro Graner, Klaus Menrath. Site analysis: Erdbaulabor, Dr Wolfgang Witten. Interior artwork: Prof. Friedrich Meckseper. Exterior artwork: Prof. Erich Reusch. Steelwork: Dyckerhoff und Widmann (phase 1); Arnold Georg (phase 2). Ironmongery: Kentzler. Steel-glass façade: MBS-Fassadenbau. Wood and aluminium windows: Lanco. Glazed roof lights: Eberspächer. Plasterwork: F. Steinrücken. Tiling: Ernst. Flooring: Riwoplan; Schaaf. Stone flooring: Vetter. Concrete floors: Kenngott. Paintwork: Wolter & Sohn. Suspended ceiling: Hoppmann und Ernst. Elevated floors: Goldbach. Partition walls: Küster-Bau; Lindner; abopart. Landscape architect: Prof. Wehberg, Lange. Eppinger, Schmidtke. Heating: Arge Büürma/Ruhstrat. Air-conditioning: Sulzer. Carpentry: Schaper. Catalogue furniture: Kaiser. Reception rotunda: Berndt. General lighting: Ruhstrat; Rodust. Table lights: Guzzini.

Queens Building, School of Engineering, De Montfort University, Leicester, UK
Architecture and interior design: Short Ford & Associates. Project team: Charles Alan Short, Brian Ford, Anne Goldrick, Catherine Hoggard; with Peter Sharratt, Garry Stewart, Mike Betts, Bruce Graham, Mark Hewitt, Patrick De Roe, Joseph Ki, Oliver Chapman, Lisa Harmey. Client: De Montfort University, School of Engineering & Manufacture, Leicester. Structural engineer: YRM Anthony Hunt Associates. Quantity surveyor: Dearle & Henderson. M & E Engineer: Max Fordham Associates. Landscape: Livingston McIntosh Associates. Coordinator: Dr Frank Mills, BDP Manchester. Main contractor: Laing Midlands. Steel fabrication: Potter Johnson.

Mechanical subcontractor: Howe Engineering Services. Electrical subcontractor: Hall & Stinson. Windows: Mellowes Archital. Ironmongery: Dryad Architectural Hardware.

Edythe and Eli Broad Center, Pitzer College, Claremont, California, USA
Architecture and interior design: Gwathmey Siegel & Associates Architects. Project team: Charles Gwathmey; Robert Siegel (partners); Gerald Gendreau (associate in charge); Greg Karn (project architect); Tom Lewis. Client: Pitzer College. Main contractor: Robert E. Bayley Construction Inc. Project management: Stegeman and Kaster Inc. Structural engineer: John A. Martin Associates. Mechanical and electrical engineers: Levine/Seegel Associates. Steelwork: Lee & Daniel. HVAC: Control Air Conditioning. Electrical: Shasta Electric. Plumbing: George Kaufman Plumbing. Landscape architects: Claremont Environmental Design Group, Inc. Civil engineers: Associated Engineers. Acoustical consultants: Purcell & Noppe & Associates. Lighting consultants: Hillmann DiBernardo & Associates, Inc. AV consultants: Brook & Chavez & Associates. Furniture dealer: The Sheridan Group. Cabinets: Wavell Huber Wood Products.

Groninger City Museum, Groningen, The Netherlands
Architectural and interior design project: Atelier Mendini. Project team: Alessandro Mendini, Francesco Mendini, Gerda Vossaert, Alexandre Mocika. Guest architects: Philippe Starck (aluminium drum); Coop Himmelblau (East Pavilion), Michele de Lucchi (archaeology exhibition design). Client: Foundation for the Construction of the new Groninger Museum. Executive development and project management: Team 4. Economy and construction management: Twijnstra Gudde NV. Structural project: Ingenieursbureau Wassenaar BV. Technical systems: Van Heugten BV. Art on drawbridge: Wim Delvoye. Carpets: Vorwerk.

Stadthaus, Ulm, Germany
Architect: Richard Meier & Partners. Project team: Richard Meier (design); Bernhard Lutz (project architect); Mary Buttrick, Martin Falke, Beat Küttel, Siobhan McInerney, Gunter R. Standke, Wolfram Wöhr. Client: City of Ulm – Building Department. Project management: City of Ulm Hochbauamt. Construction management: Becker & Partner. Heating and ventilation: Ingenieurgemeinschaft Korner, Ott & Spiess. Electrical equipment: Korner Ingenieurgesellschaft (KIG). Lighting: Ingenieurbüro Zitnik. Lifts: Stadt Ulm Hochbauamt. Quantity surveyor: Stadtmessungsamt, Ulm. Building shell: Keller Bau GmbH & Co. Metalwork: Arge Gartner/Gauss. Steel staircases: Stahl-& Metallbau, Bacher GmbH. Interior balustrades: Georg Flammer GmbH & Co., KG. Interior plastering: Wilhelm Frank GmbH & Co., KG. Floor finishing: Häcker KG. Stonework: Marmor-Industrie Keifer GmbH. Tiling: Theodor Wölpert GmbH & Co. Doors: Eberhard Lampert KG. Parquet flooring: Bembe-Parkett. Painting: Franz Dullenkopf, Malerbetriebe und Gerüstbau. Blinds: Verdunkelungen, Brichta GmbH. Counters: Matthäus Rees, Möbelwerkstätten. Furniture: Wilde & Spieth GmbH & Co. (hall tables and chairs); Behr Möbel GmbH (restaurant and ground floor tables and chairs).

Civic Arts Plaza, City of Thousand Oaks, California, USA
Design architect: Antoine Predock Architect. Project team: Antoine Predock (principal-in-charge); Geoffrey Beebe (associate-in-charge); Douglas Friend (project architect); Chris Calott, Haji Uesato, Paul

Gonzales, Deborah Waldrip, Sam Sterling, Chris Romero, David Mishler, Michael Wewerka, Joseph Andrade. Architect of record: Dworsky Associates Inc. Project team: Daniel Dworsky (principal-in-charge); Robert Rosenberg (project director); Robert Newsom (project director); Kenneth Stein (design coordinator); Kenneth Rossi (project architect); Watana Charoenrath (field architect); Paz Costelo, Ira Mann, Oscar Castelo (job captains); Janet Suen, James Noh, Celso Velarde, Virgilio Merina, Hue Tong, Fred Antonio. Client: City of Thousand Oaks. Construction manager: Lehrer McGovern Bovis. Landscape architect: EDAW Inc. Engineers: John A. Martin & Associates (structural); Nack Engineering (mechanical/ plumbing); Frederick Russell Brown & Associates (electrical); RBA Partners, Inc. (civil). Consultants: McKay Conant Brook, Inc. (acoustical); Robert M. Morris (audio/visual); Knudson & Benson Associates (theatre); Interior Architects Inc. (interior space planners); Lighting Design Alliance (lighting).

The Foyer of the New Israeli Opera House, Tel Aviv, Israel
Architecture and interior design: Ron Arad Associates. Project team: Ron Arad, Alison Brooks, Monique van den Hurk, Vincent Chang, Charles Walker, Oliver Salway, Sophie Bruere, Graham Goymour, Christophe Egret. Architect of Performing Arts Centre: Yacov Rechter. Client: Tel Aviv Performing Arts Centre. Main contractor: Ramir Construction. Main subcontractor: Israel Freyssinet Co. Ltd. Project manager: D & H Projects Development and Management Ltd. Site engineer: Moshe Zur, Tel Aviv Performing Arts Centre. Structural consultant: Michael Peri Consulting Engineers. Mechanical consultant: B. Schor & Co. Electrical consultant: Kaplan & Navot. Lighting consultant: Ingo Maurer GmbH. Acoustic consultant: John Wyckham Associates. Services consultant: Leon A. Sherman. Signage: Neville Brody Studio. Metalwork subcontractor: Marzorati Ronchetti Srl.

Museum of Contemporary Art, Tokyo, Japan
Architecture and interior design: TAK Associated Architects Inc. Project team: Basis Design; Kisaburo Kawakami. Client: City of Tokyo. Main contractors: Takenaka Corporation; Muramoto Construction; Asanuma-Gumi; Ohki Construction; Morimoto-Gumi; Sanpei Construction; Tomoe Corporation. Landscape and stonework manufacture: Masatoshi Izumi. Environmental art: Yamaguchi Katsuhiro, Kisaburo Kawakami (design); TAK Associated architects Inc. (technical).

Finnish Embassy, Washington, D. C., USA
Architecture and interior design: Heikkinen–Komonen Architects. Project team: Mikko Heikkinen, Markku Komonen, Sarlotta Narjus (project architect). Associate architect: Angelos Demetriou & Associates. Client: Ministry for Foreign Affairs. Main contractor: Chas H. Tompkins Co. Structural engineers: Matti Ollila. Engineer consultant: Smislova, Kehnemui & Associates. MPE Engineer: Joel Majurinen. Landscape architect: Lee and Liu Associates. Contractors: Sayegh International (masonry); TSI Exterior Wall Systems Inc. (metal/glass curtain walls and glass block); Armetco Systems Inc. (copper panels); Potomac Concrete Co. (concrete); South Eastern Floor Co. Inc. (cedar wood flooring); Beta Construction Co. (roofing); Criss Brothers Inc. (steel windows); United Skys Inc. (aluminium windows); TSI Exterior Wall System (glass and glazing); Brite Vue Glass System Inc. (custom-made bronze and glass doors); Swingin' Door Inc. (metal/wood/sliding doors and grills); Dominion

Applicators Inc. (ceilings and partitioning); Saunas by Erkki (cabinetwork and custom woodwork); Hudson-Shatz Mid Atlantic Painting (paintwork); Elam-Trading Oy (acoustical panelling); David Allen Company (tiles); Sayegh International (granite flooring); Southeastern Floor Co. Inc. (maple wood flooring). Furnishing: Kelkkalan Puusepäntehdas (custom-made office furniture); Herman Miller (Eames reception furniture); Matti Nyman (office chairs). Lighting contractor: Freestate Electric using Staff, Lightolier, Baflux, Edison Price, Artemide lights (interior); Bega, Prescolite (exterior) and custom-made lamps from Lightron. Mural artist: Juhana Blomstedt.

City Library, Münster, Germany
Architecture and interior design: Architekturbüro Bolles-Wilson & Partner. Project team: Julia B. Bolles-Wilson, Peter L. Wilson, Eberhard E. Kleffner (architects); Friedhelm Haas, Martin Schlüter, Andreas Kimmel (project assistants); Jim Yohe, Manfred Schoeps, Dietmar Berner, Anne Elshof, Glen Widemeier, Cornelia Nottelmann, Jens Ludolf, Laura Fogarasi, Mikkel Frost, Toshi Hisatomi, Dirk Paulsen, Stefanie Schmand, Karen Haupt, Katrin Lahusen, Jean Michel Crettaz, Thomas Müller (assistants). Client: Building Department of the City of Münster. Main contractors: Becker and Börge (basic concept); Zimmerei Sieveke (carpentry). Contractors: Fa Luft and Klima GmbH (air-conditioning); Wolfgang Korn Tief and Strassenbau GmbH (plasterwork); W. P. S. Metalbauges MbH & Co. (façade); Faro Treppenbau GmbH; Fa Wallmeyer (steelwork); Fa Niewerth (painting); Uhlenbrock & Treus GmbH (joinery); E. K. Z. GmbH (library fitings); Fa Kriger GmbH (furniture). Building supervision: Bolles-Wilson & Partner; Harms and Partner. Structural engineer: Ing.-Büro Thomas and Bökamp; Ing.-Büro Menke und Köhler. Service engineers: Ing-Büro Albers; House and Services Department of the City of Münster. Lighting consultants: Lichtdesign. Lighting: Zumtobel Staff. Acoustics: Büro Stemmer und Tonnermann. Tilework: Fa P.u.D Henrichs GmbH. Stone flooring: Fa ESS Eva-Susanne Schieckel. Landscaping: Fa Benning GmbH & Co.

Ehime Museum of Science, Ehime, Japan
Architect: Kisho Kurokawa Architect. Client: Ehime Prefecture. General contractor: Shimizu Corporation; Sumitomo; Ando and Noma. Engineers: Inuzuka Engineering Consultants (mechanical).

Hôtel du Département de la Meuse, Bar-le-Duc, France
Architecture and interior design: Dominique Perrault. Client: Conseil Général de la Meuse. Project control: Picardat; BET; SEEBI. Technical controller: Verutas Nancy. Electrical consultants: Planet et Watthom; Houve Nachel Energy. Plasterwork and partition walls: Lafarge. Soft flooring: Sommer. Floor tiling: Buchtal; A.B.K. False ceiling: Tolartois; Panel System. Sanitation: Jacob Delefon; Porcher. Plumbing: Grohe. Technical Board: Planet et Watthom. Electrical equipment: Legrand. Lighting fixtures: Mazda, Sammode, Belux. Paintwork: Tollens. Walls: Matfor; Aluxal. Woodwork and aluminium: Schüco. Cupboards: Merlin-Gerin. Wooden parquet and veneer: Ober. Glazing: Favilor; Viqualor. Heating and ventilation: CIAT.

Kemper Museum of Contemporary Art and Design, Kansas City, Missouri, USA
Architecture and interior design: Gunnar Birkerts and Associates Inc. Project team: Gunnar Birkerts (conceptual designer); Anthony Gholz (principal-in-

charge); Kevin Shultis (project architect). Interior designer: Mary Jane Williamson. Client: Kansas City Art Institute (currently Kemper Museum Foundation). General contractor: J. E. Dunn Construction. Mechanical and electrical engineer: Joseph R. Loring and Associates Inc. Structural engineer: Bob D. Campbell & Company. Civil engineer: Shafer, Kline and Warren, P. A. Lighting design consultant: Yarnell Associates Inc. Audio visual and sound consultants: Coffeen Fricke and Associates, Inc. Signage: Design GBA, created by Karmen Ltd. Sculpture court water feature: Gunnar Birkerts. Paintwork: Edmondson Painting Company. Ceiling, internal walls, partitions: Lorance Contracting Company. Glass doors and windows: NGG Ltd., Inc. Architectural hardware: Builders Specialities & Hardware. Skylights: Super Sky Products. Architectural woodwork: E. C. Wood Fixtures. HVAC: Edwards McDowell Inc. Lighting supplier: Mark One Electric Company. Lighting manufacturers: Edison Price Lighting Inc. (galleries); KIM Lighting, Inc. (exterior); Bega/US (exterior). Wood flooring: Acme Floor Company, Inc. Stainless steel roofing systems: Standard Sheet Metal Inc. Concrete: J. R. Warren Company. Granite flooring: C. A. International.

Thyssen-Bornemisza Collection, Villahermosa Palace, Madrid, Spain
Architecture and interior design: José Rafael Moneo. Project team: Luis Moreno Mansillo, Emilio Tuñón, Belén Hermida. Client: Thyssen-Bornemisza Foundation. Main contractor: Entrecanales y Tavora SA. Structural engineers: Ove Arup and Partners; Esteyco SA. Mechanical engineers: Ove Arup and Partners; J. G. Associates.

Chikatsu-Asuka Historical Museum, Osaka, Japan
Architecture and interior design: Tadao Ando. Client: Osaka Prefecture. Main contractors: Konoike Construction; Mitsubishi Construction. Consultants: Ascoral Engineering Associates (structural engineers); Setsubi Giken Engineering (electric/mechanical engineers).

Gallery of the Museum of Contemporary Furniture, Ravenna, Italy
Architect: Sottsass Associati. Project team: Ettore Sottsass, Johanna Grawunder. Collaborator: Federica Barbieró. Client: Sine Loco Snc di Raffaello Biagetti & Co. Consultant architect: Agorà S.n.c. Portico construction: Leca Blocchi. Prefabricated structure: Vibrocementi srl. Infrastructure and finishes: Adriatica Costruzioni Cervese. Heating and sanitation: TESCO srl. Electrical: Elettroimpianti Master. Air-conditioning: Tecnica di Vespignani Roberto. Marble: Sergio Francesconi – Marble and Granite. Copperwork and portico: Vincenzo Missiroli.

Restoration of the Joslyn Art Museum, Omaha, Nebraska, USA
Architect: Sir Norman Foster and Partners. Project team: Sir Norman Foster, David Nelson, Ken Shuttleworth, Graham Phillips, Nigel Dancey, Tom Leslie, Lulie Fisher, Kate Peake, Nigel Greenhill, John Ball, Justin Nichols, Hing Chan, Adele Pascal. Client: Joslyn Art Museum. Local architects and engineers: Henningson, Durham & Richardson (HDR). Main contractor: Kiewit Construction Company. Lighting: Claude Engle Lighting. Acoustics: R. F. Mahoney and Associates. Precast concrete: Kroeger Precast Concrete Inc. Structural steel: Drake-Williams Steel. Electrical engineer: Electric Company of Omaha. Mechanical engineer: Ray Martin Company of Omaha. Glass: Husker Glass Inc. Stone: J. Kapcheck & Co.

Sea Folk Museum, Mie Prefecture, Japan
Architecture and interior design: Naito Architect & Associates. Client: Foundation of Tokai Suisan Kagaku Kyokai. Main contractors: Kajima Corporation; Onishi Tanezo Construction Co. Ltd. Structural engineering: Kunio Watanabe; Structural Design Group Co. Ltd.

Shima Art Museum, Mie Prefecture, Japan
Architecture and interior design: Naito Architect & Associates. Client: Kamegawa Construction Corporation. Main contractor: Kamegawa Construction Corporation. Structural engineering: Kunio Watanabe; Structural Design Group Co. Ltd.

Finnish National Opera House, Helsinki, Finland
Architecture and interior design: Hyvämäki-Karhunen-Parkkinen Architects. Project team: Eero Hyvämäki, Risto Parkkinen, Jukka Karhunen (design); Eero Hyvämäki, Kari Piela, Tuula Mäkinen, Antti Laiho (project implementation). Client: National Board of Public Building. Main contractors: 'Ooppera': Palmberg-Ruola-Teräsbetoni (frame and structure); YIT-Yhtmä Oy (interior construction). Contractors: Ilmateollisuus Oy (air-conditioning); Yleiskylmä Oy (cooling); LVI-Karjalainen Oy (plumbing); HPY Asiakasverkot (electroincs); Sähkölähteenmäki Oy (electrics). Electrical and stage technology: Engineering Consultants Joel Majurinen Ky. Structural engineer: Engineering Consultants Mikko Vahanen Oy. HPAC: Engineering Consultants Chydeuius Ky. Subcontractors: Esko Nurmisen Maalamo Oy (painting); H. Väänänen Oy (parquet and wooden flooring); Idea-Puu Oy (wooden covering for the auditoria); YIT-Yhtymä Oy (glass elevations and roof windows); Metallirakenne Oy (metal windows and glazing); Partek Oy Ab (tile and concrete plate claddings for elevations); Alavuden Puunjalostustehdas Oy (timber doors); E. Hiltunen Oy (suspended ceilings); Kurikan Interiööri Oy (gliding doors); U. J. Saarni Oy (public area fixtures); Oy Leino-Kaluste & Co. (main auditorium seats); Avarte Oy (rehearsal stage seats); Oy Mock Ab (marquees). Acoustics: Alpo Halme. Auditorium seats: Yrjö Kukkapuro. Green arrangement design: Camilla Rosengren.

Mexican Gallery in the British Museum, London, UK
Architect: Teodoro González de León. Client: Consejo Nacional para la Cultura y las Artes; Insituto Nacional de Antropología e Historia de Mexico. Project team: Ernesto Betancourt; Miguel Cervantes. Project management: British Museum Architecture and Building Services; British Museum Design Office. Quantity surveyor: William C. Inman and Partners. Structural engineer: F. J. Samuely and Partners. Services engineer: Hoare Lea and Partners. Lighting: Fisher Marantz Renfro Stone Inc.

The Museum of Modern Art/Prefectural Museum, Wakayama, Japan
Architecture and interior design: Kisho Kurokawa Architect & Associates. Client: Wakayama Prefectural Museum. General contractors: Takenaka Corporation; Shimizu Corporation; Toda Construction Co., Ltd. Mechanical consultant: Sogo Consultants. Landscape design: Urban Design Consultants. Curtain wall: Sankyo Aluminium Industry Corporation (Art Museum); Tateyama Aluminium Industry Corporation (Prefectural Museum). Lighting: Matsushita Electronic Works Ltd. Furniture: PPM Corporation.

Begegnungsstätte Alte Synagogue, Wuppertal, Germany
Architecture and interior design: Busmann & Haberer. Project team: Busmann & Haberer (architects); Zbyszek Oksuita (interior design,

architect and sculpture); Volker Püschel (landscape design). Client: City Administration of Wuppertal. Project management: Roland Lattka Architect. Structural engineer: Bonekämper, Ingeneering, Wuppertal. Structural survey: Graner & Partner.

Kirishima International Concert Hall, Aira, Kagoshima, Japan

Architecture and interior design: Fumihiko Maki and Maki and Associates. Project team: Fumihiko Maki (principal-in-charge); Yukitoshi Wakatsuki, Yasushi Ikeda, Yoshitaka Wada, Mark Mulligan, Paul Harney, Noriko Kawamura, Yoshiki Kondo, Minoru Kudaka. Client: Kagoshima Prefectural Government. General contractor: Takenaka Corporation. Consultants: SDG Structural Design Group (structure); Sogo Consultants (mechanical and electrical); Equipe Espace (landscape); Yoichi Ando (acoustics); Nagata Acoustics (theatrical sound and lighting); Kei Miyazaki/Plants Design (carpet design).

Vancouver Library Square, Vancouver, British Columbia, Canada

Architect: Moshe Safdie & Associates Ltd/Downs Archambault & Partners. Project team: Moshe Safdie, David Galpin, Philip Matthews, Ron Beaton, Michael McKee, Michael Guran, Joe Morog, Jeff Jacoby, Chris Chan, Paul Morissette, Tony Cowan, Glenn Burwell, Kim Lannard, Doug Watts, Tony Depace. Client: Vancouver Public Library. General contractor: PCL Constructors Pacific Inc. Project manager: N. W. Fletcher & Associates Ltd. Structural consultant: Read Jones Christoffersen. Mechanical consultant: Keen Engineering Co. Ltd. Electrical consultant: Schenke/Bawol Engineering. Structural/mechanical engineering concepts: Ove Arup and Partners. Landscape consultant: Cornelia Hahn Oberlander. Acoustic consultant: Brown Strachan. Lighting consultant: Fisher Marantz Renfro Stone.

The Environment Theatre, The National Museum of Natural Science, Taichung, Taiwan

Interior designer: MET Studio Ltd. Client: The National Museum of Natural Science. Main contractor: Arrow Structures. Contractor: Carlton Beck. Naturalist/script-writer/advisor: Peter Roberts. Concept design and project management: MET Studio. Audiovisual production: Lightworks Entertainment. Audiovisual hardware and control system: Electrosonic. Lighting design: DHA. Sound design and production: The Sound Experience Consultancy. Laser system: Definitive Laser. Stills and video imaging: CAL. Graphic panel production: Photobition. Audiovisual software suppliers: New Media. Taxidermist: Derek Frampton. Rainforest diorama: Academy Studio. Model making: Bob Farrow.

Imax Theatre, Port Vell, Barcelona, Spain

Architecture and interior design: Jordi Garcés–Enric Sòria. Project team: Jordi Garcés, Enric Sòria, Joan Ignasi Quintana, Jordi Maristany. Client: Teatro Imax Barcelona SA. Quantity surveyor: Victor Serra de Rivera. Screen engineer and special structures: Jacques Prat. Installations: Ingenieria Jeroni Cabot. Acoustics: Higini Arau. Colour schemes: Anna Miquel.

Extension, Charitable Service of the Lutheran Church, Stuttgart, Germany

Architecture and interior design: Behnisch & Partner. Project team: Günter Behnisch, Winfried Büxel, Manfred Sabatke, Erhard Tränkner (partners); Gabriele Harder-Beier, Franz Harder, Carmen Lenz (project architects); Jochen Schmid, Stefanie Hehl, Kai Kniesel, Hagen Ruff, Katrin

Vogler, Christian Kandzia. Client: Charitable Service of the Lutheran Church in Württemberg e.V. Structural engineers: Schlaich, Bergermann und Partner. Electrical engineer: Schlaefle. Structural survey: Bobran Ingenieure. Construction: Jacob Thalheimer. Roofing: Holl. Heating: Surfesse. Air-conditioning: Bühr. Sanitation: Schwenk. Electrical contractor: Rudel. Elevated flooring: Mero. Office façade: Trube & Kings. Steel façade and glass roof: App. Leitkirch. Woodwork and plasterwork: Alender; Zell a; Harmersbach u Strähle. Plasterwork and insulation: Aichele. Suspended ceiling: Rienth. Basic flooring: Burkhardt. Stone flooring: Günther. Wood flooring: Ott. Carpeting: Feil. Steel construction: Ferral. Ironmongery: Integral GmbH. Steel/glass walls: Schmid & Drüppel. Carpenter: Obermüller & Gläser. Tiling: Schäfer. Paintwork: Henneberg & Oesterle. Furniture: Kohler; Nonhoff; Vereinigte Schulmöbelfabriken; Kilpper.

Shimosuwa Municipal Museum, Shimosuwa, Japan

Architecture and interior design: Toyo Ito, Toyo Ito & Associates Architects. Client: Shimosuwa-cho. Main contractors: JV of Shimizu Corporation; Shibusaki Construction. Structural engineer and planners: Toshihiko Kimura; Oak Architects Co. Ltd. HVAC engineer: Tetens Engineering Co. Ltd. Electrical engineers: Setsubi Keikaku Co. Ltd. Lighting consultant: Lighting Planners Associates.

Pavilion Hong Kong, Mobile Touring Structure

Architects: Apicella Associates. Project team: Lorenzo Apicella, James Robson, Hilary Clark, John Massey, Kate Derby, David Gausden. Clients: Hong Kong Tourist Authority; The CP Group. Main contractor: Brilliant Stages Ltd. Structural engineers: SMP Atelier One. Mechanical and electrical engineers: Atelier Ten. Glazing: Glostal. Hydraulics: 3D Design. Exhibition contractor: Modex. Air-conditioning: 'Air Cool' Engineering.

Médiathèque d'Orléans, Orléans, France

Architect: Pierre du Besset–Dominique Lyon. Project team: Pierre du Besset, Dominique Lyon, Charles-Henri de Rovira, Marie-Claude Leblond, Gary Glaser (interior decor consultant); Victor Birgin (artwork). Client: City of Orléans. Main contractor: Dalla Vera. Façade: Bel. Perforated aluminium sun screens: Gantois. Air-conditioning and heating: Sulzer. Electricity and false ceilings: Entreprise Industrielle. Paintwork: Gauthier. Interior woodwork: Quetin. Plumbing and sanitation: Mollière. Lifts: Otis. Furniture: Moinet (reception desk, custom-made tables, stainless steel lamps); Fritz Hansen (table and chairs); BCI (metal bookshelves); Casas ('Mirai' chairs); Ugap; Silvera (reading room chairs); Dactyl-Buro (cafeteria tables and chairs). Wall coverings: Hoogovens (corrugated aluminium cladding in halls); Saint-Frères (industrial tarpaulin in reading room hall); Barrisol (PCV fabric in reading room); Griffine (silver vinyl fabric in children's library, musical and video library halls).

Irish Film Centre, Temple Bar, Dublin, Ireland

Architecture and interior design: O'Donnell and Tuomey. Client: Irish Film Centre. Main contractor: Cleary and Doyle. Structural engineer: Fearon O'Neill Rooney. Services: Engineering Design Associates. Quantity surveyor: Boyd and Creed. Joinery subcontractors: JDB Design; Period Design. Furniture suppliers: O'Hagan Contracts.

Ibaraki Nature Museum, Ibaraki Prefecture, Japan

Architecture and interior design: Mitsuru Man Senda & Environment Design Institute. Client: Ibaraki Prefectural Government.

General contractors: Taisei/Mutou/Shouei; Obayashi/Nissan/Kogusuri. Structure: Kozo Keikaku Engineering Inc. Design of facilities: Kenchiku Setubi Sekkei Ken Kyuusyo; Facilities Design Research Institute. Interior decoration: Kunikazu Takatori Design Office. Lighting: TL Yamagiwa Laboratory Inc. Signage: Ryouhei Kojima Design Institute. Diorama exhibit: Tansei Co. Inc; Oni-Kobo Inc.; Nishio-Seisakusyo Inc.

The Florida Aquarium, Tampa, Florida, USA

Design architect: Hellmuth, Obata & Kassabaum (HOK), Inc. Project team: Gyo Obata, Charles M. Davis (principals-in-charge of design); Pete Karamitsanis (principal-in-charge); Alan Temple (project manager); Robert Stockdale (project designer); Jim Hastings, Foard Merriweather (project architects). Collaborating architect: Esherick Homsey Dodge and Davis (EHDD). Client: The Florida Aquarium. Main contractors: Turner Construction; Kajima International Inc. Consultants: Joseph A. Wetzel & Associates (exhibit design); Walter P. Moore & Associates (structural engineering); Syska & Hennessy (mechanical/electrical/plumbing/engineering and life support); Greiner Inc. (civil engineering). Developer: Kajima International Inc.

Bus Stop, Friedrichswall, Germany

Design: Massimo Iosa Ghini. Planning: Studio Iosa Ghini; Haack Krüger & Partner Architekten. Sponsor: Ruhrgas AG. Structural engineer: Eilers & Vogel GmbH. Quantity surveyor: Drecoll, v. Berckefeld. Construction: Philipp Holzmann AG. Roofing: Fuchs Skulpturenaufbau GmbH. Steelwork: IWZ Stahlbau GmbH. Glazing: Glascentrum Duchrow-H. Dewitz GmbH. Plasterwork: Hastrabau-Wegener. Paintwork: Peichel GmbH. Electrical engineer: Zarach Elektrotechnik. Bird cage: Anthologie Quartett. Ironwork: Eickhoff Metallbau. Gardening: Günter Steinberg.

Police Booth, Tokyo, Japan

Architecture and interior design: Norihiko Dan and Associates. Client: Tokyo Metropolitan Police Department. Main contractor: Asanuma Corporation. Structural engineer: Yutaka Aoki Structural Design Office. Mechanical engineer: Uichi Inoue Mechanical Engineering Institute. Electrical engineer: Motoi Electrical Engineering Institute. Metalwork: Nelsa-Cobo.

Index